Inspiring Leadership in Teens

Group Activities to Foster Integrity, Responsibility, and Compassion

Ric Stuecker

Research Press ■ 2612 North Mattis Avenue ■ Champaign, Illinois 61822 ■ (800) 519-2707 ■ www.researchpress.com

Composition by Jeff Helgesen
Cover design by Linda Brown, Positive I.D. Graphic Design, Inc.
Printed by Seaway Printing Co., Inc.

ISBN: 978-0-87822-639-9
Library of Congress Control Number 2010930421

*To Suze Rutherford, Ted Strader, Frank DiLallo, and all those who
inspire leadership, integrity, and compassion in youth*

Contents

Acknowledgments   ix

Introduction   1

Unit 1—Creating a Learning Community   5

Introduction   7

Activity 1.1: Forming Groups: Group Puzzles   17

Activity 1.2: Forming Groups: Name Tags   19

Activity 1.3: Learning Names   21

Activity 1.4: Learning Some Facts About Each Other   23

Activity 1.5: What We Think About   25

Activity 1.6: Rules We Can Live By   27

Activity 1.7: Rules: What Happens When . . .? What Happens
    If . . .?   30

Activity 1.8: Taking Personal Responsibility   33

Activity 1.9: Working Together: A Ball Game   36

Activity 1.10: Interviews: Presenting . . .   40

Activity 1.11: Distinguishing Types of Intelligence   44

Activity 1.12: Seven Ways to Be Smart   48

Activity 1.13: The Tree of Me   51

Activity 1.14: What I Need to Succeed   53

Evaluation Meeting   55

Unit Resources   59

**Unit 2—Studying Leadership: Researching
    Inspiring Leaders   61**

Introduction   63

Phase 1: Defining Criteria for Inspiring Leaders   71

Activity 2.1: Defining Inspiring Leadership   72

Phase 2: Assigning Students to Publishing Companies and Positions   75

Activity 2.2: Publishing Company Kickoff   76

Activity 2.3: Completing a Job Application   77

Activity 2.4: Obtaining Effective Letters of Reference   81

Activity 2.5: Creating a Strong Résumé   84

Activity 2.6: Interviewing for a Job Position   87

Activity 2.7: Creating Publishing Companies   90

Phase 3: Research   93

Activity 2.8: Finding an Inspiring Leader to Study   94

Activity 2.9: Refining Research and Writing Skills   96

Phase 4: Presentations   103

Activity 2.10: Creating and Giving a PowerPoint Presentation   104

Activity 2.11: Creating a Publishing Company Display   108

Phase 5: Evaluation and Awards   113

Activity 2.12: Evaluating Individual and Team Performances   114

Activity 2.13: Holding the BlueBerry Awards Ceremony   115

Student Guide: Your Team's Publishing Company   119

Unit Resources   125

Unit 3—Creating Leadership Portfolios   127

Introduction   129

Phase 1: Inspiring Leadership Self-Assessment Workshop   133

Activity 3.1: Taking a Leadership Self-Inventory   134

Activity 3.2: Acquiring Characteristics of Inspiring Leaders   139

Activity 3.3: Exploring Personal Integrity and Responsibility   155

Activity 3.4: Making Personal Agreements   160

Phase 2: Creating a Personal Mission Statement   167

Activity 3.5: Exploring Personal Dreams   168

Activity 3.6: Discerning What I Value in Life   172

Activity 3.7: Identifying Characteristics I Admire   174

Activity 3.8: Understanding Strengths and Roadblocks   177

Activity 3.9: Identifying Contributions I Hope to Make   179

Activity 3.10: Creating a Personal Mission Statement   182

Activity 3.11: Simplifying My Personal Mission Statement   184

Phase 3: Advertising Your Inspiring Leadership Strengths   189

Activity 3.12: Making a Personal Brochure   190

Unit Resources   194

Unit 4—Understanding Communication   195

Introduction   197

Activity 4.1: Understanding Learning Styles   201

Activity 4.2: Discovering the Learning Styles of Others   205

Activity 4.3: Negotiating One to One   207

Activity 4.4: Shutting Down Communication   209

Activity 4.5: Communicating with Head and Heart   212

Activity 4.6: Understanding Power and Influence   217

Activity 4.7: Face to Face: Using Eye Placement and Body
    Position   221

Activity 4.8: Using Your Voice   223

Activity 4.9: Using "I" Messages   226

Activity 4.10: Negotiating Agreement (Skit)   230

Activity 4.11: Negotiating Agreement (Role-Plays)   235

Unit Resources   240

Unit 5—Leading Groups   241

Introduction   243

Learning Center 1: Understanding the Stages of Team Formation   245

Activity 5.1: Understanding the Team-Building Process   246

Activity 5.2: Guiding the Team Through Stages: Strategies   249

Activity 5.3: Understanding Leadership Roles   251

Activity 5.4: Card Towers   255

Activity 5.5: Silent Puzzles   258

Activity 5.6: Great Escape   261

Learning Center 2: Understanding Leadership Styles   263

Activity 5.7: Identifying Leadership Styles   264

Activity 5.8: Experiencing Types of Leadership Styles   268

Activity 5.9: Making Team Agreements   271

Activity 5.10: Understanding Levels of Agreement   273

Activity 5.11: Holding Effective Meetings   276

Activity 5.12: Holding Effective Meetings: Practice   281

Learning Center 3: Making Presentations   285

Activity 5.13: Assessing the Audience   286

Activity 5.14: Identifying Audience Leaders
    and Barometers   289

Activity 5.15: Organizing a Presentation   293

Learning Center 4: Planning—Making Positive Changes   *299*

Activity 5.16: Developing a Compelling Vision   301

Activity 5.17: Moving from Vision to Plan   304

Activity 5.18: Identifying and Solving Constraints   307

Activity 5.19: Creating Action Plans   309

Activity 5.20: Scheduling Activities   312

Unit Resources   315

Unit 6—Living Peace   317

Introduction   319

Activity 6.1: Wellness Wheel: Personal Health
     Assessment   321

Activity 6.2: When Am I in My Power?   325

Activity 6.3: Touching My Spirit: What Is Greater
     Than I Am?   328

Activity 6.4: Personal Transformation   330

Activity 6.5: Affirmations   334

Activity 6.6: Setting Boundaries   336

Activity 6.7: Asking for Forgiveness   340

Activity 6.8: Personal Dilemmas   344

Activity 6.9: My Spiritual Journey   355

Activity 6.10: This I Believe   358

Unit Resources   361

**Appendix: Using *Inspiring Leadership in Teens* in Schools and
     in Workshop Formats   363**

About the Author   379

Acknowledgments

Inspiring Leadership in Teens was developed over a number of years, mostly when I worked as a consultant for National Training Associates, which held leadership retreats in middle and high schools throughout California, Idaho, Arkansas, and other states.

Pilot programs were developed for Saint Stephen Martyr School, Saint Nicholas Academy, and Holy Cross High School in Louisville, Kentucky.

The text of *Inspiring Leadership in Teens* was written when I was a consultant and trainer for the Council on Prevention Education: Substances (COPES, Inc.). I am extremely grateful for the support given me by Ted N. Strader, Suze Rutherford, Carol Nord, Margaret Bowen, Katherine "Kitty" Schloemer, Jim Clines, and my wife, Barbara Stuecker.

Introduction

Inspiring leaders. How do we inspire young people to look inside themselves to discover who they are as leaders? Who are the leaders in our past, in our communities, in our lives who inspire us and foster our personal aspirations to lead good lives and to act in positive ways in our families, neighborhoods, and communities? How do we inspire others by who we are, what we represent, what we teach, and how we act?

The word "inspire" means to breathe into, to touch the spirit—the spirit being our life force, our breath. The challenge each of us has as teachers and people who work with youth is to inspire them to be and to become their best selves, to set a course in the great adventure of life that is positive and bountiful, to find inside themselves the courage and stamina to lead. We inspire as role models, in what we say and do and what they observe us doing. Each of them will—as do each of us, their mentors—lead. We lead in our families—perhaps as fathers, mothers, spouses. We lead in our neighborhoods—the organizations we join, the activities we participate in. We lead in our community—as citizens of our community, state, nation, world.

How do we teach the skills of leadership? Perhaps more important, how do we foster integrity, responsibility, compassion, and peace in those we lead and mentor? *Inspiring Leadership in Teens* was developed for teachers, trainers, and youth leaders who want to foster and empower leadership skills in youth. It was developed through a number of leadership retreats and classes for middle- and high-school students. The book is designed as a field guide for those who want to create leadership classes in school or for those who develop leadership activities in organizations or at camps and retreats. The focus is on high-school students, but the material can be easily used with middle-school students.

Underlying the material in *Inspiring Leadership in Teens* is a set of beliefs. These beliefs include the following:

- Leadership skills can be taught.

- The most important learning experience in the lives of youth is the role modeling of leadership by the significant adults in their lives—teachers and trainers must walk their talk.
- Leadership ought to be based on integrity, authenticity, and compassion.
- Youth learning leadership skills ought to experience leadership and responsibility directly through in-class group dynamics and through service learning situations they develop themselves.
- Everyone will be called on to be a leader some time in his or her lifetime—as parents, as employees, as citizens.
- Leadership training is essential for all students—not just for those who appear naturally gifted as leaders.
- Effecting leaders understand the group process.
- Everyone has a leadership style and role that is important in the group dynamic when teams work toward accomplishing a common goal.
- Inspiring leadership rests on integrity, responsibility, compassion, and peace.

The material in *Inspiring Leadership in Teens* is organized for a teacher in a traditional high school or middle school. Activities are designed for classes of approximately 25 students in class periods of 45 to 50 minutes. It is assumed classes meet once daily, Monday through Friday. Included in the book, however, are outlines for creating one-, two-, three-, and five-day leadership camp workshops using many of the same activities.

The material begins with a unit on creating a learning community. It is vital to take time to create a positive community of learners who are invested in each other's success. The learning community creates its own norms, procedures, and boundaries. Rules and consequences are established by the learners themselves. Creating a learning community is of itself a lesson in leadership because it demonstrates how a group of people can come together, form a community, and achieve a set of goals. Taking time to establish a learning community fosters and empowers learning and growth for the entire enterprise of teaching leadership skills.

Following the establishment of a learning community, the class conducts team research on inspiring leaders (Unit 2). It is important to create a context for examining leadership based on a set of criteria, established by the group, to identify what is meant by an inspiring leader and by studying specific leaders who can be classified as inspirational. Youth should have role models they can trust and interact with on a daily basis, and they ought to be inspired by men and women who have lived lives of integrity, responsibility, and compassion. In Unit 2, small teams publish books of biographies, create PowerPoint presentations, and design an Inspiring Leaders Hall of Fame.

In Unit 3, students construct personal leadership portfolios. Each portfolio includes the following:

- A personal mission statement
- The eight components of inspiring leadership
- A set of personal goals to achieve
- A personal brochure highlighting the student's leadership skills, talents, and experiences

The focus in Unit 4 shifts to building communication skills. Communication skills taught include:

- Communicating one-on-one
- Communicating leader-to-group
- Understanding various learning styles
- Negotiating agreements

The bases of the communication skills include neurolinguistic programming (NLP), verbal and nonverbal strategies, and recent developments in common-ground planning such as Future Search, Search, and Open Space technologies for group planning. The activities in the unit will help students sharpen the communication skills that can enable them to build relationships of integrity with peers and others, understand group dynamics, run an effective meeting, and participate in group-planning processes.

In Unit 5, students develop skills in leading groups and making presentations. These skills include an understanding of:

- The team-building process
- Personal leadership styles
- Roles people play on teams

The unit also helps student learn how to:

- Conduct an effective meeting
- Create and give a presentations
- Develop an action plan for a project

The last unit of *Inspiring Leadership in Teens* challenges students again to look at themselves, this time to determine their spiritual strengths, personal aspirations, and what they believe.

Inspiring Leadership in Teens is a comprehensive approach to student leadership. By understanding themselves as leaders, students can be confident in their skills and continue to build on these experiences as they become leaders in school activities, athletics programs, and clubs, and then develop into good citizens, parents, members of the workforce, and participants in their local communities.

UNIT 1: CREATING A LEARNING COMMUNITY

Introduction   7

Activities

1.1   Forming Groups: Group Puzzles   17

1.2   Forming Groups: Name Tags   19

1.3   Learning Names   21

1.4   Learning Some Facts About Each Other   23

1.5   What We Think About   25

1.6   Rules We Can Live By   27

1.7   Rules: What Happens When . . . ? What Happens
       If . . . ?   30

       Handout 1.7.1: Benefits and Consequences   *32*

1.8   Taking Personal Responsibility   33

       Handout 1.8.1: Doing My Best or Just Getting By?   *35*

1.9   Working Together: A Ball Game   36

1.10   Interviews: Presenting . . .   40

       Handout 1.10.1: Interview   *42*

1.11   Distinguishing Types of Intelligence   44

1.12   Seven Ways to Be Smart   48

       Handout 1.12.1: Seven Ways to Be Smart   *49*

1.13   The Tree of Me   51

1.14   What I Need to Succeed   53

       Handout 1.14.1: What I Need to Succeed   *54*

Evaluation Meeting   **55**

       Team Evaluation   *57*

       Personal Evaluation   *58*

Unit Resources   **59**

Creating a Learning Community

Whether in a classroom or other instructional environment, it is important to create a community in which the learners invest in each other's success and the teacher functions as a catalyst and facilitator of learning experiences to help learners bond into teams, to set up observation and feedback as essential elements of learning, to foster a positive climate for learning in which individuals respect each other, and to promote both individual self-awareness and acquisition of skills needed by leaders.

Creating a learning community takes time and patience, but it ultimately brings rich results in terms of quality of both learning and outcomes that do not happen when community-building steps are ignored. It takes time to move students from a collection of individuals to a community of learners who are bonded to one another; who focus on a common set of values and beliefs; who are motivated by a common vision and set of outcomes of the learning experience; who respect the boundaries, rules, and procedures they help to create; and who communicate with each other effectively and with care and concern.

Moving a group from a set of individuals to a learning community happens in stages led by a teacher who initiates and manages learning experiences. Stage 1, often called the "I stage" or "forming stage," is when a group of individuals first meet in an unfamiliar setting. Stage 2 is reached when members form a bond and see themselves as a group. Stage 2 is called "norming" because norms for the group are established. It can also be called the "we stage" because individuals see themselves as part of a group. Stage 3, the final phase of forming a community is known as "performing." During this stage, the group functions at peak efficiency.

For a more in-depth discussion of the needs, tasks, and outcomes of each stage, see pages 10–12.

STAGE 1: FORMING

During Stage 1, the learners tend to focus on themselves and on safety issues. They want to know how they will be treated by the teacher and the other learners. They want to know what is going to happen. They wonder what the rules will be. Often there are concerns about who will sit next to whom—will they be able to work with their friends? Sometimes they are concerned about evaluation and what they need to do to get a good grade. Therefore, creating a physical environment that is consistent and easy to manage helps greatly in satisfying the "I" needs of individuals during the forming stage. Some components of an effective physical environment include the following:

- Predictable seating arrangement
- Designated areas where groups meet
- Easy-to-read signs and other visual information
- Areas, centers, materials, and resources arranged and labeled
- Specific areas for groups to post their work
- A daily routine posted
- A daily assignment posted, with easy-to-read instructions
- A consistent system for turning in completed work
- A consistent system for picking up instructions and handouts
- An announcement board

The major idea is "form follows function"—any function the teacher plans to have happen consistently needs a designated space. Consistency in where functions and activities happen creates a sense of safety and dependability for the learner.

For the *Inspiring Leadership in Teens* program, we recommend that you limit participation to 25 to 30 learners divided into five groups. If you have fewer or more students in the course, adjust small-group size as you see fit. Ideally, however, you will be able to set a limit of 25 participants, because 30 is a rather large number of students to work with, and fewer than 15 may lead to loss of an essential group dynamic.

Place groups at geographic locations in the learning area—for example, based on the four directions as well as in the middle: north, south, east, west, and center. Give each group its own space in the room for seating and for posting its work. Place each group's supplies and resources (including one computer for each group) in its meeting area.

Color code each work area—white for north, yellow for east, red for south, and black for west. These are the colors traditionally used by Native Americans to represent the four directions. Label each area: north is "visionary leadership," east is "relationships," south is "action," and west is "thought." These are the four directions of leadership energy. The center (color-coded green) represents "interior"—a connection to what is greater than the self, a person's roots, and who a person is inside.

Arrange the groups by following the suggestions in Activity 1.1 or Activity 1.2. Or simply ask the students to stand in a circle and count them off, for example, one through five or one through six, to create random groups.

STAGE 2: NORMING

Once groups are formed, you can begin to move the group toward bonding—focusing on the "we." The essential components of a bonded learning community include the following:

- Everyone knows everyone else's name.
- Everyone knows the rules of the community.
- Everyone knows and uses a process for resolving conflicts.
- Everyone learns and respects the history, culture, and background of the other learners.
- Everyone agrees to foster each other's growth.
- Everyone agrees to a common vision and mission as a group.

Once the norms are set and learners have bonded emotionally with each other, then work becomes efficient and rich. The groups are ready to move to Stage 3.

STAGE 3: PERFORMING

The final stage of creating a learning community is performing. Individuals invest in each other's successes and achievements. Leadership skills naturally grow. Each group, and the class as a whole, moves forward, enjoying the benefits of working through Stage 1 and Stage 2. In Stage 3, learners begin to understand what makes an inspiring leader, to gain inspiration from past and present leaders, to develop the skills of leadership, and to understand who they each are as leaders.

IDENTIFYING TYPES OF GROUP MEMBERS

Individuals can be categorized by how they function in a group. Three types of roles are leader, eccentric, and follower. There are several ways to "read" a group of learners and discern their roles. In general, a quick and easy way is to mentally divide them into "dogs" and "cats." Dogs are pack animals—they like to please, work for rewards, and be praised. They prefer a consistent routine and can be easily trained. Cats are said to be finicky, independent, and selective about showing and receiving affection. They often do not follow a routine and can be difficult to train. Most learners tend to be doglike. They like to be rewarded and to cooperate with others; they prefer the safety

(continued on page 13)

CREATING A LEARNING COMMUNITY: NEEDS, TASKS, AND OUTCOMES OF THE THREE STAGES

STAGE 1: FORMING

Learners are focused on their own individual needs as people and as learners. At this stage, the group is a collection of individuals, with some subgroups already formed—friends, teammates, neighbors, classmates from previous years, or other relationships developed prior to this learning experience.

NEED

In Stage 1, individuals need to feel safe. They want to know that they belong in some way, that they will be respected, that the time and space is managed well by an adult who cares about them, that they can speak and be heard, and that they have a place both in the learning environment and within the learning community.

TASK

The primary task for Stage 1 is to lead the group from a collection of individuals to a group that relates to each other in positive ways. By starting with a learning space setup that is easy to understand and function in and that is consistent and dependable, learners will feel safe and have confidence that they will learn something valuable. As the teacher, you should take some time to think through how the space will be used and how to create spaces for whole-group instruction and small-group interaction. You can take the following steps to help achieve the goals of Stage 1:

- Create a standard schedule and post it in a central area.
- Use large, easy-to-read signs to label areas of the space so that students can find resources and materials easily.
- As the community develops, post the rules and a code of ethics, announcements, and other information.
- Give each small group a space to meet in and a section of wall space to display work and findings.
- If possible, provide a resource center with a computer (with Internet access) for each group.

OUTCOMES

The outcomes for Stage 1 are for students to:

- Form small groups

- Establish group stations
- Learn each other's names
- Know the typical class schedule

STAGE 2: NORMING

During this stage, learners create relationships and form teams. Group norms are established and are clearly understood. Norms include the rules, a code of ethics, the daily schedule, operational logistics, teacher expectations, and how to operate in the learning space.

NEED

In Stage 2, learners need to establish relationships with each other and the teacher. They need to feel part of a group that has a goal and destination. Usually, students bond first with the teacher, then with each other, then with the goals and tasks of the group.

TASK

Because a key goal of Stage 2 is to have learners focused on a goal or vision and for them to feel positively bonded and invested in each other's success, the task is to create a learning community in which all learners feel valued and are working together to foster each other's growth and development as well as movement toward Stage 3. It is important to develop—with input from learners—the rules of the community, a code of ethics describing how they want to treat each other, the logistics of the team and the large group, and a set of expectations and outcomes.

To develop rapport and relationships, the sequence of learning experiences is designed to allow students to discover each other and build bonds by examining what they hold in common while allowing and honoring individual differences.

OUTCOMES

The outcomes of Stage 2 are to establish:

- A simple set of classroom/workshop rules
- A code of ethics that is easy to understand and implement
- A method for resolving conflicts that satisfies both parties
- Investment in cooperative learning, positive growth, and development of individuals within the learning community
- A consistent and caring method for observing and giving positive feedback

- An understanding of the history and culture of the individual learners
- Respect for differences and discovery of similarities among learners

STAGE 3: PERFORMING

Learners are ready and eager to do realistic tasks with significant outcomes in the real world. Learners are bonded and invested in working together toward a common goal.

NEED

In Stage 3, learners need to accomplish real objectives.

TASK

The task in Stage 3 is to lead learners to a place where they are creating realistic and doable projects. Projects should include action plans that involve all students using their strengths. Objectives should be broken down into a sequence of action steps for which various team members take responsibility. A timeline establishes a set of deadlines and includes outcomes for each step.

OUTCOMES

The outcomes of Stage 3 are learners who can:

- Accomplish a realistic project, with adult supervision and mentoring
- Identify their roles in working on the project and their talents as leaders
- Examine and critique how they might improve their own and team performance in the future
- Set personal goals and objectives for developing further as inspiring leaders
- Create a personal mission for themselves

and routine of a group and like to meet challenges as a group. On the other hand, some learners are more catlike and prefer to be independent.

Some individuals in groups are natural leaders. Leaders often come from the "catlike" group. As you get to know your class, look for the student to whom the group responds with attention. When that student asks a question, makes a comment, or answers a question, the others look at him or her, pay close attention to what he or she is saying, and often indicate with their body language (nodding, eye contact) that they agree with that student. That student is likely to be a leader.

It is good to know not only who the leaders are, but where they are leading. If they are positive leaders, if they buy into the goals and objectives of the learning experiences, find them interesting and useful, and express positive energy for the work in class, they will lead others in creating a positive atmosphere. If a leader is negative, then you will need to connect with him or her and try to get that student to work with you. Giving these students responsibilities through which they can shine and praising their successes will often encourage them to become more positive.

A second group of students with catlike ways are known as eccentrics. These students define themselves as unique and different from other members of the group. Eccentrics can sometimes be irritating. They might ask questions that are not on topic, use an annoying tone of voice, wear unusual clothing styles, state unusual opinions, or act in opposition to the group. These students can be difficult to work with. Sometimes the group grows used to the eccentric and is not bothered by his or her behavior. Other times, eccentrics annoy the group, who then look to you to intervene. This is tricky business. Often, the best you can do is to work with the eccentric and see whether the group will accept him or her. You can sometimes rephrase what the eccentric says in a way that makes his or her comments more acceptable to the group. You can also ask an eccentric a question at a time when it is most likely the answer given will be on topic.

If you connect *too* much with an eccentric, however, you might lose credibility with the group. It is best to bond first with the group and generally ignore the eccentric until the group feels safe and connected to you. Once that happens, you can take action to move the eccentric into a role in which he or she can be accepted by the group. Although it is neither necessary nor wise to ask the eccentric to change, you might privately communicate to the eccentric the consequences of his or her choices and behaviors and their effect on the group. Sometimes eccentrics then make adjustments on their own.

Eccentrics can sometimes be targets for put-downs and victims of mean-spirited behavior. This can best be handled by consistently giving consequences for these behaviors, setting clear and consistent rules and expectations, and not tolerating bullying.

ARRANGING THE LEARNING SPACE

You will want to create the most efficient space possible to work with students in large-group activities and small-group interactions. It is important, therefore, to take the time to arrange the learning space before the course begins.

1. Make a list of all the types of activities you intend to do in the space where you will most often be working.

2. On graph paper, draw the outline of your classroom or training area.

3. Sketch in possible areas according to function. Here are some areas you might want to establish:

   - An area for whole-group instruction, directions, and discussions

   - Workstations or areas for four or five groups, each with five or six members

   - A resource center for dictionaries and other reference books

   - A materials center, with art supplies such as markers, various sizes of paper, scissors, tape, crayons, rulers, and any other items you think you will be using

   - A computer area where students can access the Internet and use word processing software, PowerPoint, and other programs

   - An information area to post announcements, schedules, follow-up work, assignments, and other important information students are required to know

   - An area for distributing handouts and collecting individual and group work

   - Wall space for students to post work

4. Make of list of equipment you will want to use. Here is some equipment you might want to have available:

   - A laptop computer, screen, and projector for PowerPoint presentations and mind-mapping activities

   - One computer per group, with access to the Internet

   - A whiteboard or easel pad

   - Moveable desks and chairs that are easily converted from a large-group configuration to small-group workstations

- Tables for organizing handouts, collecting assignments, etc.
- Bookshelves

5. Make signs:

  - For the most effective signs, pair a piece of clip art with words. Visual learners will read the words. Kinesthetic learners will look at graphics. Example: a picture of a computer paired with the words "computer center."
  - Use the same font and colors throughout to create a cohesive sense of space.
  - Label all important items. Make it easy on yourself and learners to find—and return—equipment and supplies and to follow the routines you want to establish.

6. Using the floor plan you drew, set up and organize your work space. If you have a fairly small group, ask the learners to help you set things up. The advantages here are that learners will feel more at home in the space they help create, may be more ready to clean up and to keep the space orderly, can bond with each other in a natural way, and will know where everything is.

OVERVIEW OF ACTIVITIES

The activities presented in this unit have been used with secondary students in many sites—urban and rural, private and public schools, and at leadership workshops lasting several days to 2 weeks. The suggested activities for this unit may be adapted for your particular setting. You can change the sequence of activities, modify them, or add other activities and learning experiences. In fact, you can and should blend these activities with others you have used and are familiar with. The activities in this unit and their sequence are designed for high-school students but can easily be used in middle school or other settings.

Unit 1 activities are as follows:

- Activities 1.1 and 1.2 are fun ways of randomly assigning students to the small groups they will work with throughout Unit 1.
- Activity 1.3 helps students learn each other's names, and Activity 1.4 helps students learn some facts about each other.
- In Activity 1.5, students have an opportunity to share their deeper thoughts and opinions.
- Activities 1.6 and 1.7 focus on creating rules for the learning community and establishing consequences for not following group rules.

- In Activity 1.8, students explore the concept of personal responsibility.

- Activity 1.9 challenges students to work as a team to achieve a common goal.

- Activity 1.10 provides further opportunity for students to learn more about each other and gives them a chance to practice interview and presentation skills.

- Activities 1.11 and 1.12 focus on different types of intelligence and allow students to evaluate their own learning styles.

- Activity 1.13 uses a tree metaphor to help students discover more about each other's backgrounds.

- Activity 1.14 concludes the unit by asking students to make commitments to academic success.

- At the end of this unit (beginning on page 55) are instructions and worksheets for evaluation meetings to be used throughout this curriculum. After the first month, you may want to hold the team evaluation meetings every 2 or 3 weeks.

ACTIVITY 1.1

Forming Groups: Group Puzzles

Activities 1.1 and 1.2 are fun ways to assign students to random groups. Feel free to use any methods you like to establish small work groups of five or six members, or more, if necessary. Activity 1.3 is especially useful when working with groups whose learners do not know each other's names. (Keep in mind that it is not a good idea to set up groups and assign learners to them yourself. Doing so can create unnecessary resentments within the group.)

PURPOSE
To arrange groups randomly

MATERIALS
Colored paper

Markers

Scissors

Clip art pictures of animals and symbols (or postcards)

Bag or basket

PREPARATION
Obtain a different postcard for each group or select a picture of a different animal or symbol.

Cut the postcards or pictures into pieces, one piece for each student you want in the group.

Put all the pieces into a bag or basket and mix them up.

DIRECTIONS
1. Ask students to form a circle. To increase random selection, you could ask them to form a circle based on height (shortest to tallest), age (youngest to oldest), birthdate, or alphabetical order of middle name.

2. Ask each student to take one piece of the puzzle from the bag or basket.

3. When all the students have a piece of the puzzle, ask them to find all the other students who have pieces to their puzzle.

4. As groups form, ask students to choose one of the workstations to lay out their puzzle. This will be that group's work space. Or you

can place a copy of the pictures you cut up to form the puzzles at each of the stations as a guide for the groups to find their area.

DISCUSSION

- Was it easy or hard to find the other members of your group?
- Was it fun?
- How else might we form random groups?
- Did anyone show leadership in helping you find your group? Who did, and how did they show leadership?
- Why might it be important to form random groups in order to learn about leadership?

ACTIVITY 1.2

Forming Groups: Name Tags

This activity may be used as an alternative to Activity 1.1.

PURPOSE   To form random work groups

MATERIALS   Blank name tags (one per student; although more expensive, name tags that pin on or can be worn around the neck are good because they can be used for several days)

Colored markers

Bag or basket

Optional: Small stickers (a different kind for each small group)

PREPARATION   In one corner of each name tag, write a number, put a colored dot, or place a sticker. If you plan to have five students in each group, make five tags with the same number, dot, or sticker. Do not put names on the name tags.

Put the name tags in a bag or basket.

At each group's workstation, display the number, color, or sticker that matches the one on the corner of the name tags.

DIRECTIONS   1. Arrange students in a line or circle according to their birthdays, heights, ages, alphabetical order of names, or some other criterion.

2. Ask each student to draw a name tag from the bag or basket.

3. Ask students to find all the other students in the group who have the same number, color, or sticker as the one on their name tag.

4. Ask students to find the workstation that has the same number, color, or sticker as the one on their name tag.

5. Rather than making their own name tags, ask students to make tags for another member in their group by neatly printing that person's name on the tag. Students may use the colored markers to add additional decorations to the name tags.

6. Have the students give the name tag they created to the person they made it for.

DISCUSSION
- Was this a good way to divide into groups?
- Would you have preferred to design your own name tag?
- How do you feel about wearing a name tag?

ACTIVITY 1.3

Learning Names

PURPOSE   To help students learn one another's names quickly

DIRECTIONS
1. Ask students to sit in a small circle facing the other members of the work group formed in Activity 1.1 or Activity 1.2 (or the activity you used to form random groups).

2. Ask each group to select a member to lead this activity. To facilitate the selection, you might ask one student in each group to raise his or her hand. That student then points to another person in the group, who becomes the activity leader.

3. Ask the group leader to decide who will go first: the person on his or her left, or on the right. The leader should go last.

4. Explain to the students that they will be telling the group their name and one interesting fact about themselves. To make this activity more creative, you might ask students to avoid repeating what anyone else has said and to avoid naming a sport when giving a fact about themselves. Provide some examples:

   • My name is Alice, and I like to go to tea parties.
   • My name is Tom, and I like to paint fences.
   • My name is Huck, and I go rafting on the river.

5. Tell the students that not only must they say their own names and provide an interesting fact, they must also repeat all the names and facts already presented. For example, the third person in the circle might say, "My name is Alice, and I like to go to tea parties. Tom paints fences. That's Huck, and he goes rafting on the river."

6. When the activity ends, ask the group leaders to facilitate the discussion by making sure that only one person speaks at a time and that all students in their group get a chance to share their opinions.

DISCUSSION

- Was this activity difficult or easy?
- Did other people help you? If so, how?
- Is it good to help one another when you get into difficulty?
- Working together, did we all succeed?
- In a learning community, should we help one another to learn? How can we best do that?

ACTIVITY 1.4

Learning Some Facts About Each Other

PURPOSE

To give students the opportunity to get to know some basic information about each other

DIRECTIONS

1. Ask students to sit in a small circle facing the other members of the work group formed in Activity 1.1 or Activity 1.2 (or the activity you used to form random groups).

2. Ask each group to select a member to lead this activity. To facilitate the selection, you might ask one student in each group to raise his or her hand. That student then points to another person in the group, who becomes the activity leader.

3. Ask the group leader to decide who will go first: the person on his or her left, or on the right. The leader should go last.

4. The first student tells the workgroup what his or her favorite color is, then other students in the group take their turn. Ask the group to repeat the activity with these items:

   - My favorite letter of the alphabet
   - My favorite number
   - The city and state where I was born
   - The number of people in my family
   - The color of the family car(s)
   - My favorite dessert
   - My favorite place to go on vacation
   - Some place I hope to visit during my lifetime
   - Something I hope to accomplish in my lifetime
   - Something really good that I hope happens to me (besides winning the lottery)
   - Something I hope to contribute to making the world a better place

5. When the activity ends, ask the group leaders to facilitate the discussion by making sure that only one person speaks at a time and that all students in their group get a chance to share their opinions.

DISCUSSION
- What information about your teammates surprised you?
- What information about your teammates was new to you?
- Which of the stated contributions intrigued you?
- What was the most interesting information you discovered about someone in your group?

OPTION
1. At another class session, following the same directions, use this set of items, one item per round:

   - Someone in sports who inspires me
   - Someone in the *national* news who inspires me
   - Someone in the *world* news who inspires me
   - A fictional character who inspires me
   - Someone from history who inspires me
   - Someone in my life who inspires me

2. Conduct a final round, asking, "What characteristics, values, or beliefs of the people who inspire you do you wish to incorporate into your personality?"

DISCUSSION
- Who were some of the people who inspired others in your group?
- Why are these people inspirational?
- What characteristics of these inspirational people do you want to incorporate into your own personality?

ACTIVITY 1.5

What We Think About

PURPOSE   To introduce students to open-ended questions

MATERIALS   Blank sheets of 8.5 × 11-inch paper (one or two per student)

DIRECTIONS   1. Ask students to sit in a circle in their assigned work groups.

2. Ask the previous activity leader to point to someone who has not yet been a group leader. This student will be the leader of this activity.

3. Ask students whether they ever just sit and think about or ponder things. Tell them that most people do—if not every day, maybe sometimes before sleep, or while fishing or out in the woods alone, or by the ocean, or maybe when listening to music.

4. Tell students you are going to give them some time to write down their "big questions"—questions about life, the future, or other things they think about. Let them know that they will be sharing their questions with their group.

5. Give students 5 minutes (or more, if you wish) to write their answers to the following questions. If some students are still writing after the allotted time, give them 1 or 2 more minutes to finish:

   • What are three big questions about *life* you often wonder about and would like the answers to?

   • What are three big questions about the *future* you often wonder about?

   • What are three questions that begin with "Why?" that you would like to ask?

   • What are three big questions about *yourself* that you sometimes ask?

   • What are three big questions facing people your age at this time in your life?

6. Have each student select five questions he or she is willing to share with the small group. Ask each student to read the questions, one

at a time, going around the circle. Remind the group leaders to facilitate this activity by selecting which direction the questions will go (from the leader's right or left, with the leader going last), allowing each person to have a turn, and making sure the others listen while each person speaks.

7. At the end of the activity, ask the leader to facilitate a discussion within the small group about the questions that were read aloud.

DISCUSSION

- Are there any big questions that might have been asked but were not?
- Did any surprise you? If so, why?
- What do you think is the biggest question asked?

ACTIVITY 1.6

Rules We Can Live By

PURPOSE   To create rules for the learning community to follow

MATERIALS   Whiteboard or easel pad
Posterboard and colored markers

DIRECTIONS   1. Ask the students the following questions:

- Do you think it is important for a group to have rules if it is to work together? If so, why?

- Have you played on any teams or worked on any projects where the group had a common goal to achieve? Did that group have rules?

- Who made the rules for the team or group you were a part of? Were you able to make suggestions for creating the rules?

- Why might it be a good idea for the members of a team to have input in establishing its rules?

- What might be some rules that a successful team would want to follow?

- Is it important for everyone to follow the rules? Why or why not?

- How many rules do you think a team needs to be successful?

2. Read or paraphrase the following:

Most teams or groups find they need rules in order to be successful. Communities usually have rules to follow—sometimes these are called laws. In our country, we have a history and a heritage of groups coming together to create communities based on rules and laws—rules and laws the community itself either writes or agrees to follow. For this learning community to function well, we might need to make some rules for us to live by. I am going to give you three very general rules, and you are going to tell me what each rule will look like—how people will follow it in our learning community.

Rule 1: Everyone will take care of himself or herself.

If everyone in our learning community looks after and takes care of himself or herself, what will we see happen? Here are some suggestions. (Note, however, that student suggestions are more powerful and more likely to be followed; use the following suggestions only if you need a starting point.)

- Everyone will come to class with materials and assignments completed.
- Everyone will try hard.
- People will listen to one another.
- People will "put down put-downs."
- People will stay out of other people's desks and things.

Write student responses on the whiteboard or easel pad. Also ask someone in the group to write them down to save. Remind the students to be specific and to tell you and the group what everyone would be seeing and what would be happening.

3. Now read or paraphrase the following:

> Have you noticed any teams where individuals didn't seem to care about anyone but themselves? Can you give some examples of teams—even teams with some really talented members—who did not reach their full potential because they could not work together? Have you noticed any teams or groups who were able to achieve a lot because they worked together, even though they might not have had the most talent? Can you give some examples of teams that worked hard, invested in one another's success, and achieved a goal? Have you ever been on a team or in a group where most people worked together and it was important to see that everyone succeeded?

4. Present this idea to the group:

> Highly effective teams and learning communities usually work together. In highly efficient teams and learning communities, individual members care about one another, foster one another's growth, and work together toward a common goal.

Rule 2: We will care about one another.

If everyone cares about each other and invests in each other's success, what will we see happening? Some suggestions (again, ask for student responses first, then use these suggestions if necessary):

- People will be nice to one another.

- People will help one another when needed.
- There might not be too many arguments.
- We'll be more relaxed.
- We'll be working together.

Write student responses down on the whiteboard or easel pad. Also ask someone in the group to write them down to save. Remind the students to be specific and to tell you and the group what you would be seeing and what would be happening.

5. Now ask the group these questions:

    - Do you think we are taking good care of the planet?
    - Do you think we are taking good care of our city or town?
    - Why would having a neat and orderly work space be a good idea for an effective learning community?

Rule 3: We will care about our learning space.

If we care about this learning space, what will we see happening? Some suggestions (use only if necessary; encourage student responses first):

- The room will be clean.
- People will pick up after themselves.
- People will leave other people's stuff alone.
- We will put things back where they belong.

Write these responses down on the whiteboard or easel pad. Also ask someone in the class to write them down to save. Keep asking the students to be specific and to tell you and the group what you would be seeing and what would be happening.

6. Ask the students whether they could live by these rules in this learning community. If anyone suggests a difficulty, ask the class to brainstorm ways to overcome that difficulty.

7. In front of the students, make a large chart or poster stating the three rules and including the specific suggestions the students made as to how the rules will look in action in a learning community.

8. Tell the students that one part of the weekly community meeting will be a review of the rules and how the community is following them. The evaluation forms are found at the end of this unit, on pages 57 and 58. (After the first month, you may want to have community meetings every 2 or 3 weeks, at which the teams examine leadership and how they are working as a group.)

ACTIVITY 1.7

Rules: What Happens When . . . ? What Happens If . . . ?

PURPOSE

To let students determine what might happen if they follow or don't follow the rules and to let students suggest consequences for those who do not follow the rules

MATERIALS

Handout 1.7.1: Consequences (one per student)

Whiteboard or easel pad

PREPARATION

On the whiteboard or easel pad, write the group rules established in Activity 1.6.

DIRECTIONS

1. Arrange the entire group in a circle. Give each student a Consequences chart and point out the two columns at the top of the chart: "When We Follow the Rules" and "When We Don't Follow the Rules."

2. Review the group rules established in Activity 1.6. Discuss with the group why following the rules is important for a learning community to function well.

3. Ask students to list, in each column on their own chart, some suggested benefits for following the rules and consequences for not following the rules.

4. When everyone is finished, make a similar chart on the whiteboard or easel pad large enough for everyone to see. Ask the group to tell you their suggestions. List the suggestions as they give them; be sure to list all the suggestions the students offer.

5. Ask students to suggest which of the consequences for not following the rules are fair, reasonable, and doable. Circle those responses on your chart.

6. Tell the students that these will be the consequences that will occur when individuals or groups do not follow the rules.

DISCUSSION

- What do you think about establishing your own consequences for behavior? Is it fair? What do you like about establishing your own rules and consequences? What do you dislike?
- Do you think consequences are a good idea? Why or why not?
- Do you believe consequences help people become responsible?
- If there were no consequences, how could you help people become responsible?
- Are consequences easier to accept if you help develop them?

Benefits: When We Follow the Rules	Consequences: When We Don't Follow the Rules

Activity 1.8

Taking Personal Responsibility

PURPOSE   To let students think about how they can take personal responsibility for their learning

MATERIALS   Handout 1.8.1: Doing My Best or Just Getting By? (one per student)
                   Whiteboard or easel pad

DIRECTIONS   1. Arrange the large group in a circle. Ask students whether they can think of anyone—a sports figure, someone in the news, someone they know—who usually does his or her best. Make a list on the whiteboard or easel pad.

2. Ask students to identify specifically how they know that these people usually do their best.

3. Remind students that one of the rules—we all will take care of ourselves—is characterized by everyone usually doing his or her best.

4. Ask students whether they have ever noticed anyone who does just enough to get by. Do they know of any sports figures or anyone else in the news who seems to just get by or who only occasionally does their best?

5. Pass out the charts and point out the column headings at the top: "Doing My Best" and "Just Getting By."

6. Ask students to list, under each heading, specific ways they just get by and specific ways they do their best.

7. Ask students to share with the whole group some of the ways they do their best and some of the ways they just get by. You may want to chart these on the whiteboard or easel pad.

8. Ask students to rate themselves, using the scale at the bottom of the chart.

DISCUSSION   • Why do you think some students just get by?
                   • Why do you think some students usually do their best?

33

- Do you think there is pressure here from other students to just get by?
- Do you think there is pressure here from other students to do your best?
- Is it okay sometimes to just get by?
- What do you think your teachers' expectations of you are? Are these expectations realistic?
- What do you think your parents' expectations of you are? Are these expectations realistic?
- What are your expectations of yourself? Are they realistic? Are you meeting these expectations?

Doing My Best   Just Getting By

RATE MYSELF

Circle one: 3 = I usually do my best.   1 = I sometimes do my best.
                2 = I often do my best.   0 = I seldom do my best.

Working Together:
A Ball Game

PURPOSE

To present a metaphor for how a learning community works together to achieve a common goal

MATERIALS

A beach ball or other soft ball at least 12 inches in diameter (a Gurdy ball works well, as does a cloth ball with a balloon insert)

Three stopwatches (many students wear watches with sweep hands or stopwatch features, and you might be able to use those)

PREPARATION

Work in a space that is mostly free of furniture. Sitting on the floor is a possibility, but most middle- and high-school students prefer to sit in chairs.

Arrange students in a large group. Students should be able to reach out and touch another student's fingertips, but there should be no large spaces or holes between them.

DIRECTIONS

1. Tell students they are about to play a ball game. Summarize the following purpose, rules, and tips on how best to play:

   • The purpose of this game is to see how long you, as a group, can keep the ball moving around without stopping and without hitting an inanimate object. (Inanimate objects include the floor, ceiling, and any items of furniture. Inanimate objects do not include your clothes or anything else you are wearing.)

   • You must stay seated.

   • If your bottom lifts off the chair (or floor), the game stops and we start again. The ball returns to me.

   • Anyone who sees someone else's bottom lift off the chair (or floor) should call out, "Bun infraction." The game will stop, and the ball will return to me.

   • Anyone who thinks that his or her own bottom lifts off the chair (or floor) should call a bun infraction on himself or herself. The game will stop, and the ball will return to me.

- This is a game of honesty and integrity.
- If the ball hits the floor, ceiling, or any inanimate object other than your clothes, the game stops. The ball will return to me.
- If the ball stops, is held, or gets stuck, the game stops. The ball returns to me.
- Use your fingertips to control the ball. Spiking is not recommended—this is not volleyball.
- I will pick three timekeepers for each round of the game. The timekeepers will keep official time.
- Remember: This is a game of personal and group integrity and honesty.

2. Ask students whether they have any questions or whether anyone has suggestions as to how the group can be successful in this activity.

3. Tell the group that highly effective teams have been able to keep the ball moving for at least 15 minutes.

4. Select three students to keep time for each round. (Choose students who have sweep hands on their watches or provide three stopwatches.)

5. Tell students you will toss out the ball after you count down from five to one. Caution the timekeepers to be ready.

6. Count down from five to one and toss the ball anywhere in the group. Play continues until there is a bun infraction; the ball hits the floor, ceiling, or another inanimate object; or the ball stops.

7. If any of these events happen, make sure the ball comes immediately back to you. (Most groups won't be able to keep the ball going for more than a minute or so during the first several rounds.)

8. After three or four rounds, stop and ask the students for more suggestions as to how they can best work together. If necessary, you can suggest the following:

- Teams that work together and are able to achieve at least 2 minutes seem to be able to keep the ball moving for as long as they want after that. You might want to set a goal of 1 minute, then 2 minutes.
- Some groups work better if they agree to maintain silence while playing.
- Teams who stay positive, support each other, work together, resist blaming each other, and celebrate achievements are often successful.

9. Try four or five rounds. Ask students to suggest what the obstacles to their success are. Ask for more suggestions of how they

might work together to achieve the goal. You might suggest that those who have been sitting toward the outer edge move carefully to the middle of the group, while those who have been in the middle move carefully to the outside.

10. Try four or five more rounds. If the group is able to keep the ball aloft for 2 minutes, see how long the group can keep going. This will set a record for the group, which they can try to break if you play the game at other sessions. You might ask the group to see whether every member of the group is able to touch the ball at least once.

11. If the group is not able to achieve 2 minutes, tell them they have three more rounds before you stop playing. If you stop playing before the group achieves 2 minutes, tell them you will play again at another time until they achieve this goal.

12. If the group is able to attain the 2-minute goal, give them three more tosses to let them try to set their personal record.

DISCUSSION

- How is this game like groups you have been in or teams you have played on?

- Who showed leadership during the game? How?

- Did put-downs occur?

- Were you successful?

- If you were successful, what were the key elements to your success?

- If you were unsuccessful, what do you have to do to increase the possibility of success?

- How does this game relate to the three rules we set for this group to live by?

- As a learning community, what changes or adjustments might we want to make to increase our possibility of success?

- What does it mean to be honest and to have integrity?

- Were people honest during the game? Give examples.

- Did people demonstrate integrity? Who did and how?

- What does being honest and showing integrity have to do with a learning community?

NOTES

This activity is a good opportunity to evaluate the social health of the group of learners. If they do not buy into the game or its goal, this group is going to need some work on group bonding. If the group includes negative leaders—those who insist on spiking the ball, hitting it only to their friends, or leading others into not buying into the game—you will need to work with these individuals privately on positive leadership. They are natural leaders who have chosen to be negative and can be your best allies with the group if you can win them over to your objectives.

You can determine natural leaders in the group by watching the group when someone makes a positive suggestion. If the group listens and follows the suggestion, this person is a natural leader in the group.

ACTIVITY 1.10

Interviews: Presenting . . .

PURPOSE   To help students learn more about other students in the learning community and to give students the chance to develop skills in interviewing and presenting information to the group

MATERIALS   Whiteboard or easel pad

Handout 1.10.1: Interview (one per student)

DIRECTIONS 1. Arrange the whole group of students in a line or a circle, then do as follows:

- Place students in groups of three.
- Ask the groups of three to sit facing one another.
- Ask groups to designate each person A, B, or C.

2. Write who will interview and present whom on the whiteboard or easel pad:

- A and B interview and present C.
- B and C interview and present A.
- A and C interview and present B.

3. Give each student a copy of the interview handout. Explain to the group that they are going to interview one of the people in their triad. Tell them that, using notes they will take on the handout, they will write a one-page profile of the person they interviewed.

4. Explain that after writing the one-page profile, they will use it while they stand with the person at the front of the room and introduce him or her to the class.

5. Allow 5 minutes for each interview. If necessary, you can give an additional 5 minutes for students to complete the interview.

6. After the interview, give the students 15 to 20 minutes to write a one-page profile based on the notes they took.

7. You are now ready for the presentations. You can conduct them at this point or schedule them at the start of the next several meetings. (Sitting through all the presentations in one meeting might be too boring for some students.)

DISCUSSION

- Does anyone find it difficult to stand up in front of a group and give a presentation? If so, what makes it difficult?

- Raise your hand if you felt nervous introducing someone else to the group. Describe how you knew were were nervous (examples: my stomach got tight, my hands perspired, I started moving around).

- Some experts tell us that speaking in public is the greatest fear most people have. Do you agree? Why might this be so?

- Do you believe speaking in public is an important skill for a leader? If so, why?

1. *Sit in groups of three, facing one another.*
2. *Concentrate on the person you are interviewing.*
3. *Two people can interview one person, but only one person will present that interviewee to the group.*
4. *Using words and short phrases, make notes to capture the answers given by the interviewee.*

Area 1: Music

Ask the interviewee questions about the music he or she loves: favorite type of music, favorite artists, favorite CDs and songs, what the person likes to do while listening to this music, other types of music and artists the person also likes. Make sure you have at least five different things about music to report on.

_____

_____

_____

Area 2: Interests

Find out three to five activities this person loves to do in his or her free time. Make sure to get lots of details as to how, when, and how often this person gets to participate in these favorite leisure-time activities.

_____

_____

_____

Area 3: Family

Ask this person to tell you about family members that drive him or her crazy. Who in the family does this, and what do they do? Also find out at least five things the interviewee does to drive his or her parents and siblings up the wall. Ask what is his or her favorite or most creative way to do so.

_____

_____

_____

Area 4: Past

Find out about an incident or several incidents that happened to this person that were funny, exciting, odd, unexpected, unusual, or in some way interesting.

_____

_____

_____

Area 5: Future

Ask the person: If you won a lot of money in the lottery, what would you do with it? What future career do you aspire to? Why? What do you hope to accomplish in your life? Do you plan to get married? Have children? Live in this city, town, or area? If not, where do you want to live, and why? What important thing do you hope to do to make the world a better place?

_____

_____

_____

Activity 1.11

Distinguishing Types
of Intelligence

PURPOSE   To give students the opportunity to evaluate themselves as learners

MATERIALS   Large paper plates (one per student)

Colored markers (a set containing at least seven different colors for each group)

PREPARATION   Make sure each group has markers or can share them so they can write in seven colors.

You may want to make a sample paper plate to show the students as a model.

DIRECTIONS
1. Arrange students into their assigned work groups.

2. Ask the most recent group leader to raise a hand and point to someone who hasn't yet been a leader (if everyone has already been a leader, ask the recent leader to choose someone who hasn't been a leader lately.)

3. Tell the leaders that they will be facilitating group discussions after you lead a series of exercises.

4. Explain that scientists have discovered at least seven kinds of intelligence and are discovering even more. Read or paraphrase the following:

> There are many ways of being smart, and each of us is smart in a unique combination of ways. The activity for today is designed to help you identify your strengths as individuals. After you identify your strengths, you will be discussing your strengths with your teams so the team knows who does what well.

5. Give each student a paper plate. Ask students to divide their plates into seven roughly equal sections (like a pie). Tell them they can use both sides of their plates.

6. Ask them to label the pie sections as follows: *number smart, word smart, space smart, people smart, self smart, body smart,* and *music smart.*

7. Explain to the students that you are going to give them a series of exercises to demonstrate each type of "smart." Ask them to put their paper plates aside.

Exercise 1

- Ask students to calculate how many seconds it takes to make one 24-hour day. Tell them they can collaborate within their work groups. (Answer: 86,400)

- Explain to the students that if they could figure that out, they are probably *number smart.*

Exercise 2

- Ask students to repeat for the large group any famous sayings, lines from poetry, lines from speeches, or rap lyrics (caution them that the lyrics must be appropriate for the learning community—no dirty words or double meanings).

- Explain that if they could recall these words, if they like to read or write or talk, they are likely to be *word smart.*

Exercise 3

- Ask students to stand and point to the following places, indicating the direction from where they are standing right now:
  - ☐ Their house
  - ☐ The principal's office
  - ☐ The gym
  - ☐ Canada
  - ☐ A large river or lake
  - ☐ A mountain range
  - ☐ Their favorite restaurant
  - ☐ The Gulf of Mexico
  - ☐ California
  - ☐ Their best friend's house
- Explain that if they could point to those places, are good at art, or can find their way through hotels and hospitals, then they are likely to be *space smart.*

Exercise 4

- Ask students to find a partner from a *different* group. Make sure everyone has a partner. (If you are working with an odd number of students, one group can have three partners.)

- Explain that if they were able to find a partner easily, then they are probably *people smart*.

- Ask the students to stay with their partners for the next exercise.

Exercise 5

- Ask students to find out the following from their partners:

  □ Favorite breakfast food

  □ Favorite vacation spot

  □ A person living or dead with whom you would like to have dinner

  □ What you would ask that person over dinner

  □ Something about yourself most people don't know

- Explain that if you could talk about those things, you are likely to be *self smart*.

Exercise 6

- Ask students to stand up, form a large circle, and close their eyes. Say:

  > Begin walking in place. Imagine that you are barefoot. You are on a country lane, barefoot. As you walk barefoot on the country lane, the sun gets higher in the sky and the ground gets hotter and hotter—it's starting to burn your feet—so you take a small step to the right onto the cool grass. You walk in the grass for a while. It rained last night. The grass is wet and muddy. You can feel the mud between your toes.

- Ask them to open their eyes and think about whether they could feel everything you suggested. Tell them if they could and if they are usually graceful, good at sports, quick, agile, or strong, they are likely to be *body smart*.

Exercise 7

- Ask the students to sit down. Hum the following tunes and ask students to identify each one:

  □ "Dum dum dum—da" (Beethoven's Fifth Symphony)

  □ The tune from a popular commercial (McDonald's usually has a good one)

       ▫ The first line of "Twinkle, Twinkle, Little Star" (see whether they can complete the tune)

- Explain that if they could identify the tunes—if they love to play music, sing, listen to music, and make up tunes—then they are probably *music smart.*

8. Ask students to return to their assigned work groups.

9. Ask students to take out their paper plates (from step 5) and think about what they learned about each type of intelligence during the brief exercises. Have them decide which area or areas of intelligence they feel they have strong talent or interest in, or are drawn to. Then ask students to write on the paper plates something specific for each of those areas that leads them to believe that they possess this talent or are interested in developing it further. Have them use a different color of marker for each selected area. (Give students 5 to 15 minutes to finish.)

10. Ask group leaders to select the direction for their group to go in (clockwise or counterclockwise) as they share the information on their plates. Ask the leaders to give each person enough time to talk, to make sure that everyone has a turn, and to ensure that everyone listens to the person who is speaking.

11. When the groups have completed the previous step, the discussion can begin. To facilitate the discussion within the small groups, read the first question out loud, allow the groups a few minutes to discuss it, then read the next question.

DISCUSSION

- What do we usually think of when we say someone is intelligent? What skills might they have? What can they do well?

- Did most of the people in your group have the same type of intelligence and abilities?

- If so, why might this be a problem?

- Why might it be a good idea to have a group made up of people of several kinds of talents, intelligence, and abilities?

- Do you believe that the leader of a group must be the most intelligent or have the most abilities?

Seven Ways to Be Smart

PURPOSE   To help students discover the various ways to be smart

MATERIALS   Handout 1.12.1: Seven Ways to Be Smart (one per student)

DIRECTIONS
1. Arrange students into their assigned work groups.
2. Distribute the Seven Ways to Be Smart worksheet.
3. Ask participants to place a check mark next to any item they believe applies to them.
4. Ask participants to count the number of check marks they made under each category and write the total for each category.
5. Ask participants to identify someone in their class that they believe possesses each kind of intelligence or ability.
6. Ask each group to select a new leader by having the most recent leader point to another student to lead the group.
7. Ask each new group leader to facilitate discussion as each person in the group talks about the items he or she checked.
8. Use the following questions to conduct a large-group discussion.

DISCUSSION
- Did anyone check nearly all of the items in a particular category or categories?
- Did anyone check only one or two items in any category or categories?
- Did anyone select at least four or five items in *all* the areas?
- Why do you think some people have interests, skills, and abilities in only a few areas? Why might this be good? Why might this be not so good?
- Do you believe it is a good idea for someone to develop skills and talents in some areas but not in others? Is this what Olympians and other people who are successful in specific activities, sports, or professions do?

For each category, place a check mark by each item that applies to you. Then count the number of checked items in each category and write that number down on the blank line next to "Total." Finally, write the name of someone in class who you believe is smart in that way.

Word Smart

☐ I love to read.

☐ I like to tell stories.

☐ I talk on the phone for hours.

☐ I write poems sometimes.

☐ I can give good directions.

☐ I am good at Scrabble and other word games.

☐ I like to work crossword puzzles.

☐ I can remember things I read about and what other people tell me.

☐ I express myself well in words when talking.

☐ I express myself well in words when writing.

Total: _____

I believe _____ is *word smart*.

Number Smart

☐ I like solving puzzles and games that use logic.

☐ Numbers fascinate me.

☐ I like to work out problems in my head.

☐ I like math.

☐ I like to know that facts and figures are accurate.

☐ I like to test the logic of people's thinking, planning, and arguments.

☐ I like to play with numbers, do number games, add, subtract, multiply, and divide.

☐ I like puzzles like Rubik's Cube and puzzles in which you have to put things in order or make designs.

☐ It makes me uncomfortable when people don't seem to make logical sense.

☐ I like science.

Total: _____

I believe _____ is *number smart*.

Body Smart

☐ Playing sports is great.

☐ I move great on the dance floor.

☐ I'm good with tools.

☐ If I sit too long, I get uncomfortable.

☐ I think better when I'm moving, walking, or driving.

☐ I gesture a lot when I talk.

☐ I prefer to take things apart to learn how they work.

☐ I'm good at doing things with my hands.

☐ Given a choice, I prefer to play a sport or be out doing things rather than reading or sitting and talking.

☐ When I'm sitting, I find myself shifting positions a lot.

Total: _____

I believe _____ is *body smart*.

People Smart

☐ I like to watch people and try to figure out how they relate to one another.

☐ I like to work in groups on projects.

☐ I can usually tell you who the couples are at my school.

From *Inspiring Leadership in Teens: Group Activities to Foster Integrity, Responsibility, and Compassion,* © 2010 by Ric Stuecker, Champaign, IL: Research Press (800-519-2707, www.researchpress.com)

☐ I like it when people come to me for advice and counsel.

☐ I prefer team sports to individual sports.

☐ When I have a problem, I like to work it out with others.

☐ I like to be on teams, and I like to join clubs.

☐ I enjoy social events.

☐ I like tutoring and teaching others.

☐ I consider myself outgoing.

Total: _____

I believe _____ is *people smart*.

Self Smart

☐ I like spending time alone.

☐ I like to read or learn about things that will improve me.

☐ I prefer individual sports.

☐ I like to take time out to think about things.

☐ I like to make up my own mind about things.

☐ When I have a problem, I like to work it out for myself.

☐ I have only a few very close friends.

☐ I'm not comfortable in crowds.

☐ I like to express my own opinion about things.

☐ I like being strong willed and independent.

Total: _____

I believe _____ is *self smart*.

Music Smart

☐ I often have a song in my head.

☐ I find myself tapping out beats.

☐ I like to listen to music while doing other things.

☐ I play or would like to play a musical instrument.

☐ I like to dance.

☐ I often have a radio on or listen to a personal music player.

☐ I feel like I have good rhythm.

☐ I sometimes find myself singing or humming.

☐ I like to sing.

☐ I like to remember and repeat melodies.

Total: _____

I believe _____ is *music smart*.

Space Smart

☐ I find it easy to picture things in my head.

☐ I like to draw and sketch.

☐ I sometimes find myself doodling.

☐ I sometimes walk into a room and think the furniture is out of balance.

☐ I like to work with color.

☐ I like to take or look at photographs.

☐ Once I drive somewhere, I know how to get there again.

☐ Once I walk through a complicated building, I can usually find my way again.

☐ I can read a map.

☐ I like to imagine what things might look like from different angles and points of view.

Total: _____

I believe _____ is *space smart*.

ACTIVITY 1.13

The Tree of Me

PURPOSE

To allow students to discover and to honor each other's backgrounds

MATERIALS

Colored markers

Large pieces of blank paper (one sheet per student)

DIRECTIONS

1. Arrange students into their assigned work groups.

2. Tell students to think of their favorite tree. Ask some of them to tell you their favorite tree, then ask what all trees have in common (roots, trunk, branches).

3. Suggest to the students that, although there are various types of trees, each tree is unique. In the same way, we come from a variety of heritages, and each of us grows in our own unique way and direction.

4. Distribute the markers and give each student a sheet of paper. Ask students to draw the outline of a tree that fills the entire sheet. Ask them to make sure to include roots, trunk, and branches.

5. Ask students to label, on the left-hand side of their drawings, the roots, trunk, and branches. Tell them:

   • The roots represent the cultures they came from—what they inherited from their families.

   • The trunk represents them now—who they are and what the culture of their family and their life is like now.

   • The branches represent their hopes, dreams, and future.

6. Ask the students to write the following on their drawings under the three categories. Give them 15 minutes or so to complete this task:

   Roots

   • Your nationality or country of origin

   • Names of your parents, grandparents, and older relatives

51

- Anything your parents, grandparents, or older relatives have taught you
- Anything you are proud of concerning your heritage
- Special traditions and rituals you honor from your heritage

Trunk

- Members of your immediate family
- Close friends
- Sports you play
- Activities you love to do
- How you and your family celebrate special events
- Family pets
- Important events or dates

Branches

- Hopes and dreams
- Directions your life might take
- Personal spirituality
- Words you live by
- What you give or contribute to others
- Something you hope to accomplish
- Places you'd like to visit
- Future plans

7. Ask students, in their small groups, to hold their own tree in front of them and, in silence, look at each other's trees.

8. Designate a leader and a timekeeper in each group. Ask leaders to give each group member 3 minutes to explain what is on his or her drawing.

9. When the small groups are finished, ask whether anyone would like to explain his or her personal tree to the entire group. Give those students the opportunity to do so.

DISCUSSION

- What did you learn from this experience?
- Would you say you had more things in common with other people in your group or fewer things in common?
- In what part of your life did you find more things in common with others? More differences?
- Did you learn anything new or surprising about anyone here?
- Do you feel closer to the people in your group, or less close?

ACTIVITY 1.14

What I Need to Succeed

PURPOSE   To give students the opportunity to make commitments to be successful academically

MATERIALS   Handout 1.14.1: What I Need to Succeed (one per student)
Whiteboard or easel pad

DIRECTIONS   1. Arrange students into their assigned work groups.

2. Ask students to imagine a highly successful student.

3. Divide the space on the whiteboard or easel pad into three sections. Label the sections "Skills," "Attitudes," and "Behaviors."

4. Using brainstorming techniques, ask students to tell you the skills, attitudes, and behaviors successful students have. Record these on the whiteboard or easel pad.

5. Hand out the What I Need to Succeed worksheets. Give students approximately 5 minutes to complete them.

6. Designate a leader in each group. Ask the leaders to give each group member an opportunity to present to the small group the commitments he or she has made to be a successful student.

7. Ask students to post their worksheets in the display area designated for their group's work.

DISCUSSION   • Was it hard to make a commitment to be a successful student?

• What do you think will be most difficult for you to do to be successful?

• Looking at what others put on their worksheets, what do you have in common?

• How can your teachers and your small group help you to be successful?

I have the following goals to achieve in my classes:

1. _____

2. _____

3. _____

The people who can help me be successful are:

1. _____

2. _____

3. _____

4. _____

5. _____

To be successful, I will need these attitudes:

1. _____

2. _____

3. _____

I will need to use these skills:

1. _____

2. _____

3. _____

I will need to do these things:

1. _____

2. _____

3. _____

My commitment to be successful is at this level:

1	2	3	4	5
Low				High

Evaluation Meeting

PURPOSE

To allow students to reflect on their performance on teams and as leaders and to give feedback to teammates

MATERIALS

Handouts: Team Evaluation and Personal Evaluation worksheets (one each per student)

File folders (one per student and an additional folder for each team)

DIRECTIONS

1. Arrange students in teams at their workstations.

2. Hand out copies of the Team Evaluation and Personal Evaluation worksheets. Ask students to fill out both evaluation sheets privately.

3. Ask teams to select a leader for this discussion. (Teams should select a new discussion leader each week.)

4. Give students approximately 5 minutes to fill out the evaluation sheets. Allow more time if necessary.

5. Ask group leaders to begin to process the team evaluations by asking each student to read his or her evaluation to the group. Give the groups 5 minutes to read the evaluations (more if necessary).

6. When the groups are finished reading their evaluations aloud, ask group leaders to solicit reactions, comments, and feedback within their groups on the evaluations presented. Group leaders should ask whether the evaluations were accurate and fair, as well as solicit any specific feedback individuals might have to help the group work better and more cooperatively. Give groups about 5 minutes to discuss their feedback and comments.

7. Ask group leaders to process the personal evaluations by asking each team member to read his or her self-evaluation. Give students approximately 5 minutes to read their self-evaluations to their teams. Allow more time if needed.

8. When all the groups are finished, ask group leaders to solicit reactions, comments, and feedback within groups concerning the self-evaluations. Leaders should ask the groups whether they

think the individual self-evaluations were accurate and fair. They should also solicit feedback from specific individuals in the group concerning what they might want to contribute to make the group work more effectively.

9. Give the groups 5 minutes for discussing feedback (more if necessary).

10. Ask small groups to conclude their discussions. Then ask the group leaders to address the entire class and summarize what their group learned—without naming any specific members of their group or individual feedback given.

11. Ask the group leaders to put team evaluations in a file folder and hand the file to you.

12. Ask leaders to give each team member a file folder to put his or her personal evaluations in. Leaders then collect the files and hand them to you.

13. After the activity, read the files. Keep them for future reference.

Team Evaluation

Name _____ Date _____

On a scale of 1 to 10, rate how efficiently and effectively you believe this team worked this week.

        Very Poorly   1   2   3   4   5   **Very Well**

Who showed leadership on your team this week, and how did they show it?

<u>Who</u>   <u>How</u>

_____   _____

_____   _____

_____   _____

_____   _____

_____   _____

In your opinion, in what ways did your team function well this week?

_____

_____

_____

In your opinion, what specifically did your team accomplish this week?

_____

_____

_____

In your opinion, what specific obstacles does your team face in working together?

_____

_____

_____

What specific and positive suggestions do you have for overcoming these obstacles?

_____

_____

_____

From *Inspiring Leadership in Teens: Group Activities to Foster Integrity, Responsibility, and Compassion,* © 2010 by Ric Stuecker, Champaign, IL: Research Press (800-519-2707, www.researchpress.com)

Personal Evaluation

Name _____ Date _____

I would rate my level of positive participation, attitude, and concentration on the goals of my team as follows:

Very Low   1   2   3   4   5   **Very High**

I specifically contributed to my team's effort and success in the following ways:

_____

_____

_____

_____

_____

I might have contributed more by:

_____

_____

_____

_____

_____

Next week I would like to work on:

_____

_____

_____

_____

_____

From *Inspiring Leadership in Teens: Group Activities to Foster Integrity, Responsibility, and Compassion,* © 2010 by Ric Stuecker, Champaign, IL: Research Press (800-519-2707, www.researchpress.com)

Unit Resources

Armstrong, T. (1994). *Multiple intelligence in the classroom.* Alexandria, VA: Association for Supervision and Curriculum Development.

Armstrong, T. (1996). *Awakening genius in the classroom.* Alexandria, VA: Association for Supervision and Curriculum Development.

Armstrong's books are excellent materials for using multiple intelligence theories in the classroom and helping teachers plan for activities that involve using both sides of the brain.

Bodine, R. J., & Schrumpf, F. (1994). *Creating the peaceable school: A comprehensive program for teaching conflict resolution.* Champaign, IL: Research Press.

Bodine and Schrumpf's book is an excellent resource about peer negotiations, mediation, and class meetings and is a thorough model for teaching conflict resolution.

Karns, M. (1994). *How to create positive relationships with students: A handbook of group activities and teaching strategies.* Champaign, IL: Research Press.

Karns, M. (1995): *DOisms: Ten prosocial principles that ensure caring connections with kids.* Sebastopol, CA: National Training Associates.

Karns's work is outstanding for its use of games and activities to build prosocial skills and to develop a positive atmosphere in classroom learning communities.

Quaglia, R. J., Fox, K. M., & Hyatt, K. M. (1998). *Believing in achieving: Eight conditions that make a difference in the lives of all youth.* Orono, ME: National Center for Student Aspirations.

Quaglia's principles for developing realistic aspirations are fully explained in this useful resource.

Quiroz, H. C. (1997). *Start with the kids: 5 days to building a classroom community.* Santa Cruz, CA: Education Training and Research Associates.

This excellent little book for developing learning communities comes with a set of colorful posters of African saying and symbols and contains learning activities that are highly useful.

Introduction   63

Activities

Phase 1: Defining Criteria for Inspiring Leaders   71

2.1   Defining Inspiring Leadership   72

*Phase 2: Assigning Students to Publishing Companies and
    Positions*   75

2.2   Publishing Company Kickoff   76

2.3   Completing a Job Application   77

    Handout 2.3.1: Publishing Company Job Application   79

2.4   Obtaining Effective Letters of Reference   81

    Handout 2.4.1: Parts of an Effective Letter of Reference   82

    Handout 2.4.2: Sample Letter of Reference   83

2.5   Creating a Strong Résumé   84

    Handout 2.5.1: Parts of a Strong Résumé   85

    Handout 2.5.2: Sample Résumé   86

2.6   Interviewing for a Job Position   87

    Handout 2.6.1: Effective Interviewing Tips   89

2.7   Creating Publishing Companies   90

Phase 3: Research   93

2.8   Finding an Inspiring Leader to Study   94

2.9   Refining Research and Writing Skills   96

    Handout 2.9.1: Note-Taking   98

    *Handout 2.9.2: Rubric for Research Report on Your Inspiring
        Leader*   100

    Handout 2.9.3: Book Critique   101

Phase 4: Presentations   103

2.10   Creating and Giving a PowerPoint Presentation   104

    *Handout 2.10.1: Rubric for Inspiring Leaders PowerPoint
        Presentation*   106

2.11   Creating a Publishing Company Display   108

    *Handout 2.11.1: Rubric for Inspiring Leaders Hall of
        Fame Exhibit*   110

Phase 5: Evaluation and Awards   113

2.12   Evaluating Individual and Team Performances   114

2.13   Holding the BlueBerry Awards Ceremony   115

   Handout 2.13.1: Certificate of Award   117

Student Guide: Your Team's Publishing Company   119

Unit Resources   125

Studying Leadership: Researching Inspiring Leaders

The research component of *Inspiring Leadership in Teens* gives students a context within which they may better understand leadership, integrity, compassion, and inspiration. In this unit, students will research individual inspiring leaders and learn about additional leaders from the work of others. Then students will compare their own leadership development to leaders who have had an impact across a number of fields, locally, nationally, and internationally.

This unit helps you set up and oversee "publishing" companies (small groups) that each produce one book, with one chapter written by each student. Each company has three tasks:

- Task 1: Research, write, and publish a book of researched biographies of inspiring leaders.

- Task 2: Use the research to give PowerPoint presentations (one per team member) to the class.

- Task 3: Construct a display for the Inspiring Leaders Hall of Fame.

Ahead of time, be sure to read and fully understand the student guide (beginning on page 119). The guide outlines the step-by-step processes and criteria for students to follow to:

- Write a research paper, to be included as a chapter in their team's book.

- Meet requirements for their PowerPoint presentations.

- Create a team display for the Inspiring Leaders Hall of Fame.

- Construct a résumé.

- Complete a job application form.

- Obtain effective letters of reference.

There are also rubrics you may wish to use to evaluate student work.

Feel free to adapt the activities in this unit to your schedule and course objectives. Time constraints or other pressures may make it difficult for your students do all three projects. You could, for example, omit the Inspiring Leaders Hall of Fame. Although the entire process helps students gain valuable life skills, your course objectives may differ, leading you to simply assign publishing companies and job positions rather than going through the application and interviewing process. Or, if your students have limited writing skills and you are not able to spend time or find help to shore up this deficit, you may wish to substitute individual posters for the research papers. The appendix contains schedules for workshop and retreat settings, which may also give you ideas for traditional school-setting alternatives such as block scheduling.

SETTING UP THE LEARNING SPACE

With so much to accomplish during the research part of *Inspiring Leadership in Teens* (Phase 3 of this unit), it is important to transform the learning space into an efficient area for research—as well as the rest of the publishing process. Think of the space as a mini-library. Coordinating with other teachers to allow students to do some of the work in their areas will also save you space—and valuable class time. You might, for example, want to consider making arrangements with the computer lab teacher, librarian, and art teacher to do some of this work in their classes. It is possible, however, to complete this unit using computers with Internet access in your classroom or a traditional library-based approach. In addition, this unit assumes you have access to a projector for use with PowerPoint presentations, but having students create posters instead will suffice. The traditional ways still work! Obviously, every campus is different, so adapt the work to your specific resources and student needs.

Whether you direct this unit in a self-contained classroom or multiple settings will affect how you set up the learning space. In any case, however, students will need access to the Internet, the library, or both to research their chosen leaders.

In addition, as with the setup for Unit 1, you'll need team meeting areas (also good for quiet reading and writing), printing capabilities, and an art materials area for bookmaking. Add any missing bookmaking supplies: cloth, cardboard, brass tabs, glue, scissors, and blank paper. Books may be made safely in the classroom, but you may wish to engage the cooperation of an art teacher. To conserve space and keep students with other "publishing company" positions on task, limit the number of students in the art area to one or two from each team at a time. If you don't have PowerPoint presentation capability, make pieces of posterboard (16 × 20 inches or larger), markers, and other poster-making tools and supplies available.

If you do not wish to have students create books or other media while at school, assign those tasks as homework. Have students do the research and writing in the classroom then finish their other projects at home.

Creating a research library section in the classroom may help maximize class time. Students may examine and use books you have gathered from a school or public library without losing time obtaining them. As you probably know, school and public library media specialists are fantastic resources for suggestions of books and research materials, as well as teaching ideas that can help your leadership teaching flourish.

OVERVIEW OF UNIT

To conduct this unit in its entirety, you will need to guide your students through the five major phases of this project:

- Phase 1: Defining Criteria for Inspiring Leaders
- Phase 2: Assigning Students to Publishing Companies and Positions
- Phase 3: Research
- Phase 4: Presentations
- Phase 5: Evaluation and Awards

The following sections outline each phase.

Phase 1: Defining Criteria for Inspiring Leaders

A crucial first step is to construct a list of inspirational leader characteristics, or criteria. Students will use these criteria to select research subjects. In addition, these criteria will provide a framework within which students may think about how to measure (1) themselves as leaders and (2) the leaders they choose to study, honor, and emulate. (Leaders who meet the criteria set in this phase may come from any arena of human endeavor; see the research sections of the student guide, beginning on page 119, and a list of Nobel Peace Prize winners, available online at http://nobelprize.org/nobel_prizes/peace/laureates, or the website of Global Peacebuilders, at www.globalpeacebuilers.org, for some suggestions.)

Phase 2: Assigning Students to Publishing Companies and Positions

Once the criteria for inspiring leaders have been established, students will apply for job positions in simulated publishing company teams. Allow them to try for three potential positions each to give you some latitude as to whom you assign to which position. To be given a position in a publishing company, each student must fill out a job application, create an employment portfolio that includes a written résumé and three letters of reference, and be interviewed for 3 to 5 minutes by an employment committee.

The Employment Committee

Plan ahead for this committee because you should invite one or two other adults to join you. Consider asking a colleague, parent, or community member. Once the editors-in-chief have been interviewed and selected, they will also join the committee to interview applicants for other positions.

When the interviews are completed, you and the expanded committee will put together the publishing companies. First, the committee should review the employment portfolios, interview the other job applicants, then create potential companies, assigning roles. Finally, each company will be ready to work on the three major tasks, as outlined earlier.

Job Positions

In addition to editor-in-chief, you will need to assign team members to each of the following four roles within each publishing company:

- Assistant editor-in-chief
- Illustrator and bookmaker
- Proofreader
- Exhibit designer

If you need to assign one or two additional students to each company, separate the illustrator and bookmaker role into two positions or add an additional proofreader.

Phase 3: Research

Assessing and monitoring a number of factors during this phase will enhance the success of the entire unit.

Evaluating Students' Research Skills

Be sure to evaluate the research skills of your students. If skills are seriously lacking across the board, make sure you have the time and ability to teach classes on formal essay writing as well as the mechanics of presenting quoted material and citations in the manner you wish. One solution is to create an interdisciplinary alliance with an English, history, or other teacher in your school. This route will help both with the initial assessment of student skills and with getting the job done. Students could work on research and writing in other classes, extending the time you have for this undertaking.

Doing the Research

Many ways of finding inspiring leaders are at the students' fingertips. For example, have students search the Internet for halls of fame that have websites listing the people they honor along with brief biographies. Encourage students to explore people who have received the Nobel Peace Prize and select an individual (or organization) to research. Create a list of your own to share with your class, including the individuals you would especially like your students to research.

For all research projects, you might require students to use a minimum of three Internet sites and three traditional print sources from the library. In advance, decide what types of citations and notations for references you will require as well as how you want students to present quotations, take notes, and prepare an outline. You might require each student to read at least one full-length printed biography of the leader he or she is studying. For the sake of efficiency and classroom management, consider having students read while they are waiting to use computers or for teammates to finish activities.

Phase 4: Presentations

Individual PowerPoint presentations, chapters in the team books, and team exhibits should answer the following questions:

- What actions did this leader take that make him or her inspirational?
- What beliefs did this leader base his or her leadership on? What values and principles?
- Who inspired this leader?
- Where did this leader get ideas? What did he or she read or study?
- Were there any specific events in this person's life that caused him or her to become an inspiring leader?
- Were there any obstacles this leader had to overcome as a person?
- What did this leader achieve and contribute?
- Does this leader still inspire others today? If so, how? If not, why not?
- What characteristics of leadership displayed by this leader would you like to possess?

Each student will prepare and give a 5-minute PowerPoint presentation about the leader he or she has chosen to study. Although students should create and follow a script, they should not read word for word from the script. This is an excellent opportunity to begin to teach presentation skills—one of the essential leadership skills.

Allow some time for students to examine and read each other's chapters and books. If desired, create an area to display the team-created books. In addition, you may also like to ask students to critique another team's book, using the book critique form in Activity 2.9.

Designate some wall space for displaying each team's entry into the Inspiring Leaders Hall of Fame as well. Wall displays with portraits of a variety of heroes and explanatory notes may inspire your students to increase their own leadership skills.

Phase 5: Evaluation and Awards

Generalized rubrics are included in this unit (see Activities 2.9, 2.10, and 2.11) so you may—as objectively as possible—evaluate student work. Change and adapt them as you see fit. This is also another point at which involving one or more colleagues in co-teaching this unit may be especially helpful. It's a good idea for students to become familiar with the rubrics against which you will judge their work—both before and during the time they are working on their research projects and presentations. These tools will help guide students as they work.

Last, plan ahead for a gala event—the BlueBerry Awards Ceremony, more extravagantly known as the BlueBerry Awards Ceremony for Outstanding Books and Presentations. At this special event, you will present students with awards for their books and other projects.

The more lavish this presentation of awards, the more fun it will be. Some teachers wear evening gowns or tuxedos. Consider food as an option. Surprise presenters might be another option. Earning BlueBerry Awards should not be a competition; instead, recognize every student for an achievement, giving each the opportunity to approach the podium to receive an award. This is also an opportunity to inject humor and playfulness into learning. Finally, use or adapt the sample certificate provided in this unit (Activity 2.13).

UNIT PREPARATION

- Read and study the introduction to this unit.

- Make copies of the student guide (one per student) and any other information you wish to add to it.

- Plan for teaching the class as a whole group until you divide students into their publishing company work groups.

- Line up speakers from the community to speak to the class about who inspires them, how they view leadership, and how they, themselves, provide leadership to their families and the community. Appropriate speakers may include, for example, the school principal, parents, firefighters, police officers, local elected officials, reporters who write about leaders in the newspaper or other local media, coaches, members of community groups (for example, Chamber of Commerce, Lions Club), or representatives of groups that serve the community (for example, local shelters, United Way, other charities).

PHASE 1

Defining Criteria
for Inspiring Leaders

A CTIVITY 2.1

Defining Inspiring Leadership

PURPOSE

To create a list of characteristics, or criteria, that defines a leader as "inspirational"

MATERIALS

Whiteboard or easel pad

PREPARATION

Divide the whiteboard or easel pad into four sections, each labeled as follows and including some examples of leaders who:

- Lived what he or she preached
- Overcame many physical obstacles
- Led large groups of people
- Caused a change in how we treat each other

DIRECTIONS

1. Ask students to think about leaders they might identify as inspirational and write the name of one such leader on a piece of paper.

2. Ask students to list at least 10 characteristics that, in their opinion, make this leader inspirational. Refer students to the examples you listed on the whiteboard or easel pad. Give them about 5 minutes to work.

3. Have students take another look at their lists and circle the five characteristics they believe are most important in an inspirational leader. List all suggestions made on the board. (Note: There are several ways to brainstorm with students, helping them shape the criteria. In essence, you need to inspire high-energy participation and initially accept a wide range of potential answers.)

4. Ask the students to identify any suggestions that may have the same meaning. Cross off duplicates that truly have the same meanings. Then help students categorize the suggestions.

5. Ask, "Are there any items you believe don't belong on a list of criteria for inspiring leaders? Explain your reasoning." If conflict arises, ask one person to defend each side of the argument, explaining why a criterion should or should not stay on the list. After each person has finished his or her argument, ask the class to vote, with a show of hands, on whether the criterion stays or goes.

6. Tell the students:

> If I asked you to name inspiring leaders without construct-
> ing a set of criteria, you are likely to name people who are
> popular, good-looking, and good in their fields—but perhaps
> not truly inspiring. Instead, with your permission, I'd like
> to push you to think harder, go beyond the obvious, and
> refine this set of criteria. These tips should help you:
>
> • Choose an inspiring leader for study.
> • Be inspired by the leader you study.
> • Be inspired to achieve those qualities in your own life and
>   leadership endeavors.
>
> Keep in mind that these criteria will not only help you
> choose inspiring leaders for study, they will also help you:
>
> • Defend your choices in your presentations and research
>   papers.
> • Analyze your own personality for values, traits, and tal-
>   ents you have—or wish to possess—yourself.

7. Continue, "Now study the list some more. Should we add any additional criteria?" Help students construct and refine a defined set of criteria to use during this unit of leadership training.

8. When the group is satisfied that these criteria define an inspirational leader, ask someone to copy the list.

9. Type (or have a volunteer type) and make available the list of criteria to each student, titling it Inspiring Leaders Criteria (students will need this list in Activity 2.8).

PHASE 2

Assigning Students to Publishing Companies and Positions

Activity 2.2

Publishing Company Kickoff

The following five activities outline the major, but basic, lessons necessary to help ensure that students have the skills to complete this phase of this unit. Your students may have differing needs.

PURPOSE

To allow time for students to read and discuss the student guide and familiarize themselves with its content

MATERIALS

Student Guide: Your Team's Publishing Company (one per student)

PREPARATION

Use the student guide master (beginning on page 119) to make a copy of the guide for each student. If possible, have each guide comb-bound, stapled in three places along the left side, or otherwise bound securely.

DIRECTIONS

1. Distribute the student guide.
2. Ask students to read the guide silently or take turns reading it aloud in class. (If class time does not allow students to finish reading the guide, assign it as homework.)
3. Discuss and briefly clarify the information in the guide.

ACTIVITY 2.3

Completing a Job Application

PURPOSE
To help students understand and complete a job application to apply for positions in a simulated publishing company

MATERIALS
Handout 2.3.1: Publishing Company Job Application (two per student)

File folder to use as an employment portfolio (one per student)

Student guide (distributed in previous activity)

File box (or other place for storing student portfolios in class)

Whiteboard or easel pad

Optional: Overhead projector

PREPARATION
Make a large version of the job application handout on the whiteboard or easel pad, or in overhead transparency format.

DIRECTIONS
1. Distribute one copy of the Publishing Company Job Application to each student.

2. As a class, complete the large, whole-group form of the job application with sample fictional answers.

3. Have each student complete a first draft of the application with his or her own information, consulting the student guide to decide which positions to apply for.

4. Divide students into small groups of two to four.

5. Direct groups to review each other's applications and give feedback. (If necessary to remind students to be kind and helpful, review the three class rules outlined in Unit 1, Activity 1.6.)

6. Distribute a second copy of the job application to each student. Allow students time to improve their application answers, either during class or as homework. Encourage them to type or print neatly, and otherwise do their best work, on this final draft.

7. Distribute the file folders. Explain:

> Label this folder "Employment Portfolio." Store each item that may help you get a job in a publishing company.

Together, all the pieces you create for this portfolio will show as complete a picture as possible of who you are as a potential employee. Place your finalized application into your portfolio. Store your portfolio [location] so that you'll have it available each time we meet.

Print neatly in black or blue ink. Answer each question fully and accurately.

Name _____

(First Name, Middle Initial, Last Name)

Address _____

(Number and Street)

_____

(City, State, Zip Code)

Positions desired (you must list three):

1. _____

2. _____

3. _____

Education

Name and address of school

_____

_____

_____

Special skills and qualifications: List any job-related skills, training, honors, awards, and other special accomplishments.

_____

_____

_____

In three to five sentences, explain why you have applied for these positions and what makes you qualified to assume these responsibilities.

_____

_____

_____

_____

_____

From *Inspiring Leadership in Teens: Group Activities to Foster Integrity, Responsibility, and Compassion,* © 2010 by Ric Stuecker, Champaign, IL: Research Press (800-519-2707, www.researchpress.com)

References

	Name/Title	Address	Occupation
1.	_____	_____	_____
2.	_____	_____	_____
3.	_____	_____	_____

I certify that the information contained in this application is true and complete to the best of my knowledge. I understand that any false information on this application may be grounds for not hiring me or subsequently firing me.

Signature _____ Date _____

Obtaining Effective Letters
of Reference

PURPOSE   To understand the parts of an effective letter of reference, review a sample letter, and obtain three letters of reference

MATERIALS   Handout 2.4.1: Parts of an Effective Letter of Reference (one per student)

Handout 2.4.2: Sample Letter of Reference (one per student)

Employment portfolio

Student guide

DIRECTIONS 1. Distribute and have students read (silently or aloud) the Parts of an Effective Letter of Reference handout.

2. Distribute the sample letter of reference.

3. Using the first handout, guide students through identifying each part of the sample letter.

4. Discuss the strengths (and any potential weaknesses) of the sample letter.

5. Help students brainstorm potential reference letter writers: teachers, parents, an older brother or sister, real-world employers, babysitting clients, clergy, coaches, neighbors, a mentor, or the like.

6. Give students a firm deadline for turning in three letters (1 week is suggested).

7. Have students place their letters in their employment portfolios.

Ask the three people who are writing you a letter of reference to include the following:

Salutation

Use the salutation "To Whom It May Concern:"

Paragraph 1

The first paragraph of this reference letter should indicate *how* the reference knows you, *how long* he or she has known you, and *why* he or she is qualified to write a letter of reference.

Paragraph 2

This paragraph should include specific information about you (that is, the person applying for the job), state what you are capable of contributing, and explain why the person recommends you for the job.

Paragraph 3

In this paragraph, the reference should explain how your skills and experience match the job you are applying for.

Summary

The letter should conclude with a brief summary of why the reference is recommending you. The person providing the reference should state that he or she "highly recommends" you or "recommends you without reservation." The letter should close with "Sincerely," followed by the signature and typewritten name of the person providing the reference.

From *Inspiring Leadership in Teens: Group Activities to Foster Integrity, Responsibility, and Compassion,* © 2010 by Ric Stuecker, Champaign, IL: Research Press (800-519-2707, www.researchpress.com)

August 21, 2010

Mr. Edward Teacher
Wrestling Coach
City High School
City, State 00000

To Whom It May Concern:

This is a letter of reference for Jaden Q. Student. I have known Jaden since his freshman year, when he tried out for the wrestling team.

Jaden has been a hardworking member of the City High School wrestling team. He is a team player and always seems enthusiastic—both at practice and competitions. He is a leader on our team and an energetic supporter of all his teammates. During the past year, he was elected captain of our team.

I believe Jaden will be a contributing member on any team he joins. I highly recommend him.

Sincerely,

Edward Teacher

Edward Teacher

From *Inspiring Leadership in Teens: Group Activities to Foster Integrity, Responsibility, and Compassion,* © 2010 by Ric Stuecker, Champaign, IL: Research Press (800-519-2707, www.researchpress.com)

ACTIVITY 2.5

Creating a Strong Résumé

PURPOSE   To show students the elements of an effective résumé and help them create their own

MATERIALS   Handout 2.5.1: Parts of a Strong Résumé (one per student)

Handout 2.5.2: Sample Résumé (one per student)

Employment portfolio

Student guide

DIRECTIONS   1. Distribute and have students read (silently or aloud) the Parts of a Strong Résumé handout.

2. Distribute the Sample Résumé handout.

3. Using the first handout, guide students through identifying each part of the sample résumé.

4. Consulting the Parts of a Strong Résumé handout, discuss the strengths (and any potential weaknesses, such as the lack of art experience) of the sample résumé.

5. Ask the students to fill in the blanks on the Parts of a Strong Résumé handout. They will use this information to create a draft résumé.

6. Divide students into small groups of two to four students.

7. Direct groups to review each other's résumé drafts and give feedback. (If necessary to remind students to be kind and helpful, review the three major class rules outlined in Unit 1, Activity 1.6.)

8. Allow students time to improve their résumé content, either during class or as homework.

9. Assign the typing (or hand-printing) of a final résumé. Encourage students to line elements up neatly and otherwise do their best work on this final draft.

10. Have students place their final résumés in their employment portfolios.

Use this format to help design a résumé of your skills and experiences.

Full name _____

Address _____

Telephone number _____ E-mail address _____

Career objectives: To what career or position do you aspire?

_____

_____

_____

Education: List all schools attended and years of graduation.

_____

_____

_____

Experience: List any experiences you have had that might help you qualify for the positions you are seeking.

_____

_____

_____

Honors and awards: List any relevant honors or awards you have received.

_____

_____

_____

References: List the names, addresses, and phone numbers of three people who have agreed to recommend you for the positions you are applying for. (These may be the same people who are writing your letters of reference.)

_____

_____

_____

From *Inspiring Leadership in Teens: Group Activities to Foster Integrity, Responsibility, and Compassion,* © 2010 by Ric Stuecker, Champaign, IL: Research Press (800-519-2707, www.researchpress.com)

Jaden Q. Student
1300 Leadership Lane
City, State 00000
555–555–5555
StudentLeader@InternetServer.com

Career Objectives
To become an outstanding assistant editor-in-chief, proofreader, or illustrator

Education
1997 to 2003	City Elementary School
2003 to 2006	City Middle School
2006 to Present	City High School

Experience
1997 to Present	Classes in English, composition, research, spelling, and grammar
2007 to 2008	Captain of the wrestling team
2007 to 2008	Developed my own lawn-cutting business
2007 to 2008	Bagger—local supermarket

Awards and Honors
First Grade Through Sixth Grade	Perfect Attendance
Second, Fifth, Sixth, and Eighth Grade	Spelling Bee Champ

References
Ms. Paula Jones
7th Grade English Teacher
City Middle School

Mr. Edward Teacher
Wrestling Coach
City High School

Mr. James Grocer
Supervisor
Local Supermarket

From *Inspiring Leadership in Teens: Group Activities to Foster Integrity, Responsibility, and Compassion,* © 2010 by Ric Stuecker, Champaign, IL: Research Press (800-519-2707, www.researchpress.com)

Activity 2.6

Interviewing for a Job Position

PURPOSE
To allow students to learn about and practice interviewing effectively for a job

MATERIALS
Handout 2.6.1: Effective Interviewing Tips (one per student)
Employment portfolio
Student guide

DIRECTIONS
1. Ask students to recall what they learned from doing the interviewing activities in Unit 1. Remind them that this was where they interviewed each other, then presented their interviewee to the rest of the class. Then ask:
   - What do you think helped you get the most information from the interviewee?
   - What seemed to cause the person to shut down or just not give enough information?
   - As an interviewee, how did you feel? What would you have changed?

2. Continue with this statement:

   Today, we're going to practice interviewing each other, remembering to be sensitive to what it feels like to be an interviewer and an interviewee. Interviewers should keep in mind that they need to get as much information as possible in a short time.

3. Divide students into small groups of three. Direct groups to review each other's employment portfolios to prepare for interviewing each other. Allow 5 to 10 minutes for this process.

4. Distribute and review the Effective Interviewing Tips handout.

5. Ask students to follow this procedure for interviewing each other:
   - Designate each person in your group A, B, or C.
   - Have A interview B, with C observing.
   - Have B interview C, with A observing.
   - Have A interview C, with B observing.

- After each round, using the Effective Interviewing Tips hand-out, have the observer give the interviewer and interviewee feedback.
- They have 3 minutes for each interview and 30 seconds for each feedback opportunity.

6. After all three rounds, briefly allow students to share with the entire class what they did well as interviewees and what they think they need to improve.

7. Re-divide the students into new groups of three. Repeat step 5, but this time with 5 minutes per interview and 1 minute per feedback opportunity.

8. Debrief the activity through additional discussion of what students feel they did well as interviewees and what they think they need to improve. Reinforce the importance of being a good interviewer. That skill will serve editors-in-chief well when they join the employment committee.

Tips for Interviewers

- Give a warm welcome to the interviewee.

- Listen carefully to how the interviewee answers your questions. Ask follow-up questions for clarity or further information.

- Use the interviewee's résumé as a reference for your questions.

- Ask questions that help determine whether the interviewee is a good fit for the position.

- Thank the interviewee for applying for the position and give him or her an indication of when you will be making your decision.

Tips for Interviewees

- Be polite.

- Listen to the interviewer carefully.

- Look the interviewer in the eye when answering.

- Give accurate and truthful answers.

- Answer only what the interviewer asks. It is probably best not to elaborate unless the interviewer asks you to.

- If you do not understand a question, ask the interviewer to rephrase it.

- Thank the interviewer for considering you for the position.

From *Inspiring Leadership in Teens: Group Activities to Foster Integrity, Responsibility, and Compassion,* © 2010 by Ric Stuecker, Champaign, IL: Research Press (800-519-2707, www.researchpress.com)

ACTIVITY 2.7

Creating Publishing Companies

You may wish to teach Activity 2.8 first so that students not interviewing have focused research to do.

PURPOSE To provide students with experience in the job application and interviewing processes in a more formal setting

MATERIALS Employment portfolio

Effective Interviewing Tips (Handout 2.6.1 from previous activity)

Student guide

PREPARATION As outlined in the unit introduction, be sure to arrange for one, two, or more other adults to join you on the employment committee. Then confirm their availability for the specific class sessions you have set aside for the interviewing and selection process. You might need to allot two class sessions for this activity.

If appropriate for your course goals and setting, warn students in advance to dress in formal business attire, defining what you believe is appropriate and reasonable for your student population.

DIRECTIONS 1. Review and discuss the publishing company selection process as outlined in the student guide. Tell the students:

> Today, the employment committee will interview candidates for the editor-in-chief positions. The committee will then consult and choose one editor-in-chief for each company. These applicants will then join the committee. The expanded committee will interview the rest of you for other positions.
>
> Please bring your employment portfolio to your interview for the committee to review. Review the interviewing tip sheet and keep in mind what you learned from our interviewing practice in the last activity. Do your best, but keep breathing—don't get too stressed out—or you won't do as well as you could.

2. Introduce the employment committee.

3. Interview the editor-in-chief applicants.

4. Select one editor-in-chief per publishing company. Announce these choices to the class.

5. With the editors-in-chief now on the employment committee, continue interviewing applicants for the other positions.

6. Select the candidates and assign them to the other positions in the publishing companies. Announce the company rosters to the class and have companies meet for the first time.

7. Ask employees to begin exploring and preparing to perform their job duties by rereading the relevant information in the student guide. Answer any questions employees may have.

PHASE 3

Research

ACTIVITY 2.8

Finding an Inspiring Leader to Study

The following two activities outline the major, but basic, lessons necessary to help ensure that students have the skills to complete this phase of this unit. Your students may have differing needs.

PURPOSE

To provide each student with practice in collecting information from the Internet or library about potential inspiring leaders and to select an inspiring leader to write about

MATERIALS

Inspiring Leaders Criteria (one per student; completed by students during Activity 2.1)

Nobel Peace Prize Winners list (one per student; obtain a list from http://nobelprize.org/nobel_prizes/peace/laureates)

Student guide

DIRECTIONS

1. Review and discuss the research guidelines in the student guide, explaining, "We need to define what an 'inspiring leader' is in order to be able to select leaders who meet these guidelines."

2. Distribute and review the inspiring leaders criteria list.

3. Distribute and briefly discuss the Nobel Peace Prize Winners list.

4. Divide students into small groups of two to four.

5. Explain:

   With your small group, I am going to assign you 10 [or other number, dividing the list equally among all groups] of the names on this list of Nobel Peace Prize winners. Use the Internet or library to identify which area of accomplishment each of the people are (or were) leaders in—for example, chemistry, politics, or literature.

6. Allow groups to work for 20 to 30 minutes.

7. Work with the entire class to add the areas of accomplishment to each name on the Nobel Peace Prize Winners list.

8. Ask, "What area of accomplishment sounds the most interesting to you?" Pause for several students to share. Continue, "Your assignment is to find and print (or photocopy) a brief biography—one page or so—about one of the leaders listed in this area."

9. Allow students 10 to 20 minutes to do this or assign it as homework. (This is a good place to stop until the next class session.)

10. Have students take turns sharing some highlights of the biographies they gathered.

11. Now have students search for halls of fame in the same or other areas of accomplishment that interest them. Ask each student to find and print (or photocopy) two to four more brief biographies. (Note: Organizations such as the International Red Cross and Doctors Without Borders are okay to use in place of individual leaders.) If class time is not sufficient, assign this as homework.

12. Have students each share the one additional biography that they found the most interesting. Allow them to trade biographies if others are more interested in a particular leader than they are.

13. Direct students to choose one inspiring leader to study and submit their choice for your approval. If too many students select the same person, remind students that no two students in the same publishing company may select the same leader to study (however, it is okay to select the same leaders as students in *other* companies).

ACTIVITY 2.9

Refining Research and Writing Skills

PURPOSE   To help students refine and improve their research skills in note-taking, outlining, summarizing, paraphrasing, and providing proper citations, as well as drafting and editing their book chapters

MATERIALS   Handout 2.9.1: Note-Taking (seven or more forms per student)

A short (two- to five-page) research article about an inspiring leader no student chose

Handout 2.9.2: Rubric for Research Report on Your Inspiring Leader (one per student; however, you may wish to provide two copies per student, saving one for your actual assessment later in the unit)

Student guide

Handout 2.9.3: Book Critique (two per publishing company)

Prepared large format of note-taking form (written on white-board or easel pad, or on an overhead projector)

PREPARATION   If desired, arrange for a colleague to teach this lesson in your class-room or his or her classroom.

Locate a short research article about an inspiring leader no student chose.

Duplicate the research article and the note-taking form.

Create a large-group format of the note-taking form.

Later, at the appropriate stage, you will need to duplicate the Rubric for Research Report on Your Inspiring Leader and the book critique form.

DIRECTIONS   1. Briefly refer to the research guidelines in the student guide (see Research, step 7).

2. Distribute the research article. Allow students 5 to 10 minutes to read it.

3. Distribute one copy of the note-taking form to each student.

4. Guide students as they use the article to complete the form collectively. Record answers on the large-group version. Model appropriate summarizing and paraphrasing that avoids plagiarism.

5. Ask students to save this completed handout for Activity 2.10.

6. Distribute the other six copies of the note-taking form to each student or place them in a central area for students to take as needed.

7. Explain:

> You need to find at least three Internet sources and three traditional print resources. Use a new note-taking form for each source. You have [time period] to complete six or more forms fully and accurately. Let me know if you need help.

8. Revisit this lesson to teach (or have a colleague teach) additional writing skills as listed in the Purpose section of this activity.

9. Once students have completed their six note-taking forms, review the outlining information found in the student guide (see Research, step 8). Require students to each create a complete outline on their leaders.

10. Distribute and discuss the Rubric for Research Report on Your Inspiring Leader.

11. Assign the drafting, editing, and finalizing of the research papers that will become a chapter in each company's book.

12. Have each student complete a rubric on his or her individual report (book chapter), using the Research Report on Your Inspiring Leader rubric. Explain that the rubric gives students specific guidelines concerning the quality of their work and that these criteria will be used by you to evaluate each student's work. State that each report should be at least 10 pages long (you can adapt the required number of pages to reflect the ability of your students).

13. Have each company critique their own and then another company's book, using the book critique form.

Student name _____

Leader being researched _____

Information About Resource

Title of resource used _____

Author(s) _____

URL for a website resource _____

Information for a printed resource (for example, book, newspaper article, magazine article)

Publisher _____

Date of publication _____ Place of publication _____

Number of pages (if book) _____ Page number(s) where the information appears _____

Information About the Leader Chosen

Birthdate _____

Parents' names _____

Early events that shaped this leader

1. _____
2. _____
3. _____
4. _____
5. _____

Education

1. _____
2. _____
3. _____
4. _____
5. _____

Early accomplishments

1. _____
2. _____
3. _____
4. _____
5. _____

Turning points—events that changed the life of this leader

1. _____
2. _____
3. _____
4. _____
5. _____

Major accomplishments

1. _____
2. _____
3. _____
4. _____
5. _____

Honors and awards

1. _____
2. _____
3. _____
4. _____
5. _____

Legacy: Is this leader important today? Why or why not?

_____
_____
_____
_____

Student's name _____ Inspiring leader's name _____

Category	Quality			
	4	3	2	1
Internet use	Successfully uses suggested Internet links to find information. Navigates within these sites easily, without assistance.	Usually able to use suggested Internet links to find information and navigates within these sites easily, without assistance.	Occasionally able to use suggested Internet links to find information and navigates within these sites easily, without assistance.	Needs assistance or supervision to use suggested Internet links and/or to navigate within these sites.
Notes	Notes are recorded and organized in an extremely neat and orderly fashion.	Notes are recorded legibly and are somewhat organized.	Notes are recorded.	Notes are recorded only with peer or teacher assistance and reminders.
Amount of information	All topics are addressed, and all questions answered with at least two sentences each.	All topics are addressed, and most questions answered with at least two sentences each.	All topics are addressed, and most questions answered with one sentence each.	One or more topics were not addressed.
Quality of information	Information clearly relates to the main topic. It includes several supporting details and/or examples.	Information clearly relates to the main topic. It provides one or two supporting details and/or examples.	Information clearly relates to the main topic, but no details or examples are given.	Information is not offered or has little or nothing to do with the main topic.
Paragraph construction	All paragraphs include an introductory sentence, examples or details, and a concluding sentence.	Most paragraphs include an introductory sentence, examples or details, and a concluding sentence.	Paragraphs include related information but are typically not constructed well.	Paragraph structure is not clear. Sentences are not typically related to each other within the paragraphs.
Organization	Information is very well organized with well-conceived subheadings.	Information is organized. Subheadings are somewhat logical and helpful.	Information is organized, but subheadings are not especially logical or helpful.	The information appears to be disorganized.
Mechanics	The paper includes no grammatical, spelling, or punctuation errors.	The paper has a few grammatical, spelling, or punctuation errors.	The paper has some grammatical, spelling, or punctuation errors.	The paper has many grammatical, spelling, or punctuation errors.
Sources	All sources (information and graphics) are accurately documented in the desired format.	All sources (information and graphics) are accurately documented, but a few are not in the desired format.	All sources (information and graphics) are accurately documented, but many are not in the desired format.	Some sources are not accurately documented and/or none are in the desired format.

Note: Reports should be no shorter than 10 pages and no longer than 15 pages.

Names of company and members evaluating the book

_____

_____

_____

Title of book _____

Names of those who produced the book

_____

_____

_____

Rating the Cover

The cover of this book is well made and nicely put together.

                   Poor   1   2   3   4   5   6   7   Outstanding

The cover of this book is imaginative and creatively designed.

                   Poor   1   2   3   4   5   6   7   Outstanding

Rating One of the Chapters

Select one of the chapters to read and then rate the following:

The chapter was easy to understand.

                   Poor   1   2   3   4   5   6   7   Outstanding

I learned new information about this leader.

                   Poor   1   2   3   4   5   6   7   Outstanding

The illustrations (if any) were helpful.

                   Poor   1   2   3   4   5   6   7   Outstanding

The information was complete and thoroughly presented.

                   Poor   1   2   3   4   5   6   7   Outstanding

PHASE 4

Presentations

Creating and Giving a PowerPoint Presentation

The following two activities outline the major, but basic, lessons necessary to help ensure that students have the skills to complete this phase of this unit. Your students may have differing needs.

PURPOSE

To create and give a 5-minute PowerPoint presentation

MATERIALS

Handout 2.10.1: Rubric for Inspiring Leaders PowerPoint Presentation (one per student; however, you may wish to provide two copies per student, saving one for your actual assessment later in the unit)

Student guide

Collectively completed note-taking form (from Activity 2.9)

PowerPoint software with projection system and screen

Optional: Example of a short but effective PowerPoint presentation

PREPARATION

If desired, arrange for a colleague to teach this lesson.

Ensure that your PowerPoint software and presentation hardware are working properly.

DIRECTIONS

1. Refer students to the student guide section containing the requirements for PowerPoint presentations. Review and discuss this summary.

2. Distribute and discuss the Rubric for Inspiring Leaders PowerPoint Presentation.

3. If desired, show the exemplary presentation, having students critique and score it, using the content, vocabulary, and other non-speaking aspects of the rubric.

4. Project a blank PowerPoint screen onto the large-group screen and show students the mechanics of creating a PowerPoint presentation. Use the notes taken as a class in Activity 2.8 to create several slides collectively.

5. Give the following tips:

   - Due to limited space, slides force a writer to be brief and direct.

   - However, you may *say* more than you *write*—just keep your entire presentation to 3 to 5 minutes. In the software, there is a place to write additional notes to help guide your speaking, which you can see but your audience does not.

   Point this software feature out to the students.

   - You may bring in art, photos, or diagrams, but do so only if they're helpful to understanding how the leader is inspiring.

   - Follow the outline in your student guide closely, including the number of slides per section. (You can specify different numbers for the minimum and maximum slides required for the presentation.)

6. Ask each student to create a PowerPoint presentation based on his or her leader research.

7. Set and announce a firm deadline. A week is reasonable, but the deadline you choose depends on the availability of computers and other classroom factors.

Student's name _____ Inspiring leader's name _____

Category	Quality			
	4	3	2	1
Preparedness	Is completely prepared and has obviously rehearsed.	Seems fairly well prepared but might have needed a couple more rehearsals.	Is somewhat prepared, but it's clear that rehearsal was lacking.	Doesn't seem at all prepared to present.
Content	Shows a full understanding of the topic.	Shows a good understanding of the topic.	Shows a good understanding of parts of the topic.	Doesn't seem to understand the topic very well at all.
Enthusiasm	Facial expressions and body language generate a strong interest and enthusiasm about the topic in others.	Facial expressions and body language sometimes generate a strong interest and enthusiasm about the topic in others.	Facial expressions and body language are used to try to generate enthusiasm but seem somewhat faked.	Presenter uses facial expressions or body language very little. Doesn't generate much interest in the topic being presented.
Volume	Volume is loud enough to be heard by all audience members throughout the presentation.	Volume is loud enough to be heard by all audience members at least 90% of the time.	Volume is loud enough to be heard by all audience members at least 80% of the time.	Volume often too soft to be heard by all audience members.
Posture and eye contact	Stands up straight; looks relaxed and confident. Establishes eye contact with everyone in the room during the presentation.	Stands up straight and establishes eye contact with everyone in the room during the presentation.	Sometimes stands up straight and establishes eye contact.	Slouches and/or rarely or never looks at the audience during the presentation.
Speaks clearly	Speaks clearly and distinctly all the time and doesn't mispronounce any words.	Speaks clearly and distinctly all the time but mispronounces one word.	Speaks clearly and distinctly most of the time. Mispronounces no more than one word.	Often mumbles or can't be understood or mispronounces more than one word.
Vocabulary	Uses vocabulary appropriate for the audience. Extends audience vocabulary by defining words that might be new to most of the audience.	Uses vocabulary appropriate for the audience. Includes one or two words that might be new to most of the audience but doesn't define them.	Uses vocabulary appropriate for the audience. Does not include any vocabulary that might be new to the audience.	Uses several (five or more) words or phrases that are not understood by the audience.

From *Inspiring Leadership in Teens: Group Activities to Foster Integrity, Responsibility, and Compassion,* © 2010 by Ric Stuecker, Champaign, IL: Research Press (800-519-2707, www.researchpress.com)

Category	Quality			
	4	3	2	1
Stays on topic	Stays on topic all of the time.	Stays on topic most of the time.	Stays on topic some of the time.	It was hard to tell what the topic was.
Uses complete sentences	Always speaks in complete sentences.	Mostly speaks in complete sentences.	Sometimes speaks in complete sentences.	Rarely speaks in complete sentences.
Pauses	Pauses were effectively used two or more times to improve meaning and/or dramatic impact.	Pauses were effectively used once to improve meaning and/or dramatic impact.	Pauses were intentionally used but were not effective in improving meaning and/or dramatic impact.	Pauses were not intentionally used.
Time limit	Presentation is 5–6 minutes long.	Presentation is 4 minutes long.	Presentation is 3 minutes long.	Presentation is less than 3 minutes or more than 6 minutes.

ACTIVITY 2.11

Creating a Publishing Company Display

PURPOSE   To teach students the parameters for creating their publishing companies' displays for the Inspiring Leaders Hall of Fame and give them practice in working cooperatively

MATERIALS   Handout 2.11.1: Rubric for Inspiring Leaders Hall of Fame Exhibit (one per student; you may wish to make one extra copy of the rubric per team to use later in this unit when actually scoring each team's display)

Student guide

24 × 36-inch piece of posterboard (one per publishing company)

Various three-dimensional objects and additional painting or drawing supplies for creating displays

Optional: Prepared sample display

DIRECTIONS   1. Using the student guide, review the guidelines for the hall of fame exhibit.

2. Distribute and review the Rubric for Inspiring Leaders Hall of Fame Exhibit.

3. If available, guide the class in critiquing the sample display, using the rubric.

4. Discuss ways to work effectively and cooperatively to create the exhibit. If necessary, review the class rules developed in Unit 1.

5. If desired, provide (or have a qualified colleague provide) suggestions for adding creative elements to the display, such as three-dimensional objects, hand-painted or hand-drawn art, and the like. Depending on your setting, you may wish to provide some of these objects and challenge students to obtain others (e.g., vintage lightweight household objects, toys, bottle caps, and other items to represent the leaders' eras).

6. Assign the creation of a display to each company, giving a firm deadline for finalizing the project. A week is recommended, but you may adjust the deadline depending on the availability of time and materials or other classroom factors.

Student's name _____ Inspiring leader's name _____

Category	Quality			
	4	3	2	1
Graphics—clarity	Graphics are all in focus, and the content is easily viewed and identified from 6 feet away.	Most graphics are in focus, and the content is easily viewed and identified from 6 feet away.	Most graphics are in focus, and the content is easily viewed and identified from 4 feet away.	Many graphics are not clear or are too small.
Graphics—originality	Three or more of the graphics used on the poster reflect an exceptional degree of student creativity in their creation and/or display.	One or two of the graphics used on the poster reflect student creativity in their creation and/or display.	The graphics are made by the student but are based on the designs or ideas of others.	No graphics made by the student are included.
Graphics—relevance	All graphics are related to the topic and make it easier to under-stand. Each borrowed graphic has a source citation.	All graphics are related to the topic and most make it easier to understand. Each borrowed graphic has a source citation.	All graphics relate to the topic. Most borrowed graphics have their source cita-tions.	Graphics don't relate to the topic, and/or several borrowed graphics don't have their source citations.
Required elements (as outlined in the student guide)	The poster includes all required elements as well as additional helpful information.	All required elements are included on the poster.	All but one of the required elements is included on the poster.	Several required elements were missing.
Labels	All items of impor-tance on the poster are clearly labeled, with labels that can be read from at least 3 feet away.	Almost all items of importance on the poster are clearly labeled, with labels that can be read from at least 3 feet away.	Several items of impor-tance on the poster are clearly labeled, with labels that can be read from at least 3 feet away.	Labels are too small to view, or no important items were labeled.
Accuracy	At least seven accurate facts are displayed on the poster.	Five or six accurate facts are displayed on the poster.	Three or four accurate facts are displayed on the poster.	Fewer than three accurate facts are displayed on the poster.
Attractiveness	The poster is excep-tionally attractive in terms of design, layout, and neatness.	The poster is attractive, in terms of design, layout, and neatness.	The poster is accept-ably attractive, but it may be a bit messy.	The poster is distract-ingly messy or very poorly designed. It is not attractive.
Mechanics	Spelling, captialization, and punctuation are correct throughout the poster.	There is one error in spelling, capitalization, or punctuation.	There are two errors in spelling, capitalization, or punctuation.	There are more than two errors in spelling, capitalization, or punc-tuation.

From *Inspiring Leadership in Teens: Group Activities to Foster Integrity, Responsibility, and Compassion,* © 2010 by Ric Stuecker, Champaign, IL: Research Press (800-519-2707, www.researchpress.com)

Category	Quality			
	4	3	2	1
Grammar	There are no grammatical mistakes on the poster.	There is one grammatical mistake on the poster.	There are two grammatical mistakes on the poster.	There are more than two grammatical mistakes on the poster.
Knowledge gained	Can accurately answer all questions related to facts on the poster and the processes used to create the poster.	Can accurately answer more than 75% of questions related to facts on the poster and the processes used to create the poster.	Can accurately answer about 75% of questions related to facts on the poster and the processes used to create the poster.	Appears to have insufficient knowledge about the facts on the poster or the processes used to create the poster.

PHASE 5

Evaluation and Awards

ACTIVITY 2.12

Evaluating Individual and Team Performances

PURPOSE

To provide students with an opportunity to evaluate themselves and others and to receive feedback from peers and teachers

MATERIALS

The three rubrics from Activities 2.9, 2.10, and 2.11

PREPARATION

Select which rubrics you wish to use at which times. Decide which rubrics to use as self-, peer-, and teacher-evaluation tools (one, two, or all).

If you have not done so already, duplicate each rubric provided in the previous activities, as appropriate for the number of students and publishing companies you have and the types of evaluations (self-, peer-, teacher-) desired.

DIRECTIONS

1. Review each rubric as you use it.

2. Discuss appropriate ways to consider and evaluate one's self and a peer or company. For example, circle or check the box for each category that you believe accurately indicates the level achieved by the report, presentation, or poster. Give the checked or circled rubrics to the person or team that produced the report, presentation, or poster.

3. Evaluate students and companies and, as you deem appropriate, have students and companies evaluate themselves and each other.

Activity 2.13

Holding the BlueBerry Awards Ceremony

PURPOSE   To reward students for all their hard work in this unit and to reinforce their growth as leaders

MATERIALS   Handout 2.13.1: Certificate of Award (one per student)

PREPARATION   Duplicate and complete one Certificate of Award per student. Be sure to provide an award to each student to help reinforce the learning and affirm their efforts and contributions.

If desired, arrange for an evening event, food, and other trimmings (for example, parent and other dignitary invitations, formal attire, typed program) to make this event extra special.

DIRECTIONS   1. Announce the date and time of the BlueBerry Awards Ceremony. If desired, give students invitations to distribute to parents and other dignitaries.

2. Hold the BlueBerry Awards Ceremony, making it as special as possible and helping students enjoy the process.

Certificate of Award

Awarded to _____

for Outstanding Work
in the Area of

Date _____

Signed _____
Teacher

Signed _____
Principal

From Inspiring Leadership in Teens: Group Activities to Foster Integrity, Responsibility, and Compassion. © 2010
by Ric Stuecker, Champaign. IL: Research Press (800-519-2707, www.researchpress.com)

STUDENT GUIDE: YOUR TEAM'S PUBLISHING COMPANY

OVERVIEW

You and your teammates are going to form a publishing company. Your company will publish a book, create a visual display for an Inspiring Leaders Hall of Fame, and give PowerPoint presentations about the inspiring leaders you select. Each of you will:

- Write a chapter of the book about one inspiring leader of your choice

- Create a PowerPoint presentation about your chosen leader

- Create part of a hall of fame display

The chapter and presentations will be researched biographies of your chosen leader, someone you believe is inspiring and who meets the criteria of an inspiring leader (the class establishes these criteria at the beginning of this unit).

Each team member will be assigned a job in the publishing company. The jobs are:

- Editor-in-chief: Organizes and oversees the entire project of the publishing company, sees that the team meets deadlines and that the quality of work is excellent, and helps other team members with assigned tasks, if necessary.

- Assistant editor-in-chief: Helps the editor-in-chief with his or her duties and provides leadership when the editor-in-chief is absent.

  Your team has the option of dividing specific tasks between the editor-in-chief and the assistant editor-in-chief.

- Proofreader: Makes sure there are no errors in spelling, grammar, or language usage in the chapters prepared for the book. Reads and marks any changes the authors of the chapters need to make before the final version is published in the team's book. Teams may assign more than one proofreader to proofread the book.

- Illustrator-bookmaker: Selects illustrations for the book and cover, and designs and creates—or oversees the design and creation of—the cover, end pages, table of contents, and pagination. Also constructs the book or supervises the process.

  Each team is required to produce a simple book with a cloth cover over cardboard with cardboard hinges. The cover must include the book title and authors' names. Construct the book using brass tabs or yarn. One of the editors may work with the illustrator-bookmaker to construct the book.

- Exhibit designer: Coordinates the work of the publishing company to develop and produce a display of all leaders researched by the team, then creates the final look of the exhibit. One of the editors may work with the exhibit designer.

Your teacher may decide to add other roles for which you may apply. If so, he or she will give you a description of the role and its responsibilities.

HIRING THE EDITOR-IN-CHIEF AND OTHER ROLES

You will select three roles you'd like to play in the publishing company. Then you'll create a résumé, fill out a job application, and submit three letters of reference. You'll be interviewed by a employment committee (of your teacher's choosing) and hired for one of the positions, based on your interview.

Résumé

You will need to create a typed résumé to submit to the employment committee. Résumés must follow

From *Inspiring Leadership in Teens: Group Activities to Foster Integrity, Responsibility, and Compassion,* © 2010 by Ric Stuecker, Champaign, IL: Research Press (800-519-2707, www.researchpress.com)

the format explained by your teacher and shown in the sample résumé in Activity 2.5.

Job Application

You must fill out a job application listing the three jobs you are interested in doing for your publishing company team. Your teacher will give you a job application to complete.

Letters of Reference

You will need to obtain and present to the employment committee three letters of reference. These may come from such people as teachers, parents, an older brother or sister, real-world employers, babysitting clients, clergy, coaches, neighbors, a mentor, or the like.

Interviews

After submitting your résumé, job application, and letters of reference, you will be interviewed by the employment committee. You will be rated according to the following scale, with a total of 22 points possible:

    1 to 5 points for the interview

    1 to 3 points for the résumé

    1 to 5 points for the job application

    1 to 3 points for each letter of reference

Then the employment committee will place you on a publishing company team and assign your job position.

Steps in Hiring the Members of the Publishing Company

Step 1

The teacher assembles an employment committee of other teachers, administrators, staff members, community volunteers, or interested parents. The committee should include two or three (or up to five) people, including the teacher.

Step 2

Candidates for editor-in-chief submit their résumés, applications, and letters of reference. The employment committee interviews these candidates and evaluates them using the point system outlined above. After the interviews, the committee appoints one editor-in-chief to each company.

Step 3

Editors-in-chief join the employment committee. Other candidates submit applications, résumés, and letters of reference to the committee.

Step 4

The expanded employment committee interviews candidates for assistant editors-in-chief. With the advice and approval of the committee, each editor-in-chief chooses an assistant. Candidates are rated on the same scale as described earlier.

Step 5

The employment committee and the editors-in-chief interview each of the candidates for the other positions. With the advice and approval of the committee, editors-in-chief select their teams. Candidates are rated on the same scale as described earlier.

Step 6

Teams assemble and review this guide together.

RESEARCH

The newly formed publishing company teams focus on research. Using the criteria established by the class for identifying inspiring leaders, each team member selects a leader to study. No two students on the same team may choose the same leader. Students on other teams, however, may select the same leaders as students on other teams. Here are some steps you should take to write a researched biography successfully.

Step 1

Select an area of excellence you may want to select a leader from, or use the list of Nobel Peace Prize winners your teacher will provide. For now, here are some areas of human endeavor to consider:

- Historical
- International
- National
- Sports
- Politics
- Military
- Business
- Educational
- Social change, social justice
- Religious
- Peace
- State or local leaders

Step 2

Nearly every area of excellence has a hall of fame, and most halls of fame have websites. If you use a search engine such as Google, type in "hall of fame" and you'll find a multitude of halls and their websites.

Step 3

From the Nobel Peace Prize winners list, a selected hall of fame, or another list provided by your teacher, select a preliminary list of two to four people you may want to write about for your biographical chapter, present about to the class in a PowerPoint presentation, and create an exhibit about, demonstrating their leadership abilities.

Step 4

Print or photocopy and read short biographies found in your school's library or on the Internet of each of the two to four leaders you have chosen.

Step 5

Select one of the leaders to study. Make sure you can find enough biographical information about this leader in your school's library and on the Internet on which to base your research and writing.

Step 6

Find at least three sources on the Internet and three print sources for information about your leader. You may use, for example, an encyclopedia or other library reference for one print source and a book-length biography for another. (Your teacher may alter these requirements.)

Step 7

Take notes from each source about the leader you chose. You will need the notes for your book chapter, PowerPoint presentation, and hall of fame display. You should use the note-taking sheets your teacher will provide. To help you start thinking, here is a list of facts about your selected leader to include in your notes:

- Birthplace, parents, the early years
- Events that formed this person into a leader
- Influences—Who influenced the thinking, attitudes, and actions of this leader?
- Education—How did this person become educated? Did his or her education influence his or her leadership? If so, how? If not, why not?
- Leadership actions taken during the leader's life (for example, decisions a leader made, an organization a leader founded, an action a leader took that made an important difference or change).
- Turning points—Were there any major events that changed the direction of this leader's life?
- Accomplishments
- Awards and honors
- Influence of this leader today

Step 8

Adding your specific notes, write an outline for your biography. Here is a sample outline, without specific notes:

I. Introduction

In general terms, introduce the person and explain to the reader why this person is an inspiring leader.

II. Early Years

    a. Birthplace

    b. Parents and brief family history

    c. Early events that shaped this leader's life

    d. Education

    e. Early influences—What and who shaped this leader's thinking, attitudes, and behaviors?

III. Active Years

    a. Actions this person took to become a leader

    b. Events that shaped him or her as a leader

    c. Obstacles this person may have had to overcome

    d. What were the turning points in his or her life?

IV. Achievements

    a. Accomplishments

    b. Awards and honors

    c. Is this leader still important? How do his or her actions influence us today? Is this person still an inspiring leader? Why or why not?

V. Conclusions

    a. What is it about this leader that inspires you?

    b. What hopes and dreams do you have that have been influenced by this leader?

    c. How do *you* want to be remembered? For what accomplishments and contributions? Why?

Step 9

Write a draft of your paper following the outline you created. Be sure to use information directly and indirectly from your research sources. Follow your teacher's instructions on citing sources. Follow the rules to indicate when you are quoting directly from a source by using quotation marks or indentations. When you summarize or paraphrase from one of your sources, be sure to cite your source accurately and completely.

Step 10

Ask the proofreader, his or her assistant, or one of the editors to read your paper for content as well as for spelling and grammatical errors. Compare your work to the research paper rubric your teacher will provide.

Step 11

Based on the information you gained in step 10, make corrections as necessary. Rewrite your paper as many times as it takes until you and your team are satisfied your work is of excellent quality.

Step 12

Ask the illustrator-bookmaker which font he or she wants you to use for your final, typed copy and what illustrations you might include. Hand in your final version to your illustrator-bookmaker.

Your report will be evaluated by your teacher on the following criteria. Again, consult the rubric for the research report for more details:

- Content
- Writing style
- Correct spelling, punctuation, and grammar
- Correct use of citations
- Effective use of language
- Depth of research
- Your ability to analyze the character of this leader based on the leadership criteria created by the class

BOOK

You and your teammates are responsible for creating the final researched book. The illustrator-bookmaker may need your assistance. He or she will design the covers of your book and fasten it together. (See the *Make a Simple Book* instructions on page 124 in this guide.)

Your completed book will be displayed in the classroom during this research unit. It will be evaluated for possible BlueBerry Awards to be presented at the end of this unit at an awards ceremony celebrating the conclusion of your leadership research.

POWERPOINT PRESENTATIONS

The notes you took for your research report form the basis for your PowerPoint presentation. Your teacher may hold some classes to teach you how to create a PowerPoint slide show, and he or she might give you more detailed instructions than space allows here.

You can divide your presentation according to the outline you created for your paper, with each slide demonstrating a small part of the outline. Here is a generic outline for a slide show, taken from the outline for the research paper shown earlier:

Slide 1: Title of your presentation

Slides 2 Through 5: Early Years

- Birth information
- Parents
- Childhood experiences
- Early education

Slides 6 Through 10

- Later education
- Later experiences
- Early leadership roles

Slides 7 Through 15

- Chronological study of person's role as a leader
- Key turning points in his or her life
- Specific achievements

Slides 16 Through 20

- Later years
- Achievements, honors, and awards
- Legacy

Slides 21 through end

- Citation of resources and acknowledgments

Because you will present your slide show to the class, practice making your presentation ahead of time. Keep in mind that your teacher will evaluate your presentation both on the content of the slide show and on how well you speak and use presentation skills. (For specific details, see the rubric for slide shows in Activity 2.10.) Slide shows will be honored at the BlueBerry Awards ceremony.

INSPIRING LEADERS HALL OF FAME: AN EXHIBIT

You and your teammates will design and display your work in a classroom Inspiring Leaders Hall of Fame. You will be responsible for a part of your team's display. Your individual display will be about the leader you have researched and should include the following:

- At least one picture of your inspiring leader
- A time line from birth through significant events in your leader's life
- A list of accomplishments, honors, and awards
- A one-page typed biography
- A one-page discussion of why your leader demonstrates traits of inspiring leadership as defined by your class (summarized from your book chapter)

Coordinate your part of the display with the rest of your team. Remember, the exhibit designer for your team is responsible for the final look of the team's display. You will need to work cooperatively with him or her. You may use your own art materials or those provided in the art center of your classroom.

Depending on your teacher's approach, your part of your team's exhibit may be evaluated by your teacher. He or she will give you the rubric for evaluating this display (Activity 2.11). Your teacher may also evaluate your team's display for potential BlueBerry Awards.

Make a Simple Book

Materials

- Cardboard
- Cloth
- Elmer's white school glue
- Tape
- Brass tabs (three per book)
- Colored construction paper or heavyweight bond (for the inside covers)
- Paper cutter that will cut cardboard
- Colored markers
- Pencils
- Scissors
- Handheld hole punch
- 8.5 × 11-inch copy paper in a variety of colors

Instructions

1. Out of cardboard, cut two hinges and two covers as shown. The covers should be slightly larger than the paper used. If the book will use 8.5 × 11-inch paper, the cover should be approximately 9 × 11 inches.

2. Tape hinges to covers as shown below.

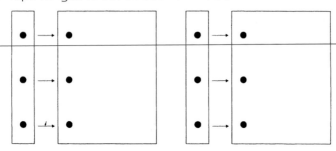

3. Cover hinges and covers with cloth. Decorate cover.
4. Glue blank paper to cover ends of cloth inside each cover.
5. Insert brass tabs into hinges as shown to the right.

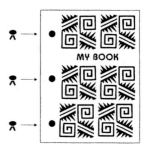

MY BOOK

From *Inspiring Leadership in Teens: Group Activities to Foster Integrity, Responsibility, and Compassion,* © 2010 by Ric Stuecker, Champaign, IL: Research Press (800-519-2707, www.researchpress.com)

Unit Resources

Search for Common Ground
www.sfcg.org

Global Peacebuilders
www.globalpeacebuilders.org

The rubrics used in Unit 2 were derived from Rubistar
(http://rubistar.4teachers.org).

UNIT 3: CREATING LEADERSHIP PORTFOLIOS

Introduction   129

Activities

Phase 1: Inspiring Leadership Self-Assessment Workshop   133

3.1   Taking a Leadership Self-Inventory   134

   Handout 3.1.1: Leadership Self-Inventory   135

   Handout 3.1.2: Transferring and Interpreting Self-Inventory Scores   137

   Handout 3.1.3: Self-Inventory Interpretation Chart   138

3.2   Acquiring Characteristics of Inspiring Leaders   139

   Handout 3.2.1: Characteristics of Inspiring Leaders   141

   Handout 3.2.2: Goal-Setting Guide   152

   Handout 3.2.3: My Goals   153

3.3   Exploring Personal Integrity and Responsibility   155

   Handout 3.3.1: Personal Integrity Assessment   157

   Handout 3.3.2: Taking On Responsibilities   158

3.4   Making Personal Agreements   160

   Handout 3.4.1: Personal Agreements   162

Phase 2: Creating a Personal Mission Statement   167

3.5   Exploring Personal Dreams   168

   Handout 3.5.1: What Is a Personal Mission Statement?   170

   Handout 3.5.2: Personal Dreams   171

3.6   Discerning What I Value in Life   172

   Handout 3.6.1: Value Statements   173

3.7   Identifying Characteristics I Admire   174

   Handout 3.7.1: Characteristics I Admire   176

3.8   Understanding Strengths and Roadblocks   177

   Handout 3.8.1: Strengths Versus Roadblocks   178

3.9   Identifying Contributions I Hope to Make   179

   Handout 3.9.1: Contributions I Can Make   181

3.10   Creating a Personal Mission Statement   182

   Handout 3.10.1: My Personal Mission   183

3.11   Simplifying My Personal Mission Statement   184

Phase 3: Advertising Your Inspiring Leadership Strengths   *189*

Activity 3.12   Making a Personal Brochure   190

   Handout 3.12.1: Personal Brochure Contents   *192*

   Handout 3.12.2: Sample Brochure   *193*

Unit Resources   **194**

Creating Leadership Portfolios

During this segment of leadership training, the focus shifts to personal reflections on the inspiring leadership qualities, talents, skills, attitudes, and behaviors each individual possesses. Students examine some qualities of inspiring leaders and assess themselves as to which qualities they possess and which they want to develop. Students learn about and examine their personal leadership styles. They construct a personal mission statement, which sets goals and inspires. They manufacture a personal brochure, detailing their mission, talents and skills, hopes and dreams, personal experiences as leaders, and goals for the future.

Through completing a leadership portfolio, students will:

- Assess themselves as leaders.

- Set personal goals to accomplish.

- Gain a realistic understanding of their personal leadership style, talents, and skills.

- Set personal skill objectives to continue to develop.

This unit consists of three phases:

- Phase 1: Inspiring Leadership Self-Assessment Workshop— Students identify their leadership strengths and weaknesses and set goals for improvement.

- Phase 2: Creating a Personal Mission Statement—Students build on what they've discovered about themselves by creating and refining a personal mission statement, exploring dreams and values, and learning ways to overcome weaknesses.

- Phase 3: Advertising Your Inspiring Leadership Strengths— Students use all of the information they have discovered and created in the first two phases to develop a personal brochure, "advertising" themselves as inspiring leaders.

COMPONENTS OF AN INSPIRING LEADER

The activities in this unit are based on the following components that many inspiring leaders possess in varying degrees. They are not meant to be a total and comprehensive list, but they are essential.

They Have Integrity

Inspiring leaders do what they say they will. Integrity means that leaders follow their own rules, have self-discipline, and speak the truth. Leaders with integrity are willing to take on any responsibility, no matter how small.

They Are Compassionate

Inspiring leaders care about others. Compassion means that a leader can "walk in the moccasins" of another person and understand the world from another's point of view. Compassion means a leader is willing to forgive others, ask for forgiveness, and move forward.

They Have a Sense of Belonging

Inspiring leaders feel they are part of a team, yet they maintain their individuality when working with others. They value the contributions of their teammates. They respect fellow team players.

They Have Aspirations

Inspiring leaders dream large dreams for themselves and for their teams. Aspiring leaders set realistic and doable goals for themselves and others. They mark their accomplishments and build on their achievements.

They Are Self-Reflective

Inspiring leaders, without being narcissistic, examine themselves and their decisions. They understand their personal skills, aptitudes, attitudes, and behaviors. They ask others for feedback and advice. They honor their own and others' accomplishments.

They Are Decisive

Inspiring leaders can make a decision. Once they have made a decision, they act on it. Having acted, they evaluate the results of their decisions and make adjustments. Inspiring leaders are able to accept the consequences of their decisions and actions.

They Are Curious and Creative

Inspiring leaders are inquisitive, ask many questions, explore many options, and seek the counsel of other members of their team. Often they seek new and different solutions, and they honor the creativity of others.

They Are Fun and Have a Sense of Humor

Inspiring leaders truly enjoy leading, being with others, and working together with enthusiasm. They enjoy a good joke, and they can laugh at themselves and with others. They often seem to have endless energy.

They Are Role Models

Inspiring leaders are people others admire and sometimes model themselves after. Leaders listen to others, make others feel comfortable, and are sometimes sought out for advice and support.

They Are Confident

Inspiring leaders put forth their best effort, have confidence in their abilities and decision-making, set high goals, and take effective actions to achieve them.

PHASE 1

Inspiring Leadership Self-Assessment Workshop

This self-assessment workshop will take three or more class meetings. It explores the 10 characteristics of inspiring leadership explained in the introduction to this unit. Students take a personal inventory of these components and assess their strengths by using an interpretive chart. Following the inventory, students are asked to evaluate how they are doing with each of the 10 components. They select an area of concern for each component and write goals and the steps they will take to improve in these areas. Finally, students construct and set short-term, medium-term, and long-term goals to increase their leadership skills, attitudes, and behaviors.

ACTIVITY 3.1

Taking a Leadership Self-Inventory

PURPOSE   To assess and interpret personal strengths and weaknesses by completing a leadership self-inventory

MATERIALS   Handout 3.1.1: Leadership Self-Inventory (one per student)

Handout 3.1.2: Transferring and Interpreting Self-Inventory Scores (one per student)

Handout 3.1.3: Self-Inventory Interpretation Chart (one per student)

DIRECTIONS
1. Distribute the Leadership Self-Inventory.
2. Ask students to take the inventory.
3. When students are finished, distribute and explain the Transferring and Interpreting Self-Inventory Scores handout. Then ask them to transfer and total the scores for each characteristic.
4. Distribute and explain the Self-Inventory Interpretation Chart. Instruct students to transfer the totals from the previous handout to this chart.
5. Encourage volunteers to share their interpretation results, discussing what they discovered from taking the inventory.

DISCUSSION
• Do you believe the self-inventory is accurate? Why or why not?
• Were you surprised by anything you learned from taking the inventory? If so, what?
• Does the inventory give you any indication of characteristics you might want to work on? If so, what might they be?

Below are 40 statements that may or may not be true for you. Read each statement and decide whether it is always true, often true, sometimes true, or never true. Allocate points as shown below. Be as honest as you can be. Respond to each item. When you have completed this inventory, you will be able to score it on an interpretation chart your teacher will give you.

Scoring Scale

The statement is always true = 3 points

The statement is often true = 2 points

The statement is sometimes true = 1 point

The statement is never true = 0 points

<u>Statement</u>   <u>Points</u>

1. I tell the truth to my team members.   _____

2. I can see other team members' points of view.   _____

3. I feel like I am a part of a team.   _____

4. I have many dreams for myself.   _____

5. I think about the consequences of my decisions.   _____

6. I can make a decision.   _____

7. I ask many questions.   _____

8. I have fun working with other team members.   _____

9. I am a positive role model.   _____

10. I am confident I will reach my goals.   _____

11. I follow the rules and standards I set for myself.   _____

12. I care about others on my team.   _____

13. I attempt to accept everyone and make them feel they are an important part   _____
of the team.

14. I set doable goals for myself and my team.   _____

15. I assess feedback others give me and make changes.   _____

16. Once I decide something, I act on it.   _____

17. I look for unique and different solutions.   _____

18. I can laugh at myself.   _____

19. My teammates ask me for my advice and support.   _____

20. I set high goals and take actions to achieve them.   _____

21. I have self-discipline.   _____

Statement	Points
22. I can forgive others.	_____
23. I value the contributions others make on my team.	_____
24. My goals are realistic and achievable.	_____
25. I ask others for feedback.	_____
26. I can accept the consequences of my decisions.	_____
27. I seek out new and different solutions from others.	_____
28. On my teams we laugh a lot.	_____
29. Others see me as a competent leader.	_____
30. I put forward my best effort.	_____
31. Others can rely on me.	_____
32. I can ask others for forgiveness.	_____
33. I feel like I am an important contributor to my team.	_____
34. I look forward to my future.	_____
35. I honor what I have accomplished.	_____
36. I can make up my mind and act.	_____
37. I like exploring and learning new things.	_____
38. I am fun to be around.	_____
39. Others respect me and give me compliments.	_____
40. I act on what I believe and think.	_____

Use the following chart to record your scores from the Leadership Self-Inventory. The small number within each block corresponds to each individual statement for which you assigned the values 0, 1, 2, or 3 on the inventory. Transfer your 40 individual item scores to the grid below. Next, add the values in each column and place the totals at the bottom of each respective column from I through X. When you have totaled the columns, transfer their values to the interpretation chart, which your teacher will give you.

Score Transfer

I	II	III	IV	V	VI	VII	VIII	IX	X
1	2	3	4	5	6	7	8	9	10
11	12	13	14	15	16	17	18	19	20
21	22	23	24	25	26	27	28	29	30
31	32	33	34	35	36	37	38	39	40

Totals

I	II	III	IV	V	VI	VII	VIII	IX	X

Transfer column totals I–X from the recording chart (on Handout 3.1.2) to the grid below.

Column	Column Score	Characteristic
I	_____	Integrity
II	_____	Compassion
III	_____	Belonging
IV	_____	Aspiring
V	_____	Self-reflection
VI	_____	Decisiveness
VII	_____	Curiosity and creativity
VIII	_____	Fun and humorous
IX	_____	Role model
X	_____	Confidence

Examine your scores. Areas for which your scores are high (compared to scores in other areas) are ones you might be strong in or that you have been focusing on. Areas with lower scores are ones that you might wish to emphasize or focus on improving.

From *Inspiring Leadership in Teens: Group Activities to Foster Integrity, Responsibility, and Compassion,* © 2010 by Ric Stuecker, Champaign, IL: Research Press (800-519-2707, www.researchpress.com)

ACTIVITY 3.2

Acquiring Characteristics of Inspiring Leaders

PURPOSE   To explore and set goals for each of the 10 characteristics of inspiring leaders

MATERIALS   Handout 3.2.1: Characteristics of Inspiring Leaders (one per student)

Handout 3.2.2: Goal-Setting Guide (one per student)

Handout 3.2.3: My Goals (one per student)

PREPARATION   If desired, have the Characteristics of Inspiring Leaders handouts (10 pages) comb-bound or stapled into a single booklet. Or keep the pages separate so that you may distribute each characteristic's description one at a time.

DIRECTIONS   1. Distribute the Characteristics of Inspiring Leaders handout if comb-bound or stapled, or hand out the integrity and compassion pages.

2. Briefly review and discuss the integrity and compassion definitions.

3. Ask students:

   • Do you agree with the definitions? Why or why not?

   • Would you like to add information or categories to either of these definitions? If so, what and why?

4. Ask students to answer the questions on the integrity and compassion handouts.

5. Distribute and review the Goal-Setting Guide and review it with students to help them understand the steps of setting a goal and the types of goals (short-term, medium-term, and long-term).

6. Distribute the My Goals worksheet.

7. Direct students as follows:

> Fill out the My Goals worksheet, which is the next step of the self-assessment. You are asked to write sentences explaining how you're doing with the integrity and compassion characteristics. Then write one area of concern you have for each. Set a goal to address each of these areas of concern. Begin to develop specific steps to reach these goals—short-term, medium-term, and long-term. The examples on the Goal-Setting Guide will help you. Establish deadlines for meeting each medium- and long-term goal. Finally, set up a way to measure whether you're meeting your goals. Pay close attention to the examples offered for each part of the process to guide you.

8. Allow volunteers to share their work to inspire and model for others who may be having a harder time.

9. Direct students to finish the goal-setting process they began in class. If they don't finish, assign it as homework.

10. For each of the next four (or more) class sessions, repeat this activity with two more characteristics, until students have explored and set goals for all 10 characteristics of inspiring leaders.

DISCUSSION

- Is it hard to write goals?
- Were any areas harder than others for you to write goals? Do you know why that might be?
- What might be the advantage of writing goals?

The following sections list characteristics that many inspiring leaders possess, at least to some degree. This is not intended to be a complete and comprehensive list, but the ones listed here are essential. The activities in this unit are based on these leadership traits:

- Integrity
- Compassion
- Belonging
- Aspiring
- Self-reflection
- Decisiveness
- Curiosity and creativity
- Fun and humor
- Role model
- Confidence

Integrity

Inspiring leaders do what they say they will. They follow their own rules, have self-discipline, and speak the truth. Leaders with *integrity* are willing to take on any responsibility—no matter how seemingly insignificant.

How Do I Show Integrity?

How do you demonstrate your integrity when working with others?

_____

_____

_____

How do you follow your own rules and show self-discipline?

_____

_____

_____

How do others know they can trust you?

_____

_____

_____

What Can I Do Better?

Identify an area of concern (example: I sometimes bend or stretch the truth).

_____

Set a goal (example: I will consciously tell the truth—exactly how it is).

_____

Decide on specific steps to take to reach your goal (example: When asked a question, I will take a breath and think about my answer).

_____

Measure your success (example: Members of my team know that I tell the truth).

_____

Summary

- Walk your talk.
- Tell the truth.
- Follow your own rules.
- Be responsible.
- Demonstrate self-discipline.

Compassion

Inspiring leaders care about others. Compassion means that you can "walk in the moccasins" of another person, seeing and understanding the world from the other's point of view. Compassionate leaders also are willing to forgive others, ask for forgiveness, and move forward.

How Do I Show Compassion?

How do I show compassion to others?

_____

_____

What do I do when I forgive someone?

_____

_____

How do I ask for forgiveness?

_____

_____

How do I show I understand and appreciate other people's points of view?

_____

_____

What Can I Do Better?

Identify an area of concern (example: I find it hard to ask for forgiveness).

_____

Set a goal (example: I will ask others to forgive me when I know I need to).

_____

Decide on specific steps to take to reach your goal (example: I will ask my team to forgive me when I make a mistake).

_____

Measure your success (example: My team members express their forgiveness).

_____

Summary

- Listen to others.
- Try harder to understand differing points of view.
- Forgive others.
- Ask for forgiveness
- Forgive yourself.

Belonging

Inspiring leaders feel they are part of a team and value the contributions of their teammates. They respect their teammates. Leaders who *belong* maintain their individuality when working with others.

How Do I Show My Sense of Belonging?

How do I show I value the contributions of others?

_____

_____

How do I show my respect for others?

_____

_____

How do I make others feel they are important?

_____

_____

How do I show pride in my team?

_____

_____

How Can I Do Better?

Select an area of concern (example: I sometimes ignore the contributions of others).

_____

Set a goal (example: I want to celebrate the contributions of others).

_____

Decide on specific steps to take to reach your goal (example: I will congratulate others when they make a contribution).

_____

Measure your success (example: I often sincerely congratulate others).

_____

Summary

- Always contribute to the success of your team.
- Congratulate and thank others who make contributions to your success.
- Respect others on your team.
- Choose to feel a part of your team.

Aspiring

Inspiring leaders dream large dreams for themselves and their teams. Aspiring leaders set realistic and doable goals for themselves and others. They celebrate accomplishments and build on achievements.

How Do I Show That I Am Aspiring?

What are my biggest dreams?

_____

_____

What goals do I have for myself?

_____

_____

What steps am I taking to fulfill my dreams and goals?

_____

_____

How do I build on my accomplishments?

_____

_____

How Can I Do Better?

Identify an area of concern (example: My goals are too hard to achieve).

_____

Set a goal (example: I will set realistic goals).

_____

Decide on specific steps to take to reach your goal (example: I will break down my goal into doable steps).

_____

Measure your success (example: I set realistic steps to achieve my goal).

_____

Summary

- Dream big.
- Break down your dreams into steps involving doable goals.
- Break down your goals into realistic steps to take toward them.
- Take action to reach your goals, step by step.
- Celebrate your accomplishments.

145

Self-Reflection

Without being narcissistic (conceited, self-absorbed), inspiring leaders examine themselves and their decisions. Self-reflective leaders understand their personal skills, aptitudes, attitudes, and behaviors. They ask others for feedback and advice. They honor their own and others' accomplishments.

How Self-Reflective Am I?

How often do I reflect on the decisions I make?

_____

_____

How well do I understand my personal leadership skills, talents, attitudes, and behaviors?

_____

_____

How do I ask for feedback and advice from others?

_____

_____

How do I celebrate and honor my own and others' accomplishments?

_____

_____

How Can I Do Better?

Identify an area of concern (example: I seldom reflect on decisions I make).

_____

Set a goal (example: I will take time to reflect on decisions I make).

_____

Decide on specific steps to take to reach your goal (example: I will discuss my decisions with a teammate).

_____

Measure your success (example: I spend more time talking over my decisions).

_____

Summary

- Take time to reflect on the decisions you make—before, during, and after making them.
- Ask others for feedback and advice.
- Review your personal skills, talents, behaviors, and attitudes.
- Honor and celebrate your own and others' accomplishments.

Decisiveness

Inspiring leaders can make decisions. Once decisive leaders have made a decision, they act on it. Having acted, they evaluate the results of their decisions and make adjustments. They are able to accept the consequences of their decisions and actions—without making excuses.

How Decisive Am I?

How do I make decisions?

_____

_____

How do I evaluate the decisions I make?

_____

_____

How do I act on the decisions I make?

_____

_____

How do I accept the consequences of my decisions?

_____

_____

How Can I Do Better?

Identify an area of concern (example: I have difficulty making up my mind).

_____

Set a goal (example: I want to make effective decisions).

_____

Decide on specific steps to take to reach your goal (example: I will discuss my decisions with a mentor).

_____

Measure your success (example: I make clear decisions, which I then act on).

_____

Summary

- Examine your options before deciding.
- Talk over options with others.
- Make clear decisions.
- Examine the consequences of decisions you make.
- Accept the consequences of decisions you make, without making excuses.

Curiosity and Creativity

Inspiring leaders are inquisitive, asking many questions, exploring many options, and seeking the counsel of other members of their teams. Curious and creative leaders often seek new and different solutions. They also honor the creativity of others.

How Curious and Creative Am I?

How curious am I?

_____

_____

How do I explore options and different solutions?

_____

_____

How often do I ask questions?

_____

_____

How do I honor the creativity of others?

_____

_____

How Can I Do Better?

Identify an area of concern (example: I seldom seek a variety of options).

_____

Set a goal (example: I will examine a number of options and different solutions).

_____

Decide on specific steps to take to reach your goal (example: I will consider several options and solutions).

_____

Measure your success (example: I ask questions and consider several solutions).

_____

Summary

- Ask a lot of questions.
- Explore many options.
- Seek new and different solutions.
- Honor your curiosity and creativity.
- Honor the creativity of others.

Fun and Humor

Inspiring leaders truly enjoy leading, being with others, and working cooperatively with enthusiasm. Fun and humorous leaders can enjoy a good joke, laughing at themselves and with others. They often seem to have endless energy.

How Fun and Humorous Am I?

How often do I laugh and have fun while working on teams?_____

_____

How do I show my enthusiasm and positive energy?_____

_____

How do I encourage fun and humor in others? _____

_____

How do I make teamwork fun and enjoyable? _____

_____

How do I avoid fun and humor that comes at others' expense? _____

_____

How Can I Do Better?

Identify an area of concern (example: I seldom have fun with my team).

_____

Set a goal (example: I will encourage fun and humor in my teammates).

_____

Decide on specific steps to take to reach your goal (example: I will encourage joke-telling on my team, making sure I avoid hurting others' feelings).

_____

Measure your success (example: My team and I often tell jokes and have fun together).

_____

Summary

- Bring a high level of energy to your team.
- Enjoy a good joke—but not at another's expense.
- Be able to laugh at yourself.
- Be able to laugh with others.
- Do your work with enthusiasm.

Role Model

Inspiring leaders are people others admire and sometimes model themselves after. Role models listen to others and make others feel comfortable. They are sometimes turned to for advice and support.

How Am I a Role Model?

How do I make others feel comfortable when working on teams?

_____

_____

How do I give support to my teammates?

_____

_____

Do others turn to me for advice and support?

_____

_____

How am I a positive role model?

_____

_____

How Can I Do Better?

Identify an area of concern (example: I want to improve how I support others).

_____

Set a goal (example: I will support other members on my team).

_____

Decide on specific steps to take to reach your goal (example: I will listen carefully to the ideas of others).

_____

Measure your success (example: Other team members share ideas with me).

_____

Summary

- Listen to the ideas of others.
- Make others feel comfortable.
- Give advice and support others when they seek it.
- Be available to work with your teammates.

Confidence

Inspiring leaders give their best efforts and have confidence in their abilities and decision-making abilities. Confident leaders set high goals for themselves and take effective actions to achieve their goals.

How Confident Am I?

How do I set high goals?

_____

_____

How do I show that I put forth my best effort?

_____

_____

How do I show I have confidence in my decision making?

_____

_____

How do I know I take effective actions?

_____

_____

How Can I Do Better?

Identify an area of concern (example: I should set higher goals).

_____

Set a goal (example: I will set higher goals).

_____

Decide on specific steps to take to reach your goals (example: I will evaluate my goals to see whether they are high enough).

_____

Measure your success (example: The goals I set are the best I can achieve).

_____

Summary

- Set high goals.
- Give projects and goals your best efforts.
- Have confidence in your abilities.
- Take effective actions to achieve your goals.
- Honor others who achieve their goals.

It's important to set goals and then take specific actions to achieve your goals. When you achieve your goals, you grow as an individual *and* as an inspiring leader. Working on goals takes time. It's a multistep process that moves from dreaming . . . to planning . . . to working step by step . . . to measuring your accomplishments . . . to examining and evaluating your outcomes.

To be successful, above all, be methodical: consciously set specific goals, measure your outcomes, evaluate your successes, and honor and celebrate your achievements.

Goal-Setting Steps

Follow these steps to set realistic and doable goals:

1. **Think and dream.** It's important to dream about the long-term goals you have for yourself—and to dream large. It may take accomplishing many smaller goals before you reach a largely dreamed objective for your life.

2. **Consider your motives.** Ask yourself why you want to accomplish the goal and what the consequences and rewards might be.

3. **Select a goal.** After considering the possibilities, choose a goal and write it down. This writing is important. It gives greater weight and reality to your goal. It also will give you a feeling of commitment to achieving the goal.

4. **Take the steps.** Write down the steps it will take to achieve your goal. Then regularly work on them.

5. **Accomplish your goal.** Do *not* quit until you have reached your goal.

6. **Celebrate your accomplishment.** Reward yourself. Ask others to celebrate with you.

7. **Set a new goal.** There are always new frontiers to explore. Continually build on your accomplishments and achievements.

Types and Examples of Goals

Short-Term Goals

A short-term goal may be accomplished in a short amount of time, usually within a week. Remember to set realistic and doable goals. Examples:

> I will give my teammates a high-five when we accomplish a team goal.

> I will write down one goal to accomplish this week.

> I will make a list of my accomplishments and add to it weekly.

Short-term goals may lead toward achieving medium-term goals.

Medium-Term Goals

A medium-term goal takes from a week to a month or more to accomplish. Remember to set realistic and doable goals, with interim goals along the way to the major goal. Examples:

> I will improve my ability to make decisions and act on them.

> I will be a role model for other members of my team.

> I will examine my goals and continually set new ones.

Medium-term goals may lead to accomplishing long-term goals.

Long-Term Goals

A long-term goal may take 6 months or more to accomplish. Long-term goals should be especially realistic and doable, with interim goals along the way to the major goal. Examples:

> I will give full effort to every team project.

> I will help my teammates in accomplishing both individual and team goals.

> I will develop a mature set of inspiring leadership skills.

Complete this worksheet to set goals for the next year. Focus on developing inspiring leader qualities, skills, and abilities. Think through the steps it will take to accomplish each goal. Make sure they are realistic and doable. Set a target date for completing each goal. Plan to celebrate your accomplishments when you achieve each goal.

Short-Term Goal

My short-term goal is _____

_____

Specific steps I will take to reach my goal

1. _____
2. _____
3. _____
4. _____
5. _____

I will accomplish this goal by (insert date) _____

Medium-Term Goal

My medium-term goal is _____

_____

Specific steps I will take to reach my goal

1. _____
2. _____
3. _____
4. _____
5. _____

I will accomplish this goal by (insert date) _____

From *Inspiring Leadership in Teens: Group Activities to Foster Integrity, Responsibility, and Compassion,* © 2010 by Ric Stuecker, Champaign, IL: Research Press (800-519-2707, www.researchpress.com)

Long-Term Goal

My long-term goal is _____

_____

Specific steps I will take to reach my goal

1. _____

2. _____

3. _____

4. _____

5. _____

I will accomplish this goal by (insert date) _____

Support

Whose support, knowledge, or advice will help me reach my goals?

_____

_____

ACTIVITY 3.3

Exploring Personal Integrity and Responsibility

PURPOSE
To further examine personal integrity, along with the related topic of how to handle responsibilities

MATERIALS
Handout 3.3.1: Personal Integrity Assessment (one per student)

Handout 3.3.2: Taking On Responsibilities (one per student)

DIRECTIONS
1. Distribute and discuss the Personal Integrity Assessment, saying, "Personal integrity means doing what you say you are going to do and having high personal standards. How does personal integrity relate to leadership?"

2. Give students about 15 minutes to complete the assessment.

3. Divide students into groups of three. Have them move their chairs together.

4. Tell the groups: "Discuss the areas of personal integrity you're most proud of. Then discuss the areas of personal integrity you think you should work on."

5. Repeat steps 1 through 3 with the Taking On Responsibilities handout, saying, "Remember that 'responsibility' means that you 'respond' to situations by doing a good job and meeting any standards at a high level."

6. Have the group move their chairs back into a whole-class formation and then lead them in a discussion using the questions that follow.

DISCUSSION
- What makes it difficult to have personal integrity?
- When you don't show integrity or responsibility, who is hurt the most?
- When others find out you have not shown integrity or been responsible, why is it embarrassing?
- When you are late, whom do you hurt or affect?
- When you fail to keep a promise, whom do you hurt or affect?

- When you spread gossip, whom do you hurt or affect?
- When you lack integrity when dealing with someone else, what can you do to get your integrity back with the person?
- What acts of service for others might help you get your integrity back?

Rate yourself on the following statements using this scale:

A = Always   S = Seldom   U = Usually   N = Never   O = Occasionally

In Part A, use the blank line under the column titled "My Rating" to put your response. The blank line under the column titled "Another's Rating" is used to record your answers in Part B of this handout.

Part A: Rating Myself

Statement	My Rating	Another's Rating
1. I show up on time to appointments, meetings, and events.	_____	_____
2. When I agree to meet someone to hang out or do something social, I show up on time.	_____	_____
3. Others can believe what I say.	_____	_____
4. If I borrow money, I pay it back quickly.	_____	_____
5. If I say I'll do something, you can count on me to do it.	_____	_____
6. If I borrow something from someone, after using it, I return it quickly.	_____	_____
7. I keep the promises I make to myself.	_____	_____
8. I keep the promises I make to others.	_____	_____
9. I tell others the truth.	_____	_____
10. I refuse to listen to gossip and spread rumors.	_____	_____
11. I refuse to pass on gossip and spread rumors told to me.	_____	_____
12. I tell the truth about others.	_____	_____
13. I respect the privacy of others.	_____	_____
14. I keep private conversations to myself.	_____	_____
15. If I promise to call someone, I make the call.	_____	_____
16. If I promise to help someone, I help them.	_____	_____
17. If I make a date, I keep it.	_____	_____
18. If I find out something embarrassing about someone, I keep it to myself.	_____	_____
19. I can be trusted not to snoop in someone else's room or home.	_____	_____
20. I leave other people's stuff alone.	_____	_____
21. I can be trusted not to steal or shoplift.	_____	_____
22. If I borrow a car, I return it with a full tank of gas.	_____	_____
23. If I break something, I own up to it and pay for it.	_____	_____
24. If I am with someone who is making a decision to do something wrong, I leave instead of going along with them.	_____	_____
25. I play sports honestly, follow the rules, and win or lose fairly.	_____	_____
26. When I play games, I follow the rules. I don't cheat.	_____	_____
27. I stand up and speak up for what I believe.	_____	_____
28. When I am wrong, I admit it.	_____	_____
29. I stand up for others.	_____	_____
30. I do what I think and believe, not what others want me to do.	_____	_____

Part B: Rating Myself as Someone Else Would

Now, go back to Part A. On the second blank after each statement, rate yourself as you believe your best friend or someone else who knows you well would rate you.

From Inspiring Leadership in Teens: Group Activities to Foster Integrity, Responsibility, and Compassion, © 2010 by Ric Stuecker, Champaign, IL: Research Press (800-519-2707, www.researchpress.com)

For each area of personal responsibility, list the specific responsibilities you have. Then, on the blank line at the right side of the page next to each item, rate yourself as to how well you believe you carry out that responsibility. Use the scale below to evaluate your performance. If you need more space, write on the back of this sheet.

> 5 = Excellent
>
> 4 = Very good
>
> 3 = Good
>
> 2 = Fair
>
> 1 = Poor

Family

What specific responsibilities do you have as a son or daughter?   <u>Rating</u>

1. _____ _____

2. _____ _____

3. _____ _____

4. _____ _____

5. _____ _____

What specific responsibilities do you have as a brother or sister?

1. _____ _____

2. _____ _____

3. _____ _____

4. _____ _____

5. _____ _____

School

What specific responsibilities do you have as a student?

1. _____ _____

2. _____ _____

3. _____ _____

4. _____ _____

5. _____ _____

Team in Class

What specific responsibilities do you have as a team player?   Rating

1. _____   _____

2. _____   _____

3. _____   _____

4. _____   _____

5. _____   _____

Activity (or Sport)

What specific responsibilities do you have as an activity (or sport team) member?

1. _____   _____

2. _____   _____

3. _____   _____

4. _____   _____

5. _____   _____

Friend

What specific responsibilities do you have as a friend?

1. _____   _____

2. _____   _____

3. _____   _____

4. _____   _____

5. _____   _____

Employment or Volunteer Work

What specific responsibilities do you have as a worker or volunteer?

1. _____   _____

2. _____   _____

3. _____   _____

4. _____   _____

5. _____   _____

Making Personal Agreements

PURPOSE

To learn about the various levels of agreement and to help students elevate their personal integrity and commitment to higher levels

MATERIALS

Handout 3.4.1: Personal Agreements (one per student)

Prepared chart (see Preparation section) on whiteboard or easel pad

PREPARATION

Set up chairs in a whole-group formation.

Write the following chart on a whiteboard or easel pad:

Commitment

Level	Agreement	Meaning
1	Yes	I'll blow it off.
2	Yes	But only under certain circumstances.
3	Yes	Okay.
4	Yes	I really agree!
5	Yes	Absolutely—no matter what!

DIRECTIONS

1. Introduce the concept of levels of agreement. Say:

   Although we often say yes when we are asked to do something, our actual intention to follow through may not be high. Looking at the chart, what do you believe will happen to an agreement agreed to at levels 1 and 2? What about level 3? What about levels 4 and 5? In a moment, I am going to give you a list of possible areas for which you might like to set an objective or make an improvement. Being honest, place a rating corresponding to the chart on the board that reflects the actual level of agreement you truly intend.

2. Raise the issue of how people often say yes—but really mean something else. Discuss the following:

   • Has anyone ever told you yes—but they were really saying no?

   • If they did, do you think they were lying? Forgetting? Didn't want to say no to you?

- Is it easier for you to break an agreement with yourself or with someone else? Why?

3. Distribute the Personal Agreements handout. Allow about 15 minutes for students to complete the handout.

4. Place students in groups of three and have them move their chairs together. Say:

> Brainstorm specific steps you can take to reach your objectives. Then rate your level of agreement for each step you agree to take. Report what areas you want to improve, what steps you're willing to take, and what level of agreement you're willing to make.

You may want to ask students to report their progress on agreements each week in this same format. Or keep a classroom chart on which students write a "+" or "–" each week, indicating whether they kept their agreements and followed their improvement plans. At the end of 6 weeks (or another time period you set), ask whether they believe they've made any measurable improvements in the areas they selected.

Consider each of the following areas. Check the areas (at least three) you would like to improve. For now, leave the blank lines in the Commitment Level column empty. You'll use them in step 4 of this handout.

<u>Objectives</u>   <u>Commitment Level</u>

☐ *My grades*

    Objective _____

    Possible steps

      1. _____ _____

      2. _____ _____

      3. _____ _____

☐ *My relationship with my parents*

    Objective _____

    Possible steps

      1. _____ _____

      2. _____ _____

      3. _____ _____

☐ *My relationships with my friends*

    Objective _____

    Possible steps

      1. _____ _____

      2. _____ _____

      3. _____ _____

☐ *My relationship with my boyfriend or girlfriend*

    Objective _____

    Possible steps

      1. _____ _____

      2. _____ _____

      3. _____ _____

From *Inspiring Leadership in Teens: Group Activities to Foster Integrity, Responsibility, and Compassion,* © 2010 by Ric Stuecker, Champaign, IL: Research Press (800-519-2707, www.researchpress.com)

<u>Objectives</u>   <u>Commitment Level</u>

☐ *My weight*

    Objective _____

    Possible steps

    1. _____   ____

    2. _____   ____

    3. _____   ____

☐ *My athletic skills*

    Objective _____

    Possible steps

    1. _____   ____

    2. _____   ____

    3. _____   ____

☐ *My fitness level*

    Objective _____

    Possible steps

    1. _____   ____

    2. _____   ____

    3. _____   ____

☐ *My temper*

    Objective _____

    Possible steps

    1. _____   ____

    2. _____   ____

    3. _____   ____

☐ *How I spend money*

    Objective _____

    Possible steps

    1. _____   ____

    2. _____   ____

    3. _____   ____

Objectives	Commitment Level

☐ *My ability to earn money*

Objective _____

Possible steps

1. _____ ____

2. _____ ____

3. _____ ____

☐ *My ability to dance*

Objective _____

Possible steps

1. _____ ____

2. _____ ____

3. _____ ____

☐ *My willingness to do family chores*

Objective _____

Possible steps

1. _____ ____

2. _____ ____

3. _____ ____

☐ *My relationship with my brother or sister*

Objective _____

Possible steps

1. _____ ____

2. _____ ____

3. _____ ____

1. Select three areas you'd like to improve in. On the lines below, write a goal you'd like to reach. Here are some examples:

   I want to improve my grades to a B average.

   I want to lose 10 pounds by the time school ends this year.

   I want to improve my football tackling skills.

_____

_____

_____

2. Meet with two other people in your class. Brainstorm specific steps you each could take to achieve your goals.

3. As you write, outline the steps you're willing to take toward improvement.

4. Using the following scale, rate the level of each step according to how strong or weak your "yes" is. Next to each of the goals you wrote in step 1, write the number (1–5) that corresponds to your commitment level. The ratings correspond to how responsible you are willing to be reaching your goal of improvement.

Commitment Level	Agreement	Meaning
1	Yes	I'll blow it off.
2	Yes	But only under certain circumstances.
3	Yes	Okay.
4	Yes	I really agree!
5	Yes	Absolutely—no matter what!

PHASE 2

Creating a Personal
Mission Statement

Many organizations and successful groups have mission statements. By creating a mission statement, these groups set a goal and establish a plan to pursue the goal. They also identify ways to measure their success. A mission statement is meant to inspire the members of the organization and to keep them focused on its purpose and goals.

Inspiring leaders often have a personal mission statement. A personal mission statement is meant to inspire an individual to lead an exemplary life.

ACTIVITY 3.5

Exploring Personal Dreams

PURPOSE
To teach students the purpose and importance of a *mission statement* and to give them an opportunity to examine and write about their hopes, dreams, and aspirations in fashioning a personal mission statement

MATERIALS
Handout 3.5.1: What Is a Personal Mission Statement? (one per student)

Handout 3.5.2: Personal Dreams (one per student)

Soft music (for example, George Winston, Mozart, or other classical or soft jazz selection)

PREPARATION
Set up the activity area so students have plenty of room to sit comfortably and write.

Select soft music to play while students are writing.

DIRECTIONS
1. Distribute and discuss the What Is a Personal Mission Statement? handout, explaining what a mission statement is and why it is important to consider your mission in life.

2. Say, "Relax—close your eyes, take a few deep breaths, and let go of any tension in your muscles." Pause for students to do so. Continue, "Activate your imagination. Imagine yourself 10 to 15 years in the future." Pause briefly.

3. At a pace that allows students to be thoughtful, ask the questions listed on the Personal Dreams handout. Instruct the students to think about the questions but to refrain from writing anything yet.

4. Continue, "Open your eyes. Now on the next handout, which I'll distribute now, jot down some thoughts you had while imagining." Distribute the Personal Dreams handout. Allow 5 minutes for students to write.

5. Say, "Now I want you to write a one-page essay, describing your hopes and dreams for your future." Allow about 15 minutes for students to write.

6. When everyone is finished writing, divide students into groups of three to five people. Ask students to read their hopes and

dreams descriptions to each other within their small groups. Allow groups about 5 minutes.

7. Allow volunteers to read their essays to the whole class.

Many organizations and successful groups have mission statements. By creating a mission statement, these groups set a goal, or direction to pursue, and establish a way to measure their success.

Effective mission statements serve these functions. For example:

- They are meant to inspire the members of the organization while keeping them focused on its purpose and goals.

- Inspiring leaders often have their own personal mission statements, meant to inspire themselves to lead exemplary lives.

- Inspiring leaders need a mission statement to help them focus their energies, inspire them when the going gets tough, and measure their impact and success.

In addition, while a mission statement may be fairly detailed and lengthy, it's often helpful to keep it quite short. Short statements are easier to memorize and remember and may more easily serve as potential "mantras" to remind you of the direction, or purpose, of your life.

Some examples of concise mission statements are:

- My mission is to foster a world in which all children are safe.

- My mission is to promote peace and harmony in my home, neighborhood, and community.

- My mission is to empower others to attain and live their dreams.

Such mission statements, however, are grandiose and difficult to accomplish. Even though they provide direction and purpose, it's unlikely a person would achieve such a mission during a lifetime.

It's helpful to add a second phrase to a mission statement, while still keeping it short. This phrase should indicate exactly how you might attempt to fulfill the vision of your mission. Here are some examples:

- My mission is to foster a world in which all children are safe by making sure the children in my life are safe, secure, and loved.

- My mission is to promote peace and harmony by remaining peaceful in my home.

- My mission is to empower others to live their dreams by encouraging them to set goals and celebrate their accomplishments.

Beyond these pointers, a mission statement needs to be practical, or usable. To do so, it's important for a person to examine:

- His or her hopes and dreams
- Principles and values to live by
- Personality characteristics to develop
- Potential obstacles in the way of living the mission
- Achievements and contributions to make

From *Inspiring Leadership in Teens: Group Activities to Foster Integrity, Responsibility, and Compassion,* © 2010 by Ric Stuecker, Champaign, IL: Research Press (800-519-2707, www.researchpress.com)

Where will you be living?

Will you be married? Dating? Living alone?

Will you have children?

What kind of job will you have? Will you like it? Why or why not?

Will you be making a lot of money? Why or why not?

What will you be doing in your spare time?

What sort of home will you have?

Who will you know? Old friends? New?

What kinds of contributions will you be making . . .

  . . . to your family?

  . . . to yourself?

  . . . to your local community?

Will you be happy? Why or why not?

From *Inspiring Leadership in Teens: Group Activities to Foster Integrity, Responsibility, and Compassion,* © 2010
by Ric Stuecker, Champaign, IL: Research Press (800-519-2707, www.researchpress.com)

ACTIVITY 3.6

Discerning What I Value in Life

PURPOSE
To allow students to examine and write about their values, explore how they might live up to them, and decide what they want from life now and in the future

MATERIALS
Handout 3.6.1: Value Statements (one per student)

DIRECTIONS
1. Distribute the Value Statements handout.

2. Ask students to read and think about the value statements on the handout. Explain that they will rate each statement as being of low value, medium value, or high value to them at this point in their lives. Allow students about 5 minutes to complete this task.

3. Give students a minute or two to select three to five statements that they value the most and mark them with a star.

4. Ask students to write a one-page description telling (1) why they value these statements the most and (2) how they plan to uphold them both now and in the future. Allow students about 15 minutes to write.

5. When everyone is finished writing, divide students into groups of three to five. Ask students to read their short essays to each other within their small groups. Allow groups about 10 minutes.

6. Ask for volunteers to read their essays to the whole class.

7. Debrief the activity with the following discussion questions.

DISCUSSION
- Were your values similar to—or different from—those of the other members of your team? Why?

- Did any person's values surprise you? Why or why not?

- Do you believe you can uphold the values you wrote about after leaving this class? Why or why not?

Rate the value to you of the following statements by circling the number that best suits your current position.

Statement	Low						High
Making a lot of money	1	2	3	4	5	6	7
Doing a job I enjoy	1	2	3	4	5	6	7
Being admired by others	1	2	3	4	5	6	7
Learning, growing as a person	1	2	3	4	5	6	7
Doing a job that pays a lot	1	2	3	4	5	6	7
Reaching for spiritual fulfillment	1	2	3	4	5	6	7
Building a family	1	2	3	4	5	6	7
Becoming famous	1	2	3	4	5	6	7
Having peace of mind	1	2	3	4	5	6	7
Contributing to the growth of others	1	2	3	4	5	6	7
Traveling to faraway places	1	2	3	4	5	6	7
Being generous to others	1	2	3	4	5	6	7
Being liked by others	1	2	3	4	5	6	7
Having lots of friends	1	2	3	4	5	6	7

ACTIVITY 3.7

Identifying Characteristics I Admire

PURPOSE

To have students consider and write about someone they know and to think about the characteristics they would like to possess personally

MATERIALS

Handout 3.7.1: Characteristics I Admire (one per student)

DIRECTIONS

1. Say, "Think about and picture in your mind someone—or several people—you admire. Think of at least one person you know well, who is currently in your life." Pause briefly.

2. Continue, "Write an essay, of at least five paragraphs, describing the person or people you chose. In specific detail, describe their characteristics that you admire." Allow 20 to 30 minutes for students to complete their essays. If necessary, assign as homework.

3. When everyone is finished writing, divide students into groups of three to five. Ask students to read their essays to each other within their small groups. Allow about 10 minutes for students to complete this process.

4. Allow volunteers to read their essays to the whole class.

5. Distribute the Characteristics I Admire handout. Say, "Think about the people you wrote about and the people you heard about. On this handout, check five of the characteristics you most admire and would like to be known for." Pause briefly. Then continue, "List each of these five characteristics on a sheet of paper. After each, come up with some ways you might develop this characteristic in yourself."

6. Debrief the activity with the following discussion questions.

DISCUSSION

- Were you surprised by any of the role models some of your classmates chose? Why or why not?

- After listening to other students' essays, did you add anyone to your list of role models? Why or why not?

- Do you believe you are a good role model? If so, who are you a good role model for? If not, are you interested in becoming one? Why or why not?
- What would you be willing to do to develop some of the characteristics you admire in others in yourself?

Check five of the characteristics you most admire and would like to be known for.

☐ Responsible	☐ Leader	☐ Ethical
☐ Respectful	☐ Funny	☐ Patient
☐ Honest	☐ Kind	☐ Intelligent
☐ Laid-back	☐ Educated	☐ Thoughtful
☐ Predictable	☐ Loyal	☐ Fair
☐ Hard-working	☐ Independent	☐ Carefree
☐ Decisive	☐ Giving	☐ Healthy
☐ Loving	☐ Wise	☐ Open
☐ Sensitive	☐ Friendly	☐ Jovial
☐ Imaginative	☐ Creative	☐ Moral
☐ Understanding	☐ Sympathetic	☐ Powerful
☐ Committed	☐ Forgiving	☐ Direct
☐ Enthusiastic	☐ Selfless	☐ Balanced

From *Inspiring Leadership in Teens: Group Activities to Foster Integrity, Responsibility, and Compassion,* © 2010 by Ric Stuecker, Champaign, IL: Research Press (800-519-2707, www.researchpress.com)

ACTIVITY 3.8

Understanding Strengths and Roadblocks

PURPOSE

To provide an opportunity for students to consider their personal strengths and potential roadblocks to achieving their goals in life, then plan how they might overcome their roadblocks

MATERIALS

Handout 3.8.1: Strengths Versus Roadblocks (one per student)

DIRECTIONS

1. Distribute the Strengths Versus Roadblocks handouts.

2. Explain, "Roadblocks are negative characteristics that may prevent a person from fulfilling his or her dreams. Roadblocks may be overcome by applying character strengths. Read and study the lists of strengths and roadblocks on the handout." Pause briefly. Continue, "Now check three to five of the characteristics that you view as your strengths and one roadblock that you're willing to work on and overcome." Pause briefly.

3. Instruct:

   Write a one-page description of why you feel these are your greatest strengths. Then, be sure to (1) describe why you feel the roadblock you chose is an obstacle and (2) how you plan to address it to make a positive change in your life, listing several potentially effective strategies.

4. Allow about 15 minutes for students to write.

5. When everyone is finished writing, divide students into groups of three to five. Ask groups to read their roadblock plans to each other within their small groups. Allow groups about 5 minutes.

6. Allow volunteers to read their roadblock plans to the whole class.

7. Debrief the activity with the following discussion questions.

DISCUSSION

- Why do you suppose it's hard to overcome roadblocks in our lives?
- Who might be able to help us overcome roadblocks and make positive changes? Why?
- How might our strengths help us to overcome roadblocks?

In the Strengths column, check three to five characteristics that you view as your strengths. In the Roadblocks column, check one roadblock that you are willing to work on to overcome.

Strengths	Roadblocks
☐ Intelligent	☐ Pessimistic
☐ Understanding	☐ Narrow-minded
☐ Optimistic	☐ Unmotivated
☐ Confident	☐ Insecure
☐ Imaginative	☐ Irresponsible
☐ Insightful	☐ Selfish
☐ Hardworking	☐ Fearful
☐ Clever	☐ Sarcastic
☐ Artistic	☐ Shy
☐ Reliable	☐ Bored
☐ Energetic	☐ Vapid (lacking liveliness or energy)
☐ Adaptable	☐ Inflexible
☐ Generous	☐ Impulsive

From *Inspiring Leadership in Teens: Group Activities to Foster Integrity, Responsibility, and Compassion,* © 2010 by Ric Stuecker, Champaign, IL: Research Press (800-519-2707, www.researchpress.com)

ACTIVITY 3.9

Identifying Contributions
I Hope to Make

PURPOSE   To have students consider and write about their potential contributions to the world

MATERIALS   Handout 3.9.1: Contributions I Can Make (one per student)

DIRECTIONS

1. Distribute the Contributions I Can Make handout.

2. Say, "Look through the list of roles on the left side of the handout. Like most people, you probably play many roles now—and will continue to do the same in the future."

3. Explain:

   We often think of money as the only way to contribute to a cause or person, but we may contribute through donating our time, talents, and energy to make a significant difference. Contributions are things and efforts you give to make the world a better place. For each area on the handout that applies to you personally, write one specific contribution you could make. Do not write something vague, such as "Be nice to others." Instead write, for example, "Help my little brother with his math homework—encouraging him instead of putting him down."

4. Allow about 10 minutes for students to write.

5. When everyone is finished writing, divide students into groups of three to five. Ask groups to read their contribution ideas to each other within their small groups. Allow groups about 5 minutes.

6. Allow volunteers to read their contribution ideas to the whole class. Facilitate peer feedback, helping students be as specific as possible.

7. Debrief the activity with the following discussion questions.

DISCUSSION

- Do you believe it's possible for an individual or a small group of people to make major changes in the world? Why or why not?

179

- Who are some individuals or small groups who have brought about major changes in the world?

- Who are some people you know who are making contributions? What specifically are they doing?

- What people in the news are making contributions? How?

- Are you aware of any organizations that make contributions to our local or global community? What do they do? Would you want to join them? Why or why not?

Role   Contribution I Can Make

Daughter or son   _____

                                               _____

Friend   _____

                                               _____

Team member   _____

                                               _____

Activity participant   _____

                                               _____

Student   _____

                                               _____

Neighbor   _____

                                               _____

Worker   _____

                                               _____

Religious community member   _____

                                               _____

Citizen   _____

                                               _____

Other: _____   _____

                                               _____

Creating a Personal Mission Statement

PURPOSE   To help students construct and present their mission statements

MATERIALS   Handout 3.10.1: My Personal Mission (one per student)
Work completed in Phase 2 of this unit

DIRECTIONS
1. Distribute the My Personal Mission handout.

2. Explain, "Today you'll be developing your own personal mission statement. Using the work you have done earlier in this unit, complete this new handout to collect your thoughts." Allow students about 10 minutes to work.

3. Continue, "Now use the notes you made on this handout to write a personal mission statement in your own words." Allow students 15 or more minutes to complete the task.

4. When everyone is finished writing, divide students into groups of three to five. Instruct the groups to read their personal mission statements aloud to each other as a sign of committing to their plans. Allow groups 5 to 10 minutes.

5. Allow volunteers to read their mission statements to the whole class.

6. Ask students to type a final version of their mission statement, using computer-generated fonts, graphics, and borders. If needed, assign this step as homework or plan an additional class period during which students may complete their work (for example, in your school's computer lab).

7. Display completed student mission statements.

DISCUSSION
- Do you find your mission statement and those of your teammates inspiring?

- Why do you think a personal mission statement might be useful?

I want to live a positive life, fulfill my dreams, and contribute to making this world a better place. To do this, I will:

Seek to fulfill the following dreams during my lifetime:

Value each of the following:

Develop the following characteristics:

Use and improve these three strengths:

Work on overcoming this roadblock:

Seek to make the following contributions:

From *Inspiring Leadership in Teens: Group Activities to Foster Integrity, Responsibility, and Compassion,* © 2010 by Ric Stuecker, Champaign, IL: Research Press (800-519-2707, www.researchpress.com)

Simplifying My Personal Mission Statement

PURPOSE

To help students create short and memorable versions of their personal mission statements

MATERIALS

Appropriate space for meditating

Prepared statement for part 2 of this activity (see Preparation, next section), written on whiteboard or easel pad

Optional: Noble and inspiring music (such as Aaron Copland's "Fanfare for the Common Man," a selection from John Williams's music composed for the Olympics, or other similar selection)

PREPARATION

Locate and set up a space where the guided meditation will not be disturbed.

Write the following phrases on a whiteboard or easel pad ahead of time, being careful to copy the punctuation exactly:

"I create a world . . ."

Example: *"I create a world of peace and harmony . . ."*

"by . . ."

Example: *" . . . by being peaceful and letting go of my anger."*

Do not reveal a line until it's needed (as explained in part 2).

If desired, select a piece of noble and inspiring music to play while students are meditating.

DIRECTIONS

1. Explain:

Now that you have a full understanding of a mission statement, today's activities will guide you in writing a simple, two-part statement you should be able to easily remember and that should inspire you as a leader. The two parts are *vision* and *action*.

The *vision* is the part of your mission statement that describes the vision you have for the world. This part of the statement is grand and eloquent. Here are some examples:

I create a world of love and truth.

I create a world of responsible leadership.

I create a world of beauty and creativity.

The *action* is what you're willing to do to achieve, at least in some small part, the vision you've described. Here are some examples:

. . . by always telling the truth.

. . . by making sure I am responsible.

. . . by exploring my creative talents.

2. Continue, "The following four activities will help you create a simple—yet inspiring—mission statement."

3. In order, conduct parts 1 through 4. Debrief the activities as you go.

Part 1: Creating the Vision: Guided Meditation

One way of helping students create a vision is to guide them through a meditation. Here are the steps for leading such a process:

1. Explain:

Have pencil or pen and a sheet of paper ready. I'll play some relaxing music to help you slow down and focus [optional]. Please sit in a comfortable, relaxing position. Today you are going to experience a guided meditation—but it's important that you avoid going to sleep, if possible.

2. If necessary, add, "This activity works best when we relax, think seriously, and act maturely."

3. Continue, "Close your eyes and listen to my voice." Pause for about 15 seconds after making each of the following statements:

Just relax and sit as comfortably as possible.

Allow any tension in your feet to relax.

Make sure your toes are relaxed.

Allow any tension in your lower legs to relax and flow out of your legs and feet.

Allow any tension in your knees and thighs to relax and flow out of your legs and feet.

Release any tension in the trunk of your body, allowing it to flow out of your body.

Let your arms go completely limp. Let any tension in your arms flow out.

Relax your hands. Allow any tension in your hands to flow out your fingers.

Relax your neck. Let any tension in your neck flow out.

Relax your head. Relax your jaw. Let any tension in your head and jaw flow out.

4. Once you see students are more relaxed, continue by making the following statements, again pausing for about 15 seconds after each statement:

Imagine you are out in a field. No one is around you. You're all alone.

It is a beautiful day. You can feel a gentle wind blowing. The sun is warm.

You're taking a walk. You're walking up a hill. It's an easy climb.

You go up higher . . . and higher . . . and higher.

It is a very high hill. As you reach the top, you see a wide valley below you.

There's a tree at the top of the hill. Sit down and rest against the tree. Feel the wind gently blowing. Feel the warmth of the sun.

You can see across a vast expanse. The scene below you is very beautiful.

As you rest and look out over the world, gradually a vision of what the world might be comes to you.

You see a vision of a world you would be willing to dedicate your life to.

Let the words come into your head, describing the world that inspires you.

Take your time. Let the words come. Relax—let the vision of this remarkable world come fully into your mind and being.

When you have completely understood the vision in your mind, stand up. Take one last look at the valley below you.

Take a deep breath and turn to walk down the hill again.

It's an easy walk down. The sun feels good.

Slowly walk all the way back down to the bottom of the hill.

When you reach the bottom, stay relaxed, but begin to return to the classroom.

Gradually open your eyes. Stretch if you want, but do *not* talk.

Pick up your pen or pencil and write a description of the vision you saw for the world from the top of the hill.

Part 2: Simplifying the Vision and Adding the Action

Follow these steps to help students come up with a simple vision phrase and then create an appropriate action phrase to follow it.

1. Display the first phrase you prepared ahead of time for this part (see Preparation section).

2. Say, "Reread the vision you just wrote, seeing whether you can find one or two key words that would generalize and summarize your vision." Reveal the first prepared example.

3. Ask each student to read his or her phrase to the class.

4. After everyone has shared, ask, "What actions could you personally take to help create the vision you've described?" Allow students to share for about 10 minutes. You might wish to list the actions on the board or an easel pad so that others may more easily consider adopting them.

5. Reveal the second half of the statement you prepared ahead of time.

6. Say, "Select the action that has the most meaning for you and add it to the vision part of your simplified mission statement. Consider the actions shared by others as well as your own." Allow about 5 minutes for students to complete the action part of their simplified mission statements.

7. Ask students to share their newly simplified statements with the class.

This is a good place to stop until the next class session.

Part 3: Honoring Your Mission Statement

1. Play an inspiring piece of instrumental music if you wish.

2. Explain:

   > This activity involves a ceremony to honor your simplified mission statements. Please stand in a circle. Make sure you can see every other student in the circle without having to move. Taking turns, let's have you each speak your mission statement loudly, proudly, and boldly.

Pause 5 to 10 seconds between each student's presentation.

Part 4: Remembering Your Mission Statement

If you have access to computers in the classroom or a computer lab, ask students to create illustrated copies of their simplified mission statements and print five copies. If you do not have access to computers, students could use colored markers and colored paper to create the illustrated copies. Another option is to assign this task as homework or an optional activity.

Explain to the students that they will now illustrate their simplified mission statements and then make five copies for themselves. Ask them to keep this important leadership training tool in places they see every day (the students can create their mission statements in various sizes):

- In a wallet or purse
- At home, on a mirror in the bathroom or bedroom
- On the inside of their locker door
- As a bookmark

DISCUSSION   Debrief the entire lesson (parts 1–4), asking the following questions:

- How did you feel during the guided meditation? Why?
- What was the hardest part for you when you were trying to describe your vision?
- Does your simplified mission statement inspire you? Why or why not?

PHASE 3

Advertising Your Inspiring Leadership Strengths

Creating individual brochures is the culminating activity for this unit of *Inspiring Leadership in Teens*. The brochure uses information from the previous activities and allows students to proudly "advertise" their achievements and mission statements.

Activity 3.12

Making a Personal Brochure

PURPOSE To allow students to consolidate the work they have done in this unit

MATERIALS Handout 3.12.1: Personal Brochure Contents (one per student)

Handout 3.12.2: Sample brochure (one per student, or enough to share)

Handouts and assignments from all previous activities in this unit

NOTE Each student's personal brochure may be made using Microsoft Word, but there are other programs that might be more useful. Talk with your school's computer teacher to get ideas for creating these brochures. If desired, arrange to team-teach with the computer teacher or team up with another colleague. In any case, students will need access to a computer and color printer, either at home or school.

DIRECTIONS 1. Discuss the characteristics of a well-made brochure and how it may be used to promote a product or service. Explain that most brochures are written in brief phrases and use bullet lists, rather than detailed paragraphs, to make their points. Brochures are usually divided into sections with prominent titles so readers can go right to the information they might be looking for. Pictures, clip art, and colors give the brochure interest.

2. Say, "You are going to make a trifold brochure describing yourself as an inspiring leader. 'Trifold' means folded into three sections."

3. Distribute the sample brochure, which was created in Microsoft Word. (That software has a number of easy-to-use brochure templates. You can also type in a search engine the words "brochure template" and find other templates to use.)

4. Referring to the Personal Brochure Contents handout, discuss the components of a complete brochure, critiquing the sample. The items on the handout are suggestions for information that might be included. Challenge students to include information that relates to leadership but also that fits them as individuals. Not

all the suggested information needs to be included. Also point out that, although there are six panels (three on front and three on back) on a trifold brochure, some people opt to leave the back center panel empty.

5. Have students create a rough draft of their brochure. Explain that they should expect to make corrections and changes as they prepare a final version. Allow about 30 minutes or until the end of the class period for students to work. If necessary, assign the draft as homework.

6. Divide students into groups of three to five. Have groups review and critique each other's draft brochures. Allow about 10 minutes for this process.

7. Assign the creation of a final version, printed in color. If necessary, have students complete this assignment as homework.

8. Create a display area for brochures. Set aside class time for students to examine each other's final brochures. Ask each student to select three brochures he or she believes accurately and positively reflect their authors. Allow time for students to find those three people and tell them what they liked about the brochures.

9. Debrief the activity with the following discussion questions.

DISCUSSION

- How does your brochure reflect you?
- Are there personal qualities you left out? How did you decide what to include or not?
- How does your motto reflect who you are?
- What personal assets and characteristics about yourself do you like the most?
- What personal assets and characteristics do you admire—in general—about others?

These items are suggestions for information that might be included in your brochure. Strive to include information that relates to leadership but also that fits you as an individual. Not all the suggested information needs to be included. Note: Although there are six panels (three on front and three on back) on a trifold brochure, you may opt to leave the back center panel empty.

Front Cover

- A graphic or piece of clip art that represents you in some way
- A photograph of yourself
- Name
- Personal motto
- Descriptive words such as "dependable," "responsible," "creative," and "energetic"

Inside Left Panel

- Personal data
- Family
- Friends
- Sports
- School activities
- Heroes and role models

Inside Center Panel

- Your simplified mission statement created in previous activities

Inside Right Panel

- Aspirations (hopes and dreams for the future)
- Leadership skills
- Special talents
- Achievements
- Awards and honors received

Back Cover

- Short description of events that have shaped you

Back Center Panel (optional)

- Additional strengths and qualifications, work and volunteer experience, and/or other information, such as how to contact you

From *Inspiring Leadership in Teens: Group Activities to Foster Integrity, Responsibility, and Compassion,* © 2010 by Ric Stuecker, Champaign, IL: Research Press (800-519-2707, www.researchpress.com)

INSIDE

About Me!

- I am 17, a junior at Valley View High School.
- My dad lives in Europe and my mom lives here. I have two younger sisters.
- I love to paint, draw and sculpt

Sports

- Baseball (Captain)
- Cross Country
- Track
- Power Lifting

Clubs

- Speech and Debate
- Pep
- Art and Sculpture

Mission

I will foster a world that is beautiful by working hard to achieve my goals, having fun with my friends, and using my talent as an artist to make beautiful objects.

Dreams

- Obtain a baseball scholarship to college
- Study art in Europe
- Become a dad like my dad
- Earn a lot of money
- Have a cool family like mine when I get married

Achievements and Awards

- Second place in regional art fair
- Most improved baseball player at Valley View High School
- First place in Valley View Patriotism Speech Contest
- Junior Class Vice President
- Boys' State

| Inside Left | Inside Center | Inside Right |

OUTSIDE

Events That Have Molded Me

- Began school at PS 101
- Voted classroom vice president in 2nd grade
- Won safety poster contest in 3rd grade
- Moved to this community in 2006
- Began to play football in 6th grade
- Elected football team co-captain in 8th grade
- Elected president of the Art Club
- Baseball team won state
- Chosen to go to Boys' State
- Won regional speakers' award from civic group
- Represented my class in Student Council
- Organized event to raise money for charity

Leadership Skills

- Able to captain teams
- Ready to lead others
- Good listening skills
- Can make good decisions
- Friendly, likable, fun to be around
- Able to let others lead when they would do a better job
- Honest and responsible

Driven to Win!

Strong!

Fearless!

Funny!

| Back Cover | Back Center | Front Cover |

Unit Resources

Covey, S. (1998). *The 7 habits of highly effective teens.* New York: Fireside.

Covey, S. R. (1989). *The 7 habits of highly effective people: Powerful lessons in personal change.* New York: Simon and Schuster.

> *Stephen R. Covey's 1989 book is required reading for anyone interested in principle-based leadership. Sean Covey's 1998 book is an excellent adaptation for teens.*

McGraw, J. (2000). *Life strategies for teens.* New York: Fireside.

Quaglia, R. J., & Fox, K. M. (2003). *Raising student aspirations: Classroom activities.* Champaign, IL: Research Press.

> *These classroom experiences take Quaglia's eight conditions for student aspirations into the school setting.*

Roberto, J. (1997). *Leadership for life: Discovering your gifts for Christian leadership.* Naugatuck, CT: Center for Ministry Development.

> *Although these materials are used in faith-based communities, these excellent leadership materials may be applied more broadly.*

Covey Leadership Center
Jamestown Square
Provo, UT 84604
Toll-free: (800) 255–0777
www.covey.com

Quaglia Institute for Student Aspirations
P.O. Box 1219
Portland, ME 04104
www.qisa.org

UNIT 4: UNDERSTANDING COMMUNICATION

Introduction   197

Activities

4.1   Understanding Learning Styles   201

Handout 4.1.1: Understanding Learning Styles   202

Handout 4.1.2: My Preferred Learning Style Inventory   203

4.2   Discovering the Learning Styles of Others   205

Handout 4.2.1: Discovering the Learning Styles of Others   206

4.3   Negotiating One to One   207

Handout 4.3.1: Tips for Negotiating One to One   208

4.4   Shutting Down Communication   209

Handout 4.4.1: Shutting Down Communication   211

4.5   Communicating with Head and Heart   212

4.6   Understanding Power and Influence   217

Handout 4.6.1: Using Power and Influence   218

Handout 4.6.2: Effective Nonverbal Communication   219

4.7   Face to Face: Using Eye Placement and Body Position   221

4.8   Using Your Voice   223

4.9   Using "I" Messages   226

Handout 4.9.1: Using "I" Messages   228

Handout 4.9.2: Formulating "I" Messages   229

4.10   Negotiating Agreement (Skit)   230

Handout 4.10.1: Negotiating an Agreement   232

Handout 4.10.2: Negotiating an Agreement Script   233

4.11   Negotiating Agreement (Role-Plays)   235

*Handout 4.11.1: Negotiating an Agreement
        Observation Chart   237*

*Handout 4.11.2: Negotiating an Agreement Role-Play
        Situation Cards   238*

Unit Resources   240

UNIT 4 INTRODUCTION

Understanding Communication

Excellent communication is critical to effective, inspirational leadership. Nearly all inspiring leaders communicate exceptionally well. Inspiring leaders are able to communicate effectively with individuals one to one and they are able to move and motivate groups of people.

The sequences of learning experiences in this unit of *Inspiring Leadership in Teens* will teach students how to understand their own and others' learning styles, how to communicate effectively with individuals, how to run a meeting, and how to create powerful presentations.

The first activities in this unit focus on learning styles. Understanding learning styles is a vital element of effective communication. There are many ways to categorize learning styles. One approach is based on research in the field of neurolinguistic programming (NLP). According to the NLP approach, *kinesthetic learners* like to be physically active in their learning and experience concepts through their bodies. *Auditory learners* like stories and discussion. *Visual learners* like to read and have information presented logically. They thrive in traditional learning environments that focus on lectures and teacher presentations, logical practice and tests, and written examinations. Kinesthetic learners and auditory learners prefer more innovative, discovery, and group-oriented learning experiences. Most of us are a combination of these styles, but we all have a dominant style or preference for absorbing and processing information.

KINESTHETIC LEARNERS

Kinesthetic learners tend to sit to the back or side of the learning space. Other students like them because they often are entertaining. They can be dramatic and comical. These learners might have a history of not doing well in school. They sometimes challenge rules and norms. When they sit, they tend to slouch in their seats. They move around a lot when sitting and are not comfortable sitting for a long time. They learn best by doing. These students will be attentive when the learning experience is active, funny, a little weird, or physically challenging. They remember what they experience.

Kinesthetic learners are likely to be leaders outside the classroom. They generally are outgoing, fun to be with, and looked up to for athletic skill. They are not always good at organizational tasks, details, creating sequences, or looking ahead. They frequently learn by trial and error and have to try things out to learn.

Kinesthetic learners respond especially well to positive relationships. Showing interest in topics and subjects they are interested in is key to connecting with them. The saying "They won't care what you know until they know you care" is especially true for kinesthetic learners. Form a relationship with a kinesthetic learner and he or she will contribute positively to the class and be energetic in supporting the class and its objectives. Do not form a positive relationship and these learners can become negative leaders. Kinesthetic leaders like praise. They enjoy working in groups and actively participating.

In a class of 25 to 30 high-school students, five or six will be predominantly kinesthetic.

AUDITORY LEARNERS

Auditory learners often sit toward the back of the room as well. They, too, are sometimes seen as difficult to teach and often have had negative experiences in school.

Auditory learners like to tell stories during class discussions. They frequently move to a beat at their desk, rocking back and forth in rhythm, or they will tap a beat with a pen or pencil. Auditory learners learn through their ears. This does not mean by listening to lectures, though. They like stories and discussion. They like songs and rhythms. They are good at music, and many play a musical instrument.

External auditory learners—who speak often and speak before being called on—are sometimes eccentrics and can be annoying to other class members.

In a class of 25 or 30 high-school students, there may be 1 or 2 auditory learners.

VISUAL LEARNERS

Teachers often like to work with visual learners. In most class situations, 80 percent or more of the instruction is designed for such learners. They are quiet, sit still, learn through their eyes, like logical presentations, and prefer organization. They often sit front and center, like to read, and sometimes prefer to work alone rather than in groups.

Visual learners prefer lectures, movies, PowerPoint presentations that are logically organized, and teacher-centered activities. They like data and details, logic and research. Visual learners are sometimes leaders and seldom are eccentrics. They usually follow the rules and procedures, and they like a dependable schedule.

In a class of 25 to 30 high-school students, the majority learn visually. By the time most students reach high school, they have adapted to traditional learning activities that are teacher centered.

Learning styles are not hard and fast. Most of us move from style to style as needed and can adapt from logical presentation to discussion to activity to evaluation. Only a few students learn according to one predominant style. Extreme kinesthetic and auditory learners might find learning in traditional settings difficult because most of the learning experiences are designed for visual learners. Extreme visual learners may find it difficult to work in groups.

OVERVIEW OF ACTIVITIES

The activities in this unit teach the skills of effective person-to-person communications. The focus is on both nonverbal and verbal communication techniques. Communications expert Michael Grinder (1995) conservatively estimates that nonverbal communication is 87 percent of all communication. Other researchers have suggested rates as high as 95 percent. To be an effective communicator, then, it is a good idea to understand the most useful and effective nonverbal strategies. The most potent nonverbal communication techniques are eye placement, body position, tone of voice, and awareness of breathing. Effective verbal communication is also important. The focus in this unit is moving from using "you" statements to "I" statements and understanding specific roadblocks that hamper communication, sometimes foster conflict, and make coming to a win/win agreement difficult.

- Activities 4.1 and 4.2 address the concept of learning styles. By understanding their own learning styles as well as those of others, students can apply specific verbal and nonverbal strategies to improve communication and foster agreement.

- The purpose of Activity 4.3 is to learn how to reach a win/win agreement—that is, an agreement in which both people get at least some of their needs met and neither feels as though he or she has lost the argument or been manipulated. Coming to a win/win agreement requires both parties to show honor, respect, and compassion for each other and to operate with integrity.

- Activity 4.4 helps students see how certain techniques can shut down communication. An important concept is that many techniques seem positive but can actually impede communication.

- The purpose of Activity 4.5 is to teach active listening skills and how to provide effective feedback. Students gain experience in communicating thoughts, facts, opinions, and feelings.

- When communicating, we have a choice to use power or to use influence. Activity 4.6 demonstrates the difference between power and influence and when each might be appropriate to use.

- Activities 4.7 and 4.8 facilitate learning about nonverbal communication (eye placement, body position, tone of voice, and awareness of breathing) and how those techniques can be used to communicate more effectively.

- In Activity 4.9, students gain skill in using "I" messages rather than "you" messages, which can shut down communication.

- In Activities 4.10 and 4.11, students have an opportunity to present a skit and then to role-play the communication skills they've learned for reaching agreements.

ACTIVITY 4.1

Understanding Learning Styles

PURPOSE   To help students learn how they and others process information

MATERIALS   Handout 4.1.1: Understanding Learning Styles (one per student)

Handout 4.1.2: My Preferred Learning Style Inventory (one per student)

DIRECTIONS
1. Distribute the Understanding Learning Styles handout. Read it with the group and discuss the concepts to ensure that students have a good understanding of the content.

2. Hand out the My Preferred Learning Style Inventory. Read the directions with the group, then give them approximately 15 minutes to answer the questions.

3. Show students how to complete and score the inventory.

4. Ask the students to discuss the learning style they most prefer, using the following questions as a basis for discussion.

DISCUSSION
- Was it easy to discover your preferred learning style?
- Do you think you use all three styles, depending on the situation?
- Are you more comfortable with one style than the others?
- Do you think you could discover the learning styles of others?

Researchers have identified three kinds of learning styles. Most of us use all three styles, but we tend to prefer one over the others. We may switch from one learning style to another according to the occasion. For example, if the situation calls for action—say, playing a pick-up basketball game with your friends—you will probably go into *kinesthetic mode*. That's because the kinesthetic mode involves processing information through the body. If you are at a concert, playing music, or singing with a friend, you will probably switch to *auditory mode*. That's because those situations involve listening. If you are at a play or listening to a fascinating lecture and taking notes, you might switch into *visual mode* because that's the mode we use for taking in logical information.

All day long, we switch our learning modes, situation by situation. Most of have preferences for how we like to learn. If you like to learn by doing, you like to learn kinesthetically. If you like to hear about things to learn about them, you prefer auditory learning. And when you like to read the instructions first, your preferred style is visual learning.

When you communicate with other people, it is a good idea to know their preferred learning style—how they like to take in, process, and store information. If you are running a meeting, it's a good idea to know the learning styles of the individuals who make up the group. If you are making a presentation, you can effectively engage your audience if you understand their learning styles and accommodate them when you speak.

Here are some characteristics of the three learning styles.

Kinesthetic Learners

- Like to do things and to learn by doing
- Take in information through their bodies
- Like repetition of physical activity
- Are physically oriented
- Prefer to be moving rather than sitting
- Like to "walk through" something to learn about it

- Use gestures and action words
- Can be extremely intuitive
- Like touching and standing close
- Are looking for relationships with others
- Understand relationships well
- Are eager to experiment and implement

Examples: Athletes, dancers, actors

Auditory Learners

- Love to listen
- Like to tell long stories
- Take in information through their ears
- Remember what they hear
- Prefer to listen to information about what they are learning
- Have a memory like a tape recorder
- Speak in a rhythmic manner
- Tend to rock rhythmically when seated
- Listen to an internal dialogue
- Often like to hear their own voices

Examples: Poets, composers, rappers, singers

Visual Learners

- Love to read
- Read everything they see
- Learn through their eyes
- Follow a speaker with their eyes
- Like individual space
- Sit up straight and tall and are still
- Like logical presentations of information
- Speak quickly, without much music to their voices
- Frequently take notes
- Prefer facts, details, and statistics
- Prefer to read about or hear a lecture about what they are learning

Examples: Professors, speakers, researchers, writers

Name _____ Date _____

Read each of the following statements and decide whether it is always true, often true, sometimes true, or never true. Allocate points as shown on the scoring scale below. Be as honest as you can. Respond to each item. When you have completed the inventory, you will be able to score it to determine your preferred learning style.

Scoring Scale

The statement is always true = 3 points

The statement is often true = 2 points

The statement is sometimes true = 1 point

The statement is never true = 0 points

Statement	*Points*
1. Give me a book—I could read all day.	_____
2. I enjoy music and listen to it whenever I can.	_____
3. I have to be doing things or I get bored.	_____
4. Show me the instructions and I can learn.	_____
5. Tell me how to do it first.	_____
6. If I can experiment with it, I can learn it.	_____
7. I find it easy to listen and take notes.	_____
8. I often find myself drumming my fingers.	_____
9. I find it hard to sit in one place for a long time.	_____
10. At a concert, I like to watch the performer.	_____
11. At a concert, I like to keep time and sing along.	_____
12. At a concert, I like to move and dance.	_____
13. My teachers think I'm a model student.	_____
14. My teachers wish I could be quiet.	_____
15. I often get in trouble at school.	_____
16. I prefer watching sports.	_____
17. I like to listen to conversations.	_____
18. I prefer to be on the field playing.	_____
19. I'd rather be in class learning.	_____
20. I'd rather be hanging out and talking with my friends.	_____
21. I'd rather be playing sports or doing something active.	_____

From *Inspiring Leadership in Teens: Group Activities to Foster Integrity, Responsibility, and Compassion,* © 2010 by Ric Stuecker, Champaign, IL: Research Press (800-519-2707, www.researchpress.com)

Transferring and Interpreting Scores

Use the following chart to record your scores. The small numbers in each block correspond to the 21 individual items for which you recorded values of 0, 1, 2, or 3 for the statements. Transfer your 21 individual item scores to the Score Transfer chart. Next, add the values in each column (I, II, and II) and place the totals at the bottom. When you have the columns totaled, transfer their values to the Score Interpretation chart that follows.

Score Transfer

I (Visual)	II (Auditory)	III (Kinesthetic)
1	2	3
4	5	6
7	8	9
10	11	12
13	14	15
16	17	18
19	20	21

Totals

Score Interpretation

My most preferred style is _____ (highest score)

My second preferred style is _____ (middle score)

My least preferred style is _____ (lowest score)

ACTIVITY 4.2

Discovering the Learning Styles of Others

PURPOSE   To help students learn to identify the learning styles of others

MATERIALS   Handout 4.2.1: Discovering the Learning Styles of Others (one per student)

DIRECTIONS
1. Distribute copies of the worksheet, then read it together to make sure everyone understands it.
2. Give students approximately 10 minutes to fill it out.
3. When all the students are finished, hold a discussion using the following questions.

DISCUSSION
- Was it difficult to find examples of each learning style?
- Do you think we use all the learning styles at different times? Can you give examples?
- Which style do we use mostly at school? Playing a game? Listening to music?

Name _____ Date _____

I believe the learning style I prefer the most is _____.

I believe this because of the following evidence:

1. _____

2. _____

3. _____

4. _____

I believe _____ prefers the visual learning style. (Select someone in the class or someone you know.)

I believe he or she is a good example because of the following evidence:

1. _____

2. _____

3. _____

4. _____

I believe _____ prefers the auditory learning style. (Select someone in the class or someone you know.)

I believe he or she is a good example because of the following evidence:

1. _____

2. _____

3. _____

4. _____

I believe _____ prefers the kinesthetic learning style. (Select someone in the class or someone you know.)

I believe he or she is a good example because of the following evidence:

1. _____

2. _____

3. _____

4. _____

From *Inspiring Leadership in Teens: Group Activities to Foster Integrity, Responsibility, and Compassion,* © 2010 by Ric Stuecker, Champaign, IL: Research Press (800-519-2707, www.researchpress.com)

Negotiating One to One

PURPOSE
To encourage learning of specific techniques for communicating on a one-to-one basis

MATERIALS
Handout 4.3.1: Tips for Negotiating One to One (one per student)

DIRECTIONS
1. Explain that sometimes leaders have to negotiate with a team member one to one.
2. Distribute the handout, then read through it with the students to ensure comprehension.
3. Hold a discussion using the following questions.

DISCUSSION
- What are some examples of situations you have been in when you negotiated with someone? For example:

   Asking a parent to borrow the car

   Asking a parent whether you can be out after curfew

   Planning a date

   Planning something to do with a friend

- What difficulties did you have in negotiating?
- Do you find you can negotiate and get what you want?
- Describe people who are difficult to negotiate with. Why are they difficult?

Kinesthetic Learners

If you are negotiating with a *kinesthetic* learner, you might want to use the following tips:

- Involve an activity.
- Take a walk together.
- Talk while he or she is driving.
- Play a game together and talk while you are playing.
- Stand or sit close, side by side or at a 90-degree angle.
- Use appropriate touch—you can touch the other person's shoulder if you want.
- When using examples, choose actions, sports, and activities.
- Make sure to shake hands on any agreements.

Auditory Learners

If you are negotiating with an *auditory* learner, you might want to use the following tips:

- Respectfully and carefully listen to any stories he or she tells.
- Wait until the person pauses before you speak.
- Put what you have to say in a story form.
- Ask respectfully whether the person can repeat what you have said to him or her.
- Talk while you are driving.
- Sit at a 90-degree angle.
- Review and repeat any agreements orally.

Visual Learners

If you are negotiating with a *visual* learner, you might want to use the following tips:

- Write down important points, ideas, or questions on a sheet of paper.
- Sit at the corner of a table, using the paper with points and questions as a focus.
- Point to each idea or question as you talk.
- Present your ideas in a logical way—outline them first.
- Take notes on any ideas or suggestions either of you make.
- Before you finish, review any agreements. Write them down.

From *Inspiring Leadership in Teens: Group Activities to Foster Integrity, Responsibility, and Compassion,* © 2010 by Ric Stuecker, Champaign, IL: Research Press (800-519-2707, www.researchpress.com)

ACTIVITY 4.4

Shutting Down Communication

PURPOSE
To help students learn what techniques tend to shut down communication

MATERIALS
Handout 4.4.1: Shutting Down Communication (one per student)

DIRECTIONS
1. Distribute the Shutting Down Communication handout. Explain that there are many ways of shutting down communication and that the handout describes a number of ways people do this. Point out that some of these techniques even seem very nice and useful—such as giving a person praise, giving advice, or sympathizing.

2. Read through the handout with the students, discussing the techniques and giving examples.

3. When you are finished discussing, have students form groups of three. Designate person A, B, and C for each group. A and B will participate. C will observe.

4. Ask person A to explain to person B one of the following:
   - My favorite way to spend a weekend
   - What's cool about my favorite sport
   - A movie I think everyone should see

5. Ask person B to use as many techniques for shutting down the conversation as possible. Ask person C to observe the interaction and to note as many techniques as he or she witnesses.

Give person A 2 minutes to speak. Person B can interrupt as often as he or she likes.

6. Make sure each person in each group of three plays each role: speaker, interrupter, and observer.

7. When all groups have had the opportunity to finish, hold a discussion, using the following questions.

DISCUSSION

- How close is this activity to what you experience in real life?
- What were the most effective ways for shutting down communication?
- Which ways seem positive but turned off communication?
- Which ways seem rude and obnoxious?
- Which ways of shutting down communication surprised you?
- How do you react when you notice your friends using these techniques on you?

Demanding and Commanding

- "Do it this way."
- "Don't ever speak to me the way you did."
- "I expect you to . . ."

Advising

- "Why don't you . . . ?"
- "If I were you, I'd . . ."

Threatening

- "Do that again and I'll . . ."
- "Be careful or I'll . . ."

Teaching and Preaching

- "What you ought to do is . . ."
- "Have you ever thought about . . .?"

Judging

- "I can't believe you did that."
- "That was really stupid."

Interpreting

- "I think you were just being careful."
- "Looks like you're afraid of . . ."

Ridiculing

- "You're just being a snob."

Questioning/Probing

- "What do you think the real reason is behind what you say?

Praising

- "You are really quite smart and clever to . . ."

Distracting

- "Did I ever tell you about the time I . . .?"

Can you think of and describe any other ways of shutting down communication?

From *Inspiring Leadership in Teens: Group Activities to Foster Integrity, Responsibility, and Compassion,* © 2010 by Ric Stuecker, Champaign, IL: Research Press (800-519-2707, www.researchpress.com)

ACTIVITY 4.5

Communicating with Head and Heart

This activity includes a series of experiences to teach active listening and effective feedback. There are several rounds.

PURPOSE
To help students learn to communicate thoughts, facts, opinions, and feelings

DIRECTIONS
1. Place students in groups of three. Ask them to designate persons A, B, and C.

2. The activity is divided into five rounds and concludes with a whole-group discussion. Follow the instructions for each round.

Round 1

1. Say:

> This is a timed activity. Do not start until I say, "Begin." Person A will speak. B and C will listen. Person A will have 45 seconds to tell B and C as many facts about himself or herself as possible in the allotted time. Here's an example:

> My name is _____ .

> I am _____ tall.

> I live on _____ Street.

> I have _____ brothers and _____ sisters.

> My favorite dessert is apple pie.

> My favorite place to travel is Florida.

Say:

> Does everyone understand? Are there any questions? When I say, "Begin," you may start. *(Pause.)* Begin.

2. At the end of 45 seconds say, "Come to a conclusion and . . . STOP."

3. Now ask B and C to repeat back to A what they heard him or her say. At the end of 30 seconds, say, "STOP."

4. Ask the A's the following questions:

   - Did you feel listened to?

   - Were B and C able to tell you what you told them?

   - If so, how did that feel?

   - B and C, did you have any difficulties listening to A? If so, what where they?

   - Was anyone so busy thinking about what to say that he or she forgot to listen?

5. Explain that being able to repeat and paraphrase for clarity is an important skill in listening and giving feedback.

6. Repeat the above procedure for persons B and C: First, A and C listen and give feedback to B. Then A and B listen and give feedback to C.

7. At the end of Round 1, ask everyone to stand up, stretch, and change seats with the others in their groups of three, then give the instructions for Round 2.

Round 2

1. Say:

   > B speaks first. A and C listen. B's, I want you to think of an opinion you hold strongly—so strongly you will fight for that opinion. For example:
   >
   > > Lunch at school should be at least an hour!
   > >
   > > Teens should be able to drink at 18!
   > >
   > > Teens should not have a curfew!
   >
   > Select something you feel strongly about. A and C, you will listen to B. Do not indicate verbally or nonverbally that you agree or disagree. Simply listen. Do not nod in agreement, shake your head, or say, "I agree." Person B, you will have 1 minute to express your strongly held opinion. Ready? *(Pause.)* Begin.

2. At the end of 1 minute, say, "Come to a conclusion . . . and STOP."

3. Give these instructions to A and C:

   > A and C, you have 30 seconds to tell B what he or she said to you. Please make sure that you do not indicate whether you agree or disagree. *(Pause.)* Begin.

4. At the end of 30 seconds, say, "STOP."

5. Repeat the procedure with C speaking and A and B listening and giving feedback. Then repeat with A speaking and B and C listening and giving feedback.

6. When everyone has spoken and been given feedback, hold a discussion, asking the following questions:

  • How did it feel to be listened to without interruption?

  • Was it difficult to listen and not indicate what you thought?

  • Was it difficult to listen and not think about what you wanted to say?

7. Say the following:

> Most of the time it is difficult to listen to someone's opinion and not respond with our own opinion. It is also difficult to listen to someone's opinion and really listen without thinking about what we want to say. Sometimes we judge other people by their opinions, and we stop listening to them and respecting them. Sometimes we believe we are being asked for our opinions or our advice when the speaker just wants us to listen.

8. Ask students to stand, stretch, and sit in a different chair within their group of three. Proceed with Round 3.

Round 3

1. Say:

> Person C will speak, and persons A and B will listen.

> Person C, I want you to imagine for a minute a person who has influenced you greatly, who has supported you in your life, who is there for you when you need him or her, and with whom you can discuss just about anything. Imagine a person you greatly admire. Take a minute and picture that person.

> Person C, if you do not have someone you greatly admire in your life, then think about what a person you would admire would be like. What characteristics would this person have?

> Person C, you have 90 seconds to describe to A and B someone you admire, who has influenced you, and who supports you. (Or you can describe what someone you might admire would be like.)

> Persons A and B, listen with an open heart. Use nonverbal communication to indicate that you understand (smiles, nods, eye contact), but do not say anything.

> Any questions? If not, begin.

2. At the end of 90 seconds, say, "Come to a conclusion and . . . STOP."

3. Give A and B these instructions:

A and B, you have 45 seconds to tell C not only what he or she said but also how it made you feel. Use feelings words. Indicate whether you have had similar experiences.

4. Repeat the above procedure with A speaking and with B and C listening and giving feedback. Then repeat with B speaking and A and C listening and giving feedback. Make sure each person gets to speak and receive feedback.

5. Hold a discussion, using the following questions:

- Was this round harder? What, if anything, made it harder?

- Was it easy or difficult to express your feelings?

- Is it difficult to talk about feelings? Is it difficult to speak from the heart?

6. If you have time, this is a good opportunity to give students a 5- to 10-minute break.

7. After the break, ask students to return to their groups of three and sit in a different chair. Then explain the following:

We often have conversations where we give facts, opinions, and descriptions. We like to "stay in our heads."

We seldom speak from the heart and talk about feelings—unless we are overwhelmed by our feelings or we are speaking with someone we trust about something important. We protect our feelings and our hearts. Describing someone we admire and who supports us takes us "into our hearts."

This next round, we are going to take the risk of speaking from the heart about our feelings. Take a minute to think about a time you were mad, sad, or afraid. You will each be given 2 minutes to talk about a time you had one of those feelings. Please be quiet while you are thinking.

8. When you have given the students some time to think, give them the following instructions for Round 4.

Round 4

1. Say:

Person A will speak first. Persons B and C will listen.

Person A, you will have 2 minutes to speak. Describe a time in your life when you were mad, sad, or afraid. Describe the event and your feelings as fully as possible. *(Pause.)* Begin.

2. At the end of 2 minutes say, "Come to a conclusion and . . . STOP." Give these instructions to B and C:

Please give person A empathetic feedback. That is, tell A
what he or she said and how you felt about what you heard.
You have 1 minute to give feedback.

3. Repeat the above procedure with B speaking and A and C listening and giving feedback, then C speaking and A and B listening
and giving feedback.

4. When everyone has spoken, discuss the following:

   • What did you learn?

   • How difficult was it for you to speak from your feelings?

   • How often do you speak from your feelings in real life?

   • To whom do you speak from the heart?

5. Ask everyone to stand and stretch and sit in their original chairs,
then ask the students to think about a time in their lives they were
really happy. Give them the following instructions for Round 5.

Round 5

1. Say:

   Think of a time you were really happy. Each of you will have
   1 minute to describe a time when something good happened
   in your life and you were really happy. Be prepared to fully
   describe the event and how you felt. We will begin with person A. *(Pause.)* Person A, begin.

2. When person A finishes, say, "STOP." Do not allow time for feedback but go right to persons B and C, giving each a minute to
speak about a time when they were happy.

3. Hold a final discussion about the entire activity, using the following questions.

DISCUSSION

• What did you like about this exercise?

• What did you dislike about this exercise?

• How do you feel about the other people in your small group?

• How do you feel about yourself?

ACTIVITY 4.6

Understanding Power and Influence

PURPOSE

To encourage learning about communication techniques that use power over others and those that use influence

MATERIALS

Handout 4.6.1: Using Power and Influence (one per student)

Handout 4.6.2: Effective Nonverbal Communication (one per student)

DIRECTIONS

1. Distribute the handouts. Read through and discuss the material, answering any questions.

2. Continue the discussion by asking the following questions.

DISCUSSION

- What sort of situations would be best for using power?

- Why wouldn't influence be useful during these situations?

- What sort of situations would be best for using influence?

- Why would using power be a bad idea during these situations?

- Have you ever experienced a leader who mostly used power? What effects did mostly using power have on the team or group?

- Have you ever experienced a leader who mostly used influence? What effects did mostly using influence have on the team or group?

- Have you ever experienced a leader who used both? Can you give examples of when the leader used power and when the leader used influence?

- Who do you believe was the most effective leader? Why do you think this?

When we are communicating, we have a choice to use our power or our influence.

Power

We can use our power in the following ways:

- By commanding, demanding, or telling someone what to do

- By getting into a power struggle in which someone wins and someone loses

- By using our position as a leader to order someone to do something

There are times when using power is important. For example, in an emergency, someone may have to take charge and give orders. In a dangerous situation such as a war, a leader may have to command and give orders to his or her troops.

Power is usually effective in the short term. It is also effective when everyone agrees that the person using power has the authority to make decisions and the situation warrants the use of power.

Power is usually ineffective for long projects or when two or more people are making a decision and carrying out tasks together. In those cases, it is often best to use influence.

Influence

We use influence when we seek a decision in situations where there is no struggle for power and when we want everyone to win. Using influence leads to long-term agreements between parties or among groups. When we use influence, we do the following:

- We value and build relationships.

- We seek consensus.

- We reach win/win agreements.

Inspiring Leaders

Inspiring leaders use both power and influence. They understand when it is important to use power and what situations demand it. They under-stand when being influential is most effective. In a leadership position, you will have to use both power and influence. Leaders build credibility with others when they are comfortable with power and use it only when necessary. Leaders build influence through relationships with others and by being approachable. Inspiring leaders are both credible and approachable.

Credibility is important because the members of a group want to know that the leader and other group members are believable, trustworthy, and knowledgeable and that they can make decisions.

Approachability is important because it encourages relationships. Relationships help when groups are working on projects where they need to work together closely over the long term. Approachability tells the other members of a group that you value them as people, that you will listen to them and consider their ideas, that you like them, and that as a team you are working together toward a common goal.

When leaders communicate through power, they increase their credibility. However, if they remain in a power mode, they will appear dictatorial, closed to other ideas, and unapproachable. Ultimately, relationships are weakened.

When a leader communicates using influence, he or she builds relationships. However, if a leader only uses influence, he or she risks being seen as indecisive, unable to take charge, lacking in knowledge, and weak.

Inspiring leaders value both approaches, use power on a limited basis when needed, and foster relationships and a team approach by using influence over the course of a project. Effective leaders know when to use power and how much to use. They calibrate, or measure, how much power the situation requires and move back to influence as soon as they can. The more a leader uses influence, the more effective his or her leadership will be.

Research has shown that more than 80 percent of all communication is nonverbal. Some studies show that as much as 95 percent of communication is nonverbal. Four powerful tools for nonverbal communication are eye placement, tone of voice, body position, and awareness of breathing. A leader can use these tools to increase his or her power and influence. The following chart indicates how to use nonverbal techniques for each effect.

	Using Power	Using Influence
Eye Placement	*Direct:* When speaking with another person, look directly into his or her eyes. When speaking to a group, make direct eye contact with individuals in the group or audience.	*Indirect:* When negotiating with another person, both people focus on a third point, such as a list of ideas. When speaking to a group, scan the group or audience or look at a chart or other visual prop.
Body Position	*Front:* The more you stand or sit face to face or front to front, the more you are using power.	*Side:* The more you move to the side of someone, the more influence you are using.
	Close: The closer you move toward someone—especially face to face—the more you are using power.	*Far:* The farther you stand or sit from a person, the more influence you are using.
	Straight and tall: If standing, balance your weight on your feet and stand tall. If sitting, sit up straight with both feet on the floor.	*Relaxed:* Standing with your weight on one leg or sitting with legs crossed or relaxed increases influence.
	Still: The more you sit or stand still, the more powerful you are.	*Moving:* When you shift stance or the way you are sitting and move in a relaxed manner, you increase influence.
Tone of Voice	*Speed:* Speak rapidly.	*Speed:* Speak slowly.
	Tone: Speak flatly and let your voice drop at the end of phrases and sentences.	*Tone:* Speak musically, with your voice going up at pauses and the end of sentences.
	Pauses: Your pauses are clear. When speaking to groups, your pauses are longer.	*Pauses:* There are no pauses, or just a quick pause that does not register, or the speaker makes noises during the pause, such as "Ah."

	Using Power	Using Influence
Breathing	When you are using power, you tend to breathe high in your chest. As you become tenser—if you are in a win/lose situation or an emergency—your breathing will become higher and higher in your chest.	When using influence, your breathing is lower, down in your belly. You breathe rhythmically, along with the person you are speaking with. The deeper the relationship, the deeper and more comfortable the breathing.
	If you notice your breathing getting higher, you are probably in a conflict with someone.	You can judge how effectively you are communicating with someone by noticing how low your breathing is.

When you use power, you are more likely to find yourself in a win/lose situation, you use more energy, and your relationships weaken. It is good to use powerful nonverbal communication when you want to establish your credibility—when you first meet someone, if you are starting a meeting, or if you are leading a negotiation with someone. If you want to close down discussion or come to a quick decision, use power techniques: direct eye contact, still and straight body, a flat tone of voice.

It is good to use influence when you want to share ideas, increase discussion, or consider options. To increase the flow of participation in a negotiation or with a group, use influence techniques: indirect eye placement, relaxed body, and a musical voice.

ACTIVITY 4.7

Face to Face: Using Eye Placement and Body Position

PURPOSE
To facilitate learning about how to use eye placement and body position effectively when communicating

DIRECTIONS
1. Have students sit in groups of three in chairs away from any tables or other furniture.
   - Ask students to designate themselves A, B, and C.
   - Ask students A and B to sit facing each other. Ask student C to observe what happens between A and B.
   - Ask A and B to look into each other's eyes and to keep looking.
   - Ask student C to watch and see how long it takes for A or B to look away. (If C doesn't have a watch, he or she can count and approximate the seconds.)
   - Ask student C to note the time and what happened.

2. Repeat the procedure, this time with C and B looking into each other's eyes and A as the observer.

3. Repeat the procedure, this time with A and C looking into each other's eyes and B as the observer.

4. Ask students A and B to sit at a 90-degree angle and discuss a favorite video game or book. After a minute, announce, "STOP."

5. Ask students B and C to sit at a 90-degree angle and discuss their favorite recent movie. After a minute, announce, "STOP."

6. Ask students A and C to sit at a 90-degree angle and discuss their favorite TV show. After a minute, announce, "STOP."

7. Explain that staying face to face often leads to arguments and power struggles and that moving to a 90-degree angle is more effective, feels more collaborative, and elicits more ideas, conversation, and agreement. It is easier to come to an agreement you both like in this position. Face to face usually means one wins and the other loses.

8. Hold a discussion, using the following questions.

DISCUSSION

- How many of you found yourselves in a struggle with someone to see who would look away first?

- How did you feel sitting facing each other? How did you feel sitting at a 90-degree angle?

- How do you think you would sit or stand if you were having an argument?

- Which would be more comfortable for negotiating an agreement?

- Have you ever been in a power struggle? (For example, your parent wants you to clean your room, but you don't.) If so, what techniques were used to win the struggle? How did it feel to be in the struggle?

- Have you ever negotiated with someone? (For example, you and your parents discussed a reasonable time to be home.) If so, what techniques were used to negotiate? Were you able to reach a win/win solution? (For example, you got to stay out later, and your parents knew where you were and when you would be home.)

A CTIVITY 4.8

Using Your Voice

PURPOSE To encourage students to learn to use tone of voice effectively

MATERIALS Whiteboard or easel pad

PREPARATION Write the following on the whiteboard or easel pad:

My name is _____.

I am a student at _____.

My dream is to someday _____.

DIRECTIONS
1. Place students in groups of three, away from tables or other furniture. Ask students to determine who is A, B, and C.

2. Explain that each person is going to introduce himself or herself to the others first by being credible, then by being approachable, and finally by mixing both. Round 1 will be credible, Round 2 will be approachable, and Round 3 will mix both.

Round 1

1. Explain that when you want to be credible you must turn your voice down at the end of each phrase and pause clearly between phrases. You also must stand straight and still and with your weight balanced. Give an example:

(Speak rapidly and turn your voice tone down at the end.)

My name is Mr. Sm i t h.

(Pause for three beats.)

I am a teacher at Jefferson High Sch o o l.

(Pause for three beats.)

My dream is to retire some day in It a l y.

2. Ask students A to stand and face students B and C. Ask them to do as follows:

   - Adjust their weight, moving their feet about 12 to 18 inches apart, toes pointed straight out.
   - Introduce themselves to B and C, using the phrases on the whiteboard or easel pad.
   - Stand completely still with their hands at their sides.
   - Pause completely and leave silence between each phrase and turn their voice down at the end of each phrase.

3. When all groups are finished, ask B and C to give A feedback:

   - Did they stand still?
   - Did they pause clearly?
   - Did they turn their voice down at the end?
   - Were they credible?

4. Ask A to repeat the introduction, using the feedback to make adjustments to become more credible.

5. Repeat the exercise with B and then C making introductions and the others giving feedback.

Round 2

1. Explain that, this time, speakers will demonstrate using an approachable style. Explain that they can shift their weight, smile, move their bodies, and make their voices musical by using tones that rise at the end of a statement. For example:

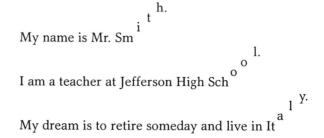

2. Ask students A to stand, face B and C, and rest their weight on one leg. Ask them to introduce themselves again, smiling and making their voices musical. Ask them not to pause between statements.

3. Ask students B and C to give A feedback:

   - Did their voices go up at the end of phrases?
   - Were their voices musical?
   - Did they smile?
   - Did they move? Shift their weight?
   - Were they more approachable?

4. Repeat this exercise with B and then C making introductions and the listeners giving feedback.

5. When everyone has introduced themselves, hold a discussion, using these questions:

   • Which method gave the speaker more authority and credibility?

   • Which seemed friendlier?

   • Which method would you want a leader of a team to use?

   • Why would a leader need to use both methods?

Round 3

1. This time, mix up credible and approachable tones of voice. Demonstrate for the class by starting credible and moving to approachable. An easy way to do this is to start by keeping your weight balanced and not smiling, then shifting your weight and smiling.

2. Ask students A to stand, introduce themselves, and move from credible to approachable.

3. Ask students B and C to give feedback on whether A moved from credible to approachable.

4. Ask A to practice until he or she is able to demonstrate both credibility and approachability.

5. Repeat this exercise with B and then C making introductions and mixing credibility and approachability.

DISCUSSION

• Which pattern was easier for you? Credible or approachable?

• If credible was easier for you, do you also tend to be a visual learner?

• If approachable was easier for you, do you tend to be an auditory or kinesthetic learner?

• How difficult was it for you to mix the two tones of voice?

• Can you think of situations where an approachable tone of voice might be preferred? If so, what sort of situations?

• Can you think of situations where a credible tone of voice might be preferred? If so, what sort of situations?

• In what situations might you want to use both?

ACTIVITY 4.9

Using "I" Messages

PURPOSE   To help students learn to use effective "I" messages instead of ineffective "you" messages

MATERIALS   Handout 4.9.1: Using "I" Messages (one per student)

Handout 4.9.2: Formulating "I" Messages (one per student)

DIRECTIONS   1. Distribute the Using "I" Messages handout. Read the handout together with the students. Ask for questions and provide clarification if necessary.

2. Hold a discussion, using the following questions:

   • Has anyone been in a power struggle or conflict over someone's behavior lately? If so, could you describe what happened?

   • Did the power struggle or conflict happen because someone used "you" messages? If so, could you give some examples?

   • Thinking back, how could you or the person you had the conflict with use an "I" message?

   • Do you believe "I" messages would be more effective in getting someone to change their behavior? If so, why?

3. Distribute the Formulating "I" Messages worksheet.

4. Ask students to rephrase each of the "you" messages as an "I" message. Remind them that "I" messages have three parts: naming the behavior, naming the feeling evoked in you, and naming the effect the behavior has on you.

5. When students have finished filling out the handout, ask for volunteers to read their answers. Explain why each is or is not a good example of an "I" message.

6. Place the students in groups of three. Ask each student to present three completely new "I" messages to his or her small group. Ask the group members to give feedback explaining why the "I" message follows the pattern or why it does not.

7. Hold a discussion, using the following questions.

DISCUSSION

- Is it hard to use "I" messages? If so, why?
- Why do you suppose using a "you" message is a way to use power?
- Why do you suppose using an "I" message is a way to use influence?
- Why do you suppose thinking about and planning an "I" message might be a good idea before confronting someone about his or her behavior?
- Are confrontations a part of leadership? Why or why not?

"You" Messages

Often, when we are speaking to or confronting others, we use "you" messages to make our point. Examples:

"You forgot to clean your room again."

"You're acting like an idiot."

"If you don't stop this behavior, I'll have to ground you."

Although they might get our point across, "you" messages usually sound to the person receiving the communication like orders, sarcasm, judgments, and threats. When people feel like they are being ordered, being made fun of, judged, or threatened, they often respond negatively and sometimes violently. At the very least, communication often shuts down. Feelings are sometimes hurt. Usually, the behavior continues as before.

"I" Messages

A more effective way to confront another person is to use an "I" message. The "I" message does not order, accuse, judge, or use sarcasm. Rather, it expresses how a person is affected by the actions of another and gives the person receiving the communication the option and responsibility of changing his or her behavior.

"I" messages consist of three parts:

1. Name the specific behavior: "When you . . ."
2. Name the feeling you have when you experience the behavior: "I feel . . ."
3. Name the effect on you the behavior has: "because . . ."

"I" messages are a lot more effective than "you" messages because they do not shut down communication. Here are some examples of effective "I" messages:

"When you arrive 15 minutes late to pick me up, I feel anxious and worried because I do not know for sure whether you are coming."

"When you fail to clean your room, I feel angry because then I have to clean it ."

"When you tell me you're coming over and then you don't show up, I feel disappointed because I think you must have found something better to do and decided to ditch me."

Read the following "you" messages and rewrite them as "I" messages. For example:

"You" message:

"You must be lazy. You never clean the kitchen up after using it."

"I" message:

(behavior) "When you leave the kitchen a mess,

(feeling) I feel angry and frustrated

(effect) because I have to clean up the kitchen myself."

1. **"You" message:**

   "Come home late again and you're grounded."

   "I" message:

   (behavior) "When _____,

   (feeling) I _____

   (effect) because _____."

2. **"You" message:**

   "Are you an idiot? I can't believe you've picked me up half an hour late."

   "I" message:

   (behavior) "When _____,

   (feeling) I _____

   (effect) because _____."

3. **"You" message:**

   "I can't believe you're incapable of telling me the truth."

   "I" message:

   (behavior) "When _____,

   (feeling) I _____

   (effect) because _____."

4. **"You" message:**

   "If you can't pull your own weight, get your act together, and contribute to the team project, you'll have to leave the team."

   "I" message:

   (behavior) "When _____,

   (feeling) I _____

   (effect) because _____."

5. **"You" message:**

   "You drive me crazy when you play with your food."

   "I" message:

   (behavior) "When _____,

   (feeling) I _____

   (effect) because _____."

From *Inspiring Leadership in Teens: Group Activities to Foster Integrity, Responsibility, and Compassion,* © 2010 by Ric Stuecker, Champaign, IL: Research Press (800-519-2707, www.researchpress.com)

ACTIVITY 4.10

Negotiating Agreement (Skit)

PURPOSE To help students learn how to effectively negotiate an agreement with another person

MATERIALS Handout 4.10.1: Negotiating an Agreement (one per student)

Handout 4.10.2: Negotiating an Agreement Script (one per student)

Optional: A small table

PREPARATION Arrange a small stage area where role-players can present a short skit to the class.

DIRECTIONS
1. Distribute the Negotiating an Agreement handout. Read the handout with the students and discuss any questions.

2. Explain each phase of the negotiation, pointing out both verbal and nonverbal techniques.

3. Select two role-players and ask one of them to be the leader. Hand out the Negotiating an Agreement script. Ask them to take a minute to read through the script. Arrange the class into a "theater" while the players are reviewing the script.

4. Prepare the role-players. Make sure the leader knows to change tone of voice, eye placement, and body position as each phase changes.

5. Position the role-players. They should have two chairs and possibly a small table. Place the chair and table at an angle so that the players can sit at a corner of the table during their negotiations and can be seen by the audience. The skit begins with both players standing.

6. Have the players present the role-play. As they do, point out each phase as the players begin it.

7. When the skit is over, thank the players and have the audience applaud the role-players.

8. Hold a discussion, asking the following questions.

DISCUSSION

- Could you follow each phase during the skit?
- How and when did the leader use a credible tone of voice?
- How, when, and why did the leader change his or her body position? Eye placement?
- Did the leader ever use "you" messages? If so, when?
- Did the leader ever use "I" messages? If so, when?
- Do you have any questions about the process of negotiating an agreement as it was presented?
- Do you have any questions before you role-play a negotiation?

Sometimes it is important for a leader to sit down with a teammate and hold a conference to negotiate an agreement to do something for the team or for a project. Or a leader might have to confront a team member concerning his or her behavior and ask for an agreement to change. When negotiating, you should use both power and influence, remain aware of your nonverbal communication techniques (remember, they're 80 percent or more of the communication!), and use "I" messages.

Conferences to negotiate an agreement usually have five specific parts, or phases.

Phase 1: Why Are We Meeting?

As the person who has asked for a conference, you should frame or describe the purpose of the meeting and the points you would like to discuss. This way, you set the limits of the negotiation and you propose some possible outcomes. You might begin by saying, "Thank you for coming . . ."

During Phase 1, you want to be credible. Use direct eye contact and a credible tone of voice and face the person directly.

Phase 2: Gathering Information

During this phase, you gather any information necessary to reach an agreement. You say, "I am wondering . . ."

You want to be approachable. You could take notes—looking at the note paper rather than directly at the person. You could move to the side, to a 90-degree angle with the person. Possibly you could sit at the corner of a table.

Phase 3: Creating Options

During this phase, you explore possible options. You say, "Let's explore what might work for us both."

You want to stay approachable.

Phase 4: Deciding

During this phase, you ask for the decision the person is willing to make. Strive to achieve a win/win position, where the person meets your needs and chooses an option that is agreeable to him or her. You say, "So you would be willing to . . ."

At this point, you want to return to credible techniques: Make eye contact, use a credible tone of voice, sit up straight, and be still.

Phase 5: Thank You

Shake hands, looking into the person's eyes, and thank him or her for working with you. Say, "Thank you for being so supportive."

From *Inspiring Leadership in Teens: Group Activities to Foster Integrity, Responsibility, and Compassion,* © 2010 by Ric Stuecker, Champaign, IL: Research Press (800-519-2707, www.researchpress.com)

Phase 1: Why Are We Meeting?

Leader (*standing, looking the team member in the eye, using a credible tone of voice*): Thank you, _____ [name], for meeting with me today. I have a few things I'd like to go over with you, and I am hoping you can help me out.

Team member: No problem. I'm willing to help however I can.

Leader: Good. Let's get started.

The two sit down at the corner of a table. Leader uses an approachable tone of voice.

Phase 2: Gathering Information

Leader: I am wondering whether you might have some time to take on an extra task for our project. When you take on a task, I feel confident because I know it will get done, be done well, and be done on time.

Team member: Thanks for the compliment. It's possible, although I have things to do at home, and I have practice for the team.

Leader: Do you think you would have time to proofread our brochure and take it to the printer?

Team member: My dad works next door to the printer. I could ask him to drop it off on his way to work.

Leader: Great! Would you also have time to proofread it first?

Team member: Maybe, if I don't have too much homework, I finish with my chores, and I'm not too tired from practice.

Phase 3: Creating Options

Leader (*continuing to use approachable voice but shifting in the chair and taking a new, more relaxed position*): Could I come over and help you with your chores?

Team member: Maybe. You know, we're not having practice on Wednesday.

Leader: That would be a good night. Do you need some help with the proofreading? Mary Ann said she might be able to go over the text with you.

Team member: I really don't have a lot to do on Wednesdays—and it might be a good idea if Mary Ann helped proofread. She's a sharp editor, and we could get it done fast. I'd be confident that I didn't miss anything. Plus, maybe we could study together.

Phase 4: Deciding

Leader (*sitting straight and still, looking directly at the team member, and shifting to a credible tone of voice*): Cool. So, you will ask your dad to drop the brochure at the printer on his way to work?

Team member: Right.

Leader: I will ask Mary Ann to come over Wednesday night to help you proofread the brochure.

Team member: Great!

Leader: If I can't get Mary Ann, I could come by and look it over with you.

Team member: That could work.

Leader: But either way, the brochure will be proofed and ready to go on Wednesday night, and your dad can take it to the printer on Thursday morning.

Team member: Sure, that works for me.

Leader: Sounds like a plan. Let me know if something comes up.

Team member: Absolutely.

Leader: Great. Here's the brochure. I really appreciate you taking this on, _____ [name].

Team member: No problem.

Phase 5: Thank You

Leader and team member stand up. Leader shakes the team member's hand, making direct eye contact.

Leader: Thanks _____ [name], thanks again.

Negotiating Agreement (Role-Plays)

PURPOSE

To give students the opportunity to practice negotiating agreements

MATERIALS

Handout 4.11.1: Negotiating an Agreement Observation Chart (one per student)

Handout 4.11.2: Negotiating an Agreement Role-Play Situation Cards (one set for each team of three students)

DIRECTIONS

1. Explain that there will be three rounds of role-plays. In each role-play, one student will play the leader. The leader has a need to complete a project that he or she and a group of students are working on. Another student will play a team member. The leader and the team member will sit down to meet and come to a win/win agreement.

2. Explain that the leader and the team member will need to use both verbal and nonverbal negotiation strategies: eye placement, body positions, and tone of voice.

3. Explain that the third student in the group will observe the interaction. The observer will use the observation chart and take notes during the role-play.

4. Explain that each role-play will end when a decision is made. Ask the class whether there are any questions and provide clarification if needed.

5. Place students into groups of three. Ask the students to determine who will be A, B, and C, with different roles being assigned according to the round.

Round 1

A is the leader.

B is the team member.

C is the observer.

Round 2

>A is the team member.
>
>B is the observer.
>
>C is the leader.

Round 3

>A is the observer.
>
>B is the leader.
>
>C is the team member.

6. Hand out the sets of role-play situation cards. Give students 3 to 4 minutes to study and rehearse the role-play and to familiarize themselves with the observation chart.

7. Begin the role-plays within the groups. Ask the observers to wait until a role-play ends to begin giving feedback.

8. Give the groups a signal to begin.

9. When all the groups have finished the first role-play, have them start the feedback process. Give the observers 3 minutes to provide feedback.

10. Repeat the process for Rounds 2 and 3.

11. When the teams have finished all the role-plays, hold a discussion using the following questions.

DISCUSSION

- What did you learn?
- How hard was it to come to a win/win agreement?
- Did anyone settle for an agreement he or she didn't like? If so, why and what happened?
- Did any group fail to reach an agreement?
- What do you think are the most important points to remember when negotiating for a win/win agreement?

Observer _____ Round observed _____

1. Did the role-players reach an agreement?

2. Was the agreement win/win?

3. What did the leader win?

4. What did the team member win?

5. If one of them lost, who lost and what did he or she lose?

6. What nonverbal techniques did the leader use?

7. What nonverbal techniques did the team member use?

8. What verbal techniques did the leader use?

9. What verbal techniques did the team member use?

10. If a win/win agreement was reached, what factors, in your opinion, allowed the agreement to be reached?

11. If a win/lose agreement was reached—or no agreement was reached—what factors, in your opinion, prevented a win/win agreement from being reached?

From *Inspiring Leadership in Teens: Group Activities to Foster Integrity, Responsibility, and Compassion,* © 2010 by Ric Stuecker, Champaign, IL: Research Press (800-519-2707, www.researchpress.com)

Round 1: Leader

You have discovered that one of your teammates is moving to another state soon and will not be able to complete his or her part of the project. You want _____ [name] to join your team. He or she has been on teams and projects with you in the past and is really talented. Not only is _____ [name] popular, but you know he or she is very busy and often commits to too many responsibilities. However, you believe he or she is the most qualified to help out your team on this project. You will have to negotiate a win/win here. You have asked _____ [name] to meet with you.

Round 1: Team Member

You are very busy. In fact, you've been thinking lately that you are overextended and need to cut back on some of your activities. However, you like the leader, the project is really cool, and the team includes some of your best friends, who really want you to join them. Also, it's possible that you might need some tutoring, and the leader or one of the teammates could give you some extra homework help. You could also decide not to join the group. Make sure you do what is in your best interest.

Round 1: Observer

Your job is to watch the interaction between the leader and the team member closely. Note as many verbal and nonverbal strategies as you can for each person during the negotiation. Be prepared to give both of them feedback. See whether you can tell which strategy won over the team member (or how the team member was able to refuse).

Round 2: Leader

You have some equipment you need to move from a storage place to school in order to work on your project. _____ [name], one of your team members, has a truck he or she loves and drives to school every day. It would be great if _____ [name] would agree to use the truck to help you move the equipment. Otherwise, your team might have to rent a truck, which would mean everyone would have to chip in to pay for it. You have asked _____ [name] to help you out.

Round 2: Team Member

You worked hard to buy your new truck, and you are proud of it. You seldom use it to carry anything, wash and wax it weekly, and watch out for dents and scratches. A lot of people have asked you to use the truck, and you're getting tired of it. However, the leader is a really good friend and a teammate on a school athletic team. In fact, all the teammates are friends of yours. In addition, you've been looking for a study buddy to help you prepare for a big math test. Several team members are excellent math students and are taking your math class. Make sure to do what's in your best interest.

From *Inspiring Leadership in Teens: Group Activities to Foster Integrity, Responsibility, and Compassion,* © 2010 by Ric Stuecker, Champaign, IL: Research Press (800-519-2707, www.researchpress.com)

Round 2: Observer

Your job is to watch the interaction between the leader and the team member closely. Note as many verbal and nonverbal strategies as you can for each person during the negotiation. Be prepared to give both of them feedback. See whether you can tell which strategy won over the team member (or how the team member was able to refuse).

Round 3: Leader

You and everyone on your team really likes _____ [name]. He or she is fun to be around. He or she tells a lot of jokes, keeps things light, and is popular. However, _____ [name] sometimes fails to follow through on his or her part of your project. He or she laughs and promises to get things done, but there is always an excuse. Some of your team members are worried that your team will not be ready by the deadline and that the project will not be completed. You have known _____ [name] for a long time, and you have to admit that sometimes he or she comes through and sometimes doesn't. It's time for you to confront _____ [name]. If he or she cannot agree and start supporting the team, you will have to ask him or her to leave the project. Your project is really cool, and a lot of others wanted to be on your team.

Round 3: Team Member

Although you laugh a lot and are fun to be around, your life is far from happy. And, lately, tensions and your responsibilities at home have risen to the point where it is hard for you to balance your home responsibilities, schoolwork, team practice, and the project. Being on the project team is really important to you because some of your close friends are on it. You would hate to have to drop off the team, but it's really hard to do your part. You've been making promises and keeping things light, but that isn't really working. You know you will have to find a way to work things out with the team or you'll be asked to leave.

Round 3: Observer

Your job is to watch the interaction between the leader and the team player closely. Note as many verbal and nonverbal strategies as you can for each person during the negotiation. Be prepared to give both of them feedback. At what point was an agreement reached (or at what point was the decision made that _____ [name] would leave the team)?

Unit Resources

Grinder, M. (1991). *Righting the educational conveyor belt.* Portland, OR: Metamorphous Press.

Grinder, M. (1995). *ENVoY: Employing non-verbal yardsticks.* Battle Ground, WA: Michael Grinder and Associates.

Grinder's materials for teachers are based on neurolinguistic programming (NLP). Understanding learning styles and nonverbal communication are invaluable skills for any leader.

Strader, T. N., Noe, T. D., & Mann, W. C. (2002). *Creating lasting family connections: Getting real.* Louisville, KY: Resilient Futures Network.

This book takes refusal skills to a whole new level and raises communication skills for "getting real" to an art form.

Border Health Foundation
3365 N. Campbell Avenue, Suite 141
Tucson, AZ 85719
Toll-free: (877)749–3727

Excellent training and consulting in overcoming cultural boundaries in communication

Council on Prevention and Education: Substances, Inc. (COPES)
845 Barret Avenue
Louisville, KY 40204
(502) 583–6820
www.copes.org

Excellent training in communication skills for parents, youth, and families

Michael Grinder and Associates
16303 NE 259th Street
Battle Ground, WA 98604
(360) 687–3238
www.michaelgrinder.com

Excellent training in nonverbal communication skills and presentation skills

UNIT 5: LEADING GROUPS

Introduction   243

Activities

*Learning Center 1: Understanding the Stages of
    Team Formation   245*

5.1   Understanding the Team-Building Process   246

    Handout 5.1.1: Stages of a Team   247

    Handout 5.1.2: Stages of a Team—Analysis   248

5.2   Guiding the Team Through Stages: Strategies   249

    Handout 5.2.1: Stages of a Team—Strategies   250

5.3   Understanding Leadership Roles   251

    Handout 5.3.1: Leadership Roles Inventory   252

    Handout 5.3.2: Understanding Leadership Roles   254

5.4   Card Towers   255

    Handout 5.4.1: Leadership Roles Identification   257

5.5   Silent Puzzles   258

5.6   Great Escape   261

Learning Center 2: Understanding Leadership Styles   263

5.7   Identifying Leadership Styles   264

    Handout 5.7.1: Understanding Leadership Styles   265

    Handout 5.7.2: Analyzing Leadership Styles   266

5.8   Experiencing Types of Leadership Styles   268

    Handout 5.8.1: Leadership Description Cards   270

5.9   Making Team Agreements   271

    Handout 5.9.1: Team Agreement Statement   272

5.10   Understanding Levels of Agreement   273

    Handout 5.10.1: Levels of Agreement   275

5.11   Holding Effective Meetings   276

    Handout 5.11.1: Meeting Role-Play Cards   278

    Handout 5.11.2: Effective Meetings   279

    Handout 5.11.3: Nonverbal Communication Techniques   280

5.12   Holding Effective Meetings: Practice   281

Learning Center 3: Making Presentations   285

5.13   Assessing the Audience   286

Handout 5.13.1: Who's in the Audience?   287

Handout 5.13.2: Audience Assessment   288

5.14   Identifying Audience Leaders and Barometers   289

Handout 5.14.1: Leaders and Barometers   290

Handout 5.14.2: Identifying Leaders and Barometers   292

5.15   Organizing a Presentation   293

Handout 5.15.1: Organizing a Presentation   296

Handout 5.15.2: Planning a Presentation   297

Handout 5.15.3: Evaluating a Presentation   298

Learning Center 4: Planning—Making Positive Changes   299

5.16   Developing a Compelling Vision   301

5.17   Moving from Vision to Plan   304

5.18   Identifying and Solving Constraints   307

5.19   Creating Action Plans   309

Handout 5.19.1: Action Plan   311

5.20   Scheduling Activities   312

Handout 5.20.1: Calendar   313

Unit Resources   315

UNIT 5 INTRODUCTION

Leading Groups

It is important that leaders understand the dynamics of teams and groups: how they form; how they reach a group identity; how they establish visions, missions, and goals; how they create norms to work by; and how they most effectively accomplish tasks. Teams and other groups move from an "I" stage to a "we" stage to a "task" stage. Effective and inspiring leaders can facilitate the movement of the group from stage to stage.

When a team is formed, team members often find the role they prefer to play on the team. Some players like to get moving and go right to the task. These are called *Doers.* Doers often take charge and energize the group. *Planners* like to think through projects and put together strategies. When conflicts arise, *Peacemakers* mediate among the opposing teammates, make sure everyone is heard, and keep the team feeling comfortable. *Visionaries* see the big picture. They often remind the group where it is headed when the team gets bogged down with details.

OVERVIEW OF UNIT

This unit is presented as a series of four "learning centers" that teach the communication skills necessary for effective and inspiring group leadership. Each learning center contains a number of activities that focus on a specific aspect of group leadership.

Learning Center 1—Understanding the Stages of Team Formation

The first learning center consists of six activities that develop and reinforce the team-building process.

- Activity 5.1 helps students understand the three stages of team development, and Activity 5.2 provides strategies for guiding a group through these stages.

- Activity 5.3 explains the various functions that leaders play on a team and helps students identify their preferred leadership roles.

- Activities 5.4, 5.5, and 5.6 are challenges that give students an opportunity to develop their team roles and understand the benefits of working as a team.

Learning Center 2—Understanding Leadership Styles

Learning Center 2 provides six activities about three leadership styles and the variations that exist within those styles.

- In Activity 5.7, students learn to identify three types of leadership, while Activity 5.8 further develops that concept and helps students understand when it is appropriate to use each style.

- Activities 5.9 and 5.10 focus on establishing team agreements and the process by which agreements are negotiated.

- Activities 5.11 and 5.12 give students information and practice in conducting effective meetings.

Learning Center 3—Making Presentations

Good presentation skills are vital to leadership. The activities in this learning center teach students how to organize and give presentations.

- Activities 5.13 and 5.14 focus on assessing an audience and its needs and using that information effectively in a presentation.

- Activity 5.15 provides a simple format for organizing and evaluating a short presentation.

Learning Center 4—Planning: Making Positive Changes

Finally, the five activities in Learning Center 4 are designed to open students' minds to the new possibilities and positive changes that can be realized under inspiring leadership. The activities lead students through the process of creating a vision to carrying out action plans.

- In Activity 5.16, students visualize an ideal, successful, and compelling future.

- In Activity 5.17, students begin an action plan for reaching their goals.

- Activity 5.18 helps students identify and solve constraints to fulfilling their plans.

- In Activities 5.19 and 5.20, students develop an action plan and schedule.

Understanding the Stages of Team Formation

Experts in group dynamics sometimes divide team formation and development into three stages: forming, norming, and performing. These stages are also described as the "I" stage, when individuals are mostly concerned about their own individual needs within the group; the "we" stage, when boundaries, procedures, and goals are set and the team members feel they are a part of a team; and, finally, the "task" stage, when a team is working well together and is meeting their established goals.

It is important for leaders to learn to recognize where a team is in this development process in order to understand the dynamic, to make suggestions that might move the process along to the next stage, to make sure each stage is performed well to maximize the outcomes the team is seeking, and to guide the team in a positive direction. During each stage, it is possible that new leaders will emerge as their specific talents come into play. For example, if a student is strong in negotiating skills and is able to mediate when sides form, that student could play an invaluable role in helping the group form the norms and goals it hopes to attain.

The activities in this learning center are designed to help students understand the process of group development and team building.

ACTIVITY 5.1

Understanding the Team-Building Process

PURPOSE

To provide students with information about the stages of team building

MATERIALS

Handout 5.1.1: Stages of a Team (one per student)

Handout 5.1.2: Stages of a Team—Analysis (one per student)

Whiteboard or easel pad

DIRECTIONS

1. Distribute Stages of a Team handout.

2. Read the handout with the students. Ask students whether they have any questions about the information on the handout.

3. Ask students to think about and remember a team they have played on or a group they have worked with on a project. Ask them to remember a team or group that was successful in reaching its goal.

4. Distribute and ask students to fill out the Stages of a Team—Analysis handout.

5. Ask for volunteers to read their answers and to discuss their team experiences.

6. Divide a whiteboard or easel pad into four sections titled "Key Components," "Roadblocks," "Overcoming Roadblocks," and "Moving from 'I' to 'We' to 'Task.'" Hold a discussion based on the questions below and record student responses. Later, transfer the responses to four individual posters (or have student volunteers create the posters). Display the posters in the classroom and refer to them as you work through the team-building activities.

DISCUSSION

- What do you believe are the key components of a successful team?

- What are the roadblocks to successful team development?

- What are some ways of overcoming these roadblocks?

- What steps can leaders take to help move a team from "I" to "we" to "task"?

246

When teams are formed, some of the team members might want to get to work immediately. Often, these team members prevail and the team quickly decides on a project and drives to complete it—sometimes with disastrous endings.

When teams take the time to build relationships, become a bonded group, value the outcome of the project, understand the boundaries the team sets, plan an approach that makes sense, and work together toward a common goal, they not only produce an outcome that is often valuable but the process used to complete the project is enjoyable and enriching.

Team building takes time and an awareness of the process. Most teams follow a three-stage process in completing the task successfully. When a player leaves a team or when a new player comes on board, the dynamic of the group often changes. The team sometimes goes back to the "I" stage, and agreements have to be re-examined and commitments made again. In other words, the team has to take the time to go back through the process stage by stage in order to work efficiently and effectively.

When teams skip steps, conflicts arise. For example, if "I" needs are not satisfied during the "I" stage, individuals might hold resentments and could sabotage the efforts of the team. If the agreements are not made with a high level of agreement—or if people say they agree but in their heart they really don't, the team is in for rough sailing. By taking the process step by step; being willing to "storm" (team members freely opining their thoughts and feelings, keeping conflicts in the open, and making compromises); and making commitments to the goals, the process of reaching those goals, the logistics, and other decisions made during the "we" stage, teams can perform with style and grace.

Stage 1: The "I" Stage—Forming

In Stage 1, individuals come together to form the team. At this point in the team-forming process,

members are focused on their own needs (the "I" stage):

- Will I be safe?
- Will I have fun?
- Will I be heard?
- Do I like the others?
- Will there be food?
- What are we going to do, and can I do it?

There are as many needs as there are individuals. When the "I" needs are met, a team can begin to think as a group.

Stage 2: The "We" Stage—Norming and Storming

In this stage, individuals work out compromises about team goals and strategies, and the team bonds and builds an alliance. Individuals choose to be a part of the team or not. The group forms an identity—members feel a part of something they are creating that has a valuable outcome, and they are proud of their team. During this phase, the team:

- Establishes a vision, outcome, or goal
- Chooses strategies for reaching the outcome or goal or achieving the vision
- Definines roles: who will do what
- Decides on logistics
- Establishes rules and consequences
- Makes commitments to the team and outcome
- Implements conflict-resolution strategies

When these decisions are made, the team can focus on the task stage.

Stage 3: The Task Stage—Performing

During this stage, the team gets to work and produces the envisioned outcome. Work is efficient and effective.

Think about a team you have been a member of in the past. This might be a sports team, a task group with an assignment to fulfill, a project group, or any other team of individuals working together for a common goal. Answer each of the following questions.

What was the purpose of the team?

What were the team's goals?

Which goals did the team achieve?

Which goals eluded the team?

Was playing with or working with the team fun and enjoyable? Why or why not?

Would you want to be on the same team for the same purpose again? Why or why not?

How effective was the leadership, and what did the leaders do?

How did the team move from "I" to "we"?

How did the team move from "we" to "task"?

If the team got stuck, why did it get stuck? How did it get unstuck?

From *Inspiring Leadership in Teens: Group Activities to Foster Integrity, Responsibility, and Compassion,* © 2010 by Ric Stuecker, Champaign, IL: Research Press (800-519-2707, www.researchpress.com)

ACTIVITY 5.2

Guiding the Team Through Stages: Strategies

PURPOSE

To teach strategies for moving a group from one stage of team development to the next

MATERIALS

Handout 5.2.1: Stages of a Team—Strategies (one per student)

DIRECTIONS

1. Ask students to imagine they are the leader of a team. It might be an athletic team or a team that has a task to perform.
2. Review the stages of team development.
3. Distribute copies of the Stages of a Team—Strategies handout.
4. Ask students to identify the goals of their imaginary team and to suggest strategies they might use to move from stage to stage.
5. When all students have filled out the handout, discuss the following questions.

DISCUSSION

- What strategies do you believe are most effective in moving from "I" to "we"?
- What strategies do you believe are most effective in moving from "we" to "task"?
- What would you do if you lost a key player?
- How would you integrate a new player onto the team?
- What criteria should a team use to define its success?

What is the purpose or goal of your team? _____

_____

What strategies would you use to move your team from the "I" to the "we" stage?
1. _____
2. _____
3. _____
4. _____
5. _____

What strategies would you use to move your team from "we" to "task"?
1. _____
2. _____
3. _____
4. _____
5. _____

What criteria will determine that your team was a success?
1. _____
2. _____
3. _____
4. _____
5. _____

What strategies would you use if you lost a key player?
1. _____
2. _____
3. _____
4. _____
5. _____

What strategies would you use to integrate a new player onto your team?
1. _____
2. _____
3. _____
4. _____
5. _____

ACTIVITY 5.3

Understanding Leadership Roles

Leadership is a group process. To be successful, all the players on a team must work together, each one bringing his or her own set of skills, talents, attitudes, and behaviors to enhance and support the work of the team. It is a good idea to understand the talents everyone on the team brings and the roles each prefers to perform. This activity helps students identify their preferred leadership roles. A questionnaire helps with the identification process and is followed by descriptions of the roles found on teams.

PURPOSE

To help students learn the various roles leaders play on a team

MATERIALS

Handout 5.3.1: Leadership Roles Inventory (one per student)

Handout 5.3.2: Understanding Leadership Roles (one per student)

DIRECTIONS

1. Hand out the Leadership Roles Inventory.
2. Ask students to answer the inventory questions.
3. Ask students to score and interpret the inventory.
4. Hold a discussion to see whether the students agree with the interpretation of the inventory.
5. Distribute the Understanding Leadership Roles handout. Read and discuss the information with students, making sure they understand each role.
6. Place the students in small groups according to their preferred roles. That is, make sure each group has at least one Doer, one Planner, one Peacemaker, and one Visionary.
7. Ask each group to hold a discussion in which each person explains the role he or she prefers, why he or she likes this role, and how he or she performs this role when working in small groups.

This inventory contains 32 statements that may or may not be true for you. Read each statement and decide whether it is always true, often true, sometimes true, or never true when you work or play on teams. Be as honest as you can be. Respond to each item. When you have completed the inventory, you will be able to score it on an interpretive chart.

Scoring Scale

The statement is always true = 3 points   The statement is sometimes true = 1 point

The statement is often true = 2 points   The statement is never true = 0 points

<u>Statement</u>   <u>Points</u>

1. I like to accomplish tasks quickly and effectively.   _____
2. I like to think things through and come up with several strategies.   _____
3. I like to make sure everyone on a team is respected.   _____
4. I can usually see the final outcome of most projects.   _____
5. I am very task oriented.   _____
6. I can put together facts, information, opinions, and ideas and come up with a plan.   _____
7. I try to make sure everyone's opinion is heard.   _____
8. Even when working on small tasks, I can see the final outcome.   _____
9. I get frustrated when we talk on and on.   _____
10. I get frustrated when we don't seem to have a plan.   _____
11. Conflicts among teammates make me uneasy.   _____
12. I like to dream big dreams.   _____
13. Getting the job done is my priority.   _____
14. I often propose ways of accomplishing tasks.   _____
15. I try to find ways to relieve tensions and conflicts.   _____
16. I sometimes remind my team what our final goal is.   _____
17. I can tell other people what to do.   _____
18. I believe there are several ways of accomplishing a task.   _____
19. People ask me to help them resolve conflicts.   _____
20. I have hopes and dreams for my life.   _____
21. Tasks have to make sense to me.   _____
22. I can help people analyze and figure out a direction.   _____
23. I welcome people and encourage participation.   _____
24. I like to know the purpose before I commit to participate.   _____

From *Inspiring Leadership in Teens: Group Activities to Foster Integrity, Responsibility, and Compassion,* © 2010 by Ric Stuecker, Champaign, IL: Research Press (800-519-2707, www.researchpress.com)

Statement	Points
25. I prefer to act rather than talk.	_____
26. I like to think and solve puzzles.	_____
27. I enjoy working with people.	_____
28. I enjoy imagining possibilities.	_____
29. I like to be in charge.	_____
30. Finding different solutions intrigues me.	_____
31. I enjoy making people around me comfortable.	_____
32. I can imagine lots of cool things groups can do.	_____

Transferring and Interpreting Scores

Use the following chart to record your scores. The small number in each block corresponds to the 32 individual items for which you recorded values of 0, 1, 2, or 3 for the preceding statements. Transfer your 32 individual item scores to the Score Transfer chart. Next, add the values in each column (columns I through IV) and place the totals at the bottom. When you have the columns totaled, transfer their values to the Score Interpretation chart that follows.

Score Transfer

I	II	III	IV
1	2	3	4
5	6	7	8
9	10	11	12
13	14	15	16
17	18	19	20
21	22	23	24
25	26	27	28
29	30	31	32

Totals

I	II	III	IV

Score Interpretation

Transfer the values from each column on the Score Transfer chart to the Column Score lines below.

Column	Column Score	Component
I	_____	Doer
II	_____	Planner
III	_____	Peacemaker
IV	_____	Visionary

Groups requiring leadership are groups who have a purpose, a mission, something to accomplish. Athletic teams, for example, usually have the goal of winning a championship. The prom committee, for another example, has the task of putting on a prom. Leadership comes in several forms. During the process of accomplishing tasks, different people often perform different roles of leadership at various times. Groups that effectively accomplish tasks often have leaders performing the following roles.

Doers

Although everyone on the team needs to participate, Doers really like to be active—and they encourage others to be active. Doers are able to tell other people what to do, and they encourage energetic participation. Sometimes, Doers get frustrated when teams spend a lot of time planning and talking. Doers are often identified as leaders because they like to make decisions and act on them, they like to direct others, and they usually don't mind conflict so long as they are moving toward completion of the task. Doers are important on a team because they keep the project going, move others, make decisions, and push the project toward its outcome. Without effective Doers, projects get stalled.

Planners

Planners like to think things through, solve puzzles, and come up with solutions. They often see several ways a task might be accomplished. Planners like to ask how and why and want to know the logic and reason behind decisions and how a decision will affect the final outcome of the task. Planners can figure out how to get to the destination, but they may have to rely on Doers to move and direct the project. Without Planners, a project can move ineffectively and without direction.

Peacemakers

Sooner or later during most projects, conflicts arise. Peacemakers like everyone to be comfortable with the process of working together. Peacemakers welcome all players, make sure their voices and opinions are heard, are open to a variety of points of view, solicit involvement from all players, and seek common ground among differing opinions. When a conflict arises, they attempt to mediate a solution that is fair to all parties. Without Peacemakers, feelings would be hurt, people would feel left out of the process, and conflicts might prevent the team from accomplishing its task.

Visionaries

Visionaries see the big picture and the final outcome. They like to dream large, and they like to see the many possibilities a project can have. Sometimes teams become focused on immediate tasks and forget their final direction. During the process, it's important for Visionaries to remind the group where it is going.

Each of you will have a preferred role—that is, the role you like and feel most comfortable playing on a team. It feels natural to you, and you are likely to be quite good at it. You will also have one or two "can do" roles. These are roles you will take on if necessary for team success. Although you might prefer a different role, you don't mind taking these other roles on. Finally, there is the role you least prefer. It may be that, if absolutely necessary, you would take on this role, but you would really rather someone else take it on. You might not feel comfortable, truly competent, or well fit for this role.

Complete the paragraph below, specifying what you believe are your preferred, can do, and least preferred roles on a team.

> When playing or working on a team, the role I truly like, enjoy, and prefer is _____.
> If someone else has taken that role, or if my team needs me to take a different role, I can take on the roles of _____ or _____.
> I would rather not take on the role of _____ unless absolutely necessary for the success of my team.

ACTIVITY 5.4

Card Towers

It's a good idea to test out the roles students play on a team by giving them activities that challenge them as a team. Students may find that the challenge changes their understanding of their role on the team. Activities 5.4, 5.5, and 5.6 are three different team challenges. In addition to the participants, you should designate observers for each team challenge to watch and describe the process used to solve the challenge and to describe which players took which roles (Doer, Planner, Peacemaker, or Visionary) during the process.

PURPOSE
To help students understand how the roles on a team work in a challenging team activity

MATERIALS
300 to 500 colored 5 × 8-inch index cards per team

Handout 5.4.1: Leadership Roles Identification (one per team)

Understanding Leadership Roles (Handout 5.3.2 from Activity 5.3) for reference (one per team)

NOTE
This activity works best in a large room without furniture.

DIRECTIONS
1. Create random groups of five to eight people. For each group, designate one or two members as observers. The others will be participants.

2. Give these instructions to the participants:

   • Your task is to create a structure at least 10 stories high.

   • You can fold the cards in the middle widthwise. Please do not otherwise fold, spindle, or mutilate the cards in any way.

   • Use all the cards you are given.

   • This will be a silent activity. From this point on, no talking. Please remain silent until I give a signal to speak. If you have any questions, please ask them now.

   • Begin.

3. Give these instructions to the observers:

   - Your job is to stand nearby and observe how the team works.
   - As you observe, keep in mind the four leadership roles and see whether you can tell who are the Doers, the Planners, the Peacemakers, and the Visionaries.

4. Allow about 20 minutes for the building of the towers.

5. Signal the teams to stop.

6. Ask teams to fill out the Leadership Roles Identification handout. (Note: You can use this handout anytime you do a group activity and want to analyze the leadership process.)

7. Lead a group discussion based on the following questions. Be sure to solicit answers from participants as well as observers.

DISCUSSION

- What did you learn?
- Was it difficult working in silence, or was it helpful?
- Who provided the team with direction and played the role of the Doer?
- Who provided the team with a plan to build the tower?
- Were there any conflicts? If so, how were they resolved?
- Did anyone have a vision for what the tower would look like? Did the tower you built resemble the vision you had in mind?

Use the following questions to examine who played the various leadership roles in your group.

Activity name _____

Who played the role of Doer by taking charge and organizing the group?

_____

List several actions this person did that indicate he or she was the Doer.

1. _____

2. _____

3. _____

Planners come up with strategies and/or solutions. Who played the role of the Planner?

_____

List several actions this person did that indicate he or she was the Planner.

1. _____

2. _____

3. _____

Who played the role of the Peacemaker by resolving any conflicts?

_____

List several actions this person did that indicate he or she was the Peacemaker.

1. _____

2. _____

3. _____

Visionaries see the big picture and can visualize the outcome of an activity. Who played the role of the Visionary?

_____

List several actions this person did that indicate he or she was the Visionary.

1. _____

2. _____

3. _____

A CTIVITY 5.5

Silent Puzzles

PURPOSE

To learn more about the roles played by team members during a team challenge

MATERIALS

One set of puzzles per team

Large envelopes for puzzle pieces (one per team)

Understanding Leadership Roles (Handout 5.3.2 from Activity 5.3) for reference (one per team)

Leadership Roles Identification (Handout 5.4.1 from Activity 5.4) for reference (one per team)

PREPARATION

You will need to prepare a set of five puzzles for each small group. It is best to make them out of white or other single color of card stock, but 8.5 × 11-inch copy paper will work.

The puzzles should look like this (actual puzzle pieces should be bigger than shown):

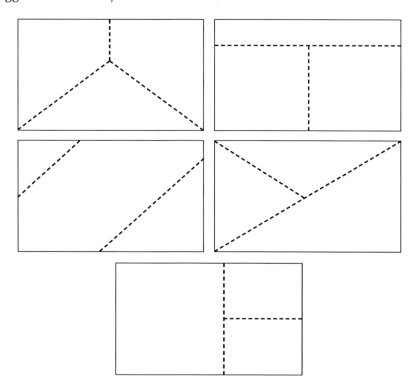

Put the pieces for all five puzzles in a large mailing envelope—one set of puzzles per envelope.

Provide a table and five chairs for each team.

DIRECTIONS

1. Create random groups of six people. Five will be working on puzzles, and one will be an observer (you can assign more observers, if necessary).

2. Ask five people on each team to raise their hands. These five will work the puzzles. Ask them to sit down at the table.

3. The remaining team member(s) will observe the process. Tell them their job is stand nearby and observe how their team works. Tell them to keep the roles of a team in mind as they observe and see whether they can tell who are the Doers, Planners, Peacemakers, and Visionaries.

4. Hand an envelope of puzzle pieces to one person at each table.

5. Ask them to wait to open the envelopes. Give the teams these instructions:

   • Inside the envelope you will find the pieces for five puzzles.

   • At the end of the activity, each of you should have in front of you a puzzle that forms a rectangle.

   • This is a silent activity. You may not talk until I announce the end of the activity.

   • You may not take anyone else's puzzle pieces. However, you may hand puzzle pieces to each other.

   • When I say "begin," the person on your team with the puzzle pieces will hand them out to you like he or she is dealing cards—one at a time to each player plus himself or herself.

   • Your team is not finished until each player has a completed puzzle sitting in front of him or her.

   • Remember, no talking at any time, and you may not take anyone else's puzzle pieces.

   • Begin.

6. Some teams will solve the puzzles faster than others. As teams finish, they may silently watch the other teams, observing how they are working together.

7. When all teams have finished, announce that the activity is finished.

8. Ask teams to fill out the Leadership Roles Identification handout for this activity.

9. Lead a group discussion based on the following questions.

DISCUSSION   Ask the observers:

- Who in your opinion played the roles of Doer? Planner? Peacemaker? Visionary? How could you tell?

- How well do you think the team you observed worked? Did they have any obstacles to overcome? Who helped the process? Who hindered the process?

Ask the players:

- Do you think the comments of the observers are correct?

- How did you feel about working with this team? What was fun? What was frustrating? Do you feel successful? If you did this activity again or another one that is similar, what would you do differently?

- What did you learn?

ACTIVITY 5.6

Great Escape

PURPOSE
To learn more about the roles played by team members during a team challenge

MATERIALS
Ball of yarn 40 feet long (enough to form a 10 × 10-foot square, one per team)

Understanding Leadership Roles (Handout 5.3.2 from Activity 5.3) for reference (one per team)

Leadership Roles Identification (Handout 5.4.1 from Activity 5.4) for reference (one per team)

PREPARATION
It is best to play this activity outside on grass or inside standing on mats, in a large space without furniture

DIRECTIONS
1. Place students in groups of 10 or 12.

2. Ask four members from each team to form a large square using the yarn to define the square: One person stands at each corner of the square holding the yarn waist high and stretching it taut.

3. Ask the remaining team members to assemble in the middle of the square. Tell them to imagine that the yarn is the top of a fence. The fence extends to the ground.

4. Explain that the square is a prison. To escape, they must help their teammates over the fence without touching it. (Note: If anyone touches the fence at any time, all team members, including those who have successfully escaped, must return to the center of the square and start over.)

5. The four people holding yarn form the fence and are not part of the escape. They also observe how the team works together to escape and identify who plays which team roles.

6. As teams finish, they can watch the remaining teams.

7. Ask teams to fill out the Leadership Roles Identification handout for this activity.

8. Lead a group discussion based on the following questions.

DISCUSSION   Ask the observers:

- Who in your opinion played the role of Doer? Planner? Peacemaker? Visionary? How could you tell?

- How well do you think the team you observed worked? Did they have any obstacles to overcome? Who helped the process? Who hindered the process?

Ask the players:

- Do you think the comments of the observers are correct?

- How did you feel about working with this team? What was fun? What was frustrating? Do you feel successful? If you did this activity again or another one that is similar, what would you do differently?

- What did you learn?

Understanding Leadership Styles

The six activities in this learning center focus on the styles leaders use when working in a group. Essentially, there are three styles with variations within each style: leader controlled, hands off, and shared power.

This learning center provides a set of activities to allow students to discover, evaluate, and understand leadership styles.

ACTIVITY 5.7

Identifying Leadership Styles

PURPOSE   To learn more about the three leadership styles and decide when it is appropriate to use each of them

MATERIALS   Handout 5.7.1: Understanding Leadership Styles (one per student)

Handout 5.7.2: Analyzing Leadership Styles (one per student)

DIRECTIONS   1. Distribute copies of the Understanding Leadership Styles handout and read it with the students. This handout reviews the concepts and will help make sure all students use a similar definition of the three styles.

2. Hand out copies of the Analyzing Leadership Styles worksheet.

3. You might want to use an overhead projector or computer display of the worksheet and fill in the items as you discuss them with your students.

4. Ask students to accurately describe each style and suggest times and situations where each style might be used. You might need to prompt students and provide feedback to ensure they understand the styles and can identify appropriate situations for use.

5. Ask students to name the style they are most comfortable using and the style they are least comfortable using.

Essentially there are three styles: leader controlled, hands off, and shared power. Each style has variations within it.

In a *leader-controlled* style, only the leader makes decisions. The leader might ask for ideas and input from other team members or ask for a critique of the decision, but he or she is the person who decides. Sometimes this leader simply announces to the group that a decision has been made. At other times, he or she might ask for ideas but make the decision alone. Or the leader might make a decision and ask for questions of clarification. If he or she allows members to make a decision, he or she reserves veto power. There are times when it is important to use a leader-controlled style. In an emergency—for example, when people are in a building that is on fire, it would be important for a leader to direct others in the safest way out of the building.

Leaders who are *hands off* abdicate decision-making power and allow team members to do whatever they want. This may not be a good style when a group is trying to make a decision. However, it may be an excellent style once all information is known, a decision has been made, and all the team members know and can accomplish their tasks. It might also be a good style if team members have specialized abilities and can make decisions for themselves in these special areas.

When a leader's style is *shared power,* he or she runs meetings and sets boundaries and limits but allows discussion and solicits information and expertise from members of the team. Although it might be the leader's responsibility to make a final decision, this leader solicits the opinion and expertise of the team. In some cases, a shared-power leader seeks the consensus of the group and allows decisions to be made by the group.

Leader Controlled

Characteristics

1. _____

2. _____

3. _____

Examples

1. _____

2. _____

3. _____

When is the best time to use this style?

When is this style not effective?

I would ___ would not ___ like to use this style.

Hands Off

Characteristics

1. _____

2. _____

3. _____

Examples

1. _____

2. _____

3. _____

When is the best time to use this style?

When is this style not effective?

I would ___ would not ___ like to use this style.

From *Inspiring Leadership in Teens: Group Activities to Foster Integrity, Responsibility, and Compassion,* © 2010 by Ric Stuecker, Champaign, IL: Research Press (800-519-2707, www.researchpress.com)

Shared Power

Characteristics

1. _____

2. _____

3. _____

Examples

1. _____

2. _____

3. _____

When is the best time to use this style?

When is this style not effective?

I would ____ would not ____ like to use this style.

ACTIVITY 5.8

Experiencing Types of Leadership Styles

PURPOSE
To identify three types of group leadership: leader controlled, hands off, and shared power

MATERIALS
3 × 5-inch index cards

Handout 5.8.1: Leadership Description Cards

PREPARATION
Students will be working in groups of five or six. Prepare a set of Leadership Description Cards using the master that follows this activity. Copy and cut out enough leadership descriptions so that each team will have one, then paste a description to an index card. If you have six groups, make two index cards for each description. Adjust as necessary for the number of groups

DIRECTIONS
1. Randomly place students into groups of five or six.

2. Ask each group to select a leader. Ask the selected leaders to see you privately.

3. Ask each leader to pick one of the leadership cards without reading it first. This will be the leadership style he or she must exhibit during the activity.

4. Make sure each leader understands the role and knows how to act in his or her group.

5. When the leaders return to their teams, announce the task:

   Your task in the next 15 to 20 minutes is to design a proposal for a class party. At the end of the planning period, you will present your idea to the entire class. Only one party idea will be chosen. Make sure you include a party theme, music, and type of food.

6. Once all groups have presented their ideas, ask students to vote on the proposal they believe is best.

7. At the end of the planning time, hold a discussion based on the questions that follow.

DISCUSSION

- How well did your group work together?
- Do you like the plan that you came up with?
- Do you like how your leader ran your group? Was it a good way to come up with a plan?
- Ask each group to identify the style their leader used. If necessary, first review the three different leadership styles.

As the head of a leader-controlled group, you will dictate to your group without taking any suggestions whatsoever. You are in charge. You will make all decisions. You will decide everything about the party you are planning. You will announce your decision—and your team will do it your way.

As a hands-off leader, you will have no opinion and make no suggestions. Do not in any way organize this party-planning session. Let everyone in your group do what they want.

As a shared-power leader, you will organize the conversation, run the meeting, make sure everyone gets to speak, and help your team work together to come up with a plan that everyone is involved in and agrees to.

Note: If there are more than three groups, duplicate enough cards to give to the leaders of the additional groups.

From *Inspiring Leadership in Teens: Group Activities to Foster Integrity, Responsibility, and Compassion,* © 2010 by Ric Stuecker, Champaign, IL: Research Press (800-519-2707, www.researchpress.com)

Activity 5.9

Making Team Agreements

Teams function, or don't function, based on the agreements and levels of agreement that members make with each other. Activities 5.9 and 5.10 in this learning center provide practice in establishing team agreements.

PURPOSE

To learn about various levels of agreement

MATERIALS

Handout 5.9.1: Team Agreement Statement (one per student)

Whiteboard or easel pad

DIRECTIONS

1. Distribute the Team Agreement Statement. Ask the students to read the statement and think about what it means.

2. Conduct a group discussion based on the questions that follow. Use a whiteboard or easel pad to record student responses to the last discussion question, below, for use in the next activity.

DISCUSSION

- When you look at the Team Agreement Statement, what stands out to you?

- Thinking about the statement, what feelings, if any, might come up about people working on teams? For example, does it bother you that your ideas might not be used? Would you rather do something yourself than depend on the work of others?

- Thinking about a time when you were on a successful team, what were the essential elements of your successful team? What specific things contributed to your feelings of success on that team?

- Based on what we have learned about each other and what has worked for us through prior experiences on successful teams, what simple agreements could we propose that will help a team be successful? *(Save these proposed agreements for use in Activity 5.10.)*

Teams seem to have a will of their own. Because of the group dynamic, teams are often in a state of flux, or change. Each person brings his or her own set of experiences, ideas, and perceptions—which change as the team grows and changes. Team building and the team process are based on the agreements each person makes and the level of commitment each person brings. When team members are committed and live up to their commitments, the team functions well.

Understanding Levels
of Agreement

PURPOSE

To understand the levels of commitment people have when they make agreements

MATERIALS

Proposed team agreements from Activity 5.9

Handout 5.10.1: Levels of Agreement (one per student)

DIRECTIONS

(Note: This is a whole-group activity.)

1. Tell the students that they are members of a group whose purpose is important to them as individuals and/or to their group.

2. State that it is their task as a group to establish a set of agreements the group can function under in order to be a success.

3. Explain that agreements that work best are specific, measurable, and easy to follow. Here is an example of an agreement that is not specific:

   Members of the team will show respect for each other in group discussion.

   This agreement is not specific because "showing respect" may mean very different things to each member of the group. Here is an example of an agreement that is well formed and specific:

   Members of the team will show respect for each other in group discussions: One person speaks at a time—no cross talking. People listen to ideas and ask questions for clarification of intent before criticizing an idea.

   Discuss what this agreement means and why it is specific. Ask: What are the advantages of forming specific agreements?

4. Tell the group that they will be challenged to examine the agreements they made in the last activity and to revise them to be more specific and meaningful.

5. Post the list of agreements where everyone can see it.

6. Ask whether there are any additional agreements that need to be stated. Add those to the list.

7. Ask the group whether any agreements can be combined. If so, rewrite to combine them.

8. Give the students a copy of the Levels of Agreement handout. Point out the five levels of agreement and what they mean.

9. Explain that people often will agree to something and then not follow through. They might have been embarrassed to say no to the group. They may decide later that following the agreement wasn't such a good idea. They may find it constricting to follow the agreement when it is actually put into use. There are a lot of reasons why someone would make an agreement and then not follow it. Under those circumstances, yes actually means no.

10. Explain that people sometimes put contingencies, or "buts . . ." on their agreements. This is not a true agreement. In this case, the agreement is not firm.

11. Explain that for a team to be successful, all agreements must be at least level 3 in the eyes of all teammates and that the goal is to create a set of agreements that encourages success and that all team members support.

12. Challenge each of the listed agreements from Activity 5.9 for their importance. Here is an example of how to challenge an agreement:

    Is this an important agreement that will support the success of our team?

13. Challenge each of the listed agreements for specificity. Ask the group to make each one, if necessary, more specific and measurable. You might ask, "What changes would make this agreement more specific? How could you measure it?"

14. Challenge each of the listed agreements for consensus. Ask whether anyone could not make this agreement at least a level 3. If anyone is reluctant to agree, ask, "What changes would make this agreement more acceptable?"

15. If, after discussion and possible modification, consensus cannot be reached, move on. The idea is to create agreements that the team will support—not to debate specific agreements.

16. Summarize the list of agreements. (Save any agreements that did not reach consensus for later review and evaluation.)

17. Ask each student to sign the adopted agreements.

It is important that every member of a team is clear about what the agreements mean and what level of agreement each member has with the team and its agreements.

Commitment Level	Statement	Intention
1	Says yes	Means NO!
2	Says yes	Maybe, but . . .
3	Says yes	Agrees
4	Says yes	I totally agree!
5	Says yes	This is my dream!

From *Inspiring Leadership in Teens: Group Activities to Foster Integrity, Responsibility, and Compassion,* © 2010 by Ric Stuecker, Champaign, IL: Research Press (800-519-2707, www.researchpress.com)

ACTIVITY 5.11

Holding Effective Meetings

PURPOSE

To demonstrate the behaviors that can interfere with successful decision making in a meeting

MATERIALS

Handout 5.11.1: Meeting Role-Play Cards (one set per team)

Handout 5.11.2: Effective Meetings (one per student)

Handout 5.11.3: Nonverbal Communication Techniques (one per student)

Whiteboard or easel pad

PREPARATION

Copy the Meeting Role-Play Cards and cut out a set for each group of eight students.

DIRECTIONS

1. Arrange the group into teams of eight.

2. Explain to the group that they are going to be on a planning team. They are meeting to plan a fund-raiser for the class. Tell them you will use the best ideas.

3. Tell the students that they will be given roles to play during the planning process. Ask them not to share what role they are playing until after the planning meeting.

4. Hand out the roles and let students prepare for about 2 minutes.

5. Ask the students who received the role of leader to raise their hands.

6. Tell the leaders that they will begin when you say "start."

7. Say, "start." Give the groups at least 5 minutes for their role-plays.

8. Stop the groups. Collect the role cards.

9. Ask each player to explain to the group what role he or she was given.

10. Ask the students:

    • Has anyone ever experienced a similar meeting in real life? Could you give examples?

    • What needs to happen for your group to function well? (Record the responses on a whiteboard or easel pad.)

11. Inform the groups that they will now hold a second meeting. Ask the groups to use the suggestions listed and to behave in ways that promote group decision making, consensus, and a positive solution.

12. Start the second meeting. Give the groups 15 minutes to propose a fund-raising activity.

13. Distribute the Effective Meetings and Nonverbal Communication Techniques handouts. Review these with students and discuss the following question.

DISCUSSION

- Which of the recommendations on the Effective Meetings handout seem to be most crucial? Why?

Player 1

You are the leader. Call the meeting to order. Make sure to structure the meeting. Make sure everyone is heard. The purpose of the meeting is to organize an event to raise money for your project. Ask the group to consider several possible ideas and come to a group agreement about one of them.

Player 2

You are impatient. Meetings bore you, and you have lots of other uses for your time. You want the meeting to end as soon as possible.

Player 3

You are childish. Play around and take nothing seriously.

Player 4

You support every idea put forward. They all sound great to you.

Player 5

You are a complainer. Keep complaining about whatever you can think of to complain about, whether it is on topic or not.

Player 6

Keep asking questions. Ask as many as you can think of.

Player 7

You have idea after idea and are eager to express all your ideas. Keep adding to the idea mix.

Player 8

You talk to everyone around you. Keep up as many side conversations with people on your team as possible.

Effective meetings generally have a purpose and a leader who directs the meeting to achieve that purpose. Several steps can be taken to give meetings a focus and help them run smoothly.

1. **Prepare an agenda.** It is often helpful to prepare a suggested agenda and distribute it before the meeting. Ask team members to suggest additional items before creating the final agenda. Then send out a final agenda, listing any items not included in the current meeting agenda as possible topics for future meetings. Establishing an agenda helps limit the number of issues that can be discussed within the time allotted for the meeting, allows members to arrive with their ideas focused, and shows that you honor members' ideas even if you cannot fit them into the present meeting.

2. **Follow a plan.** Effective meetings follow a plan. Most effective meetings have the following stages:

   Getting attention: The leader calls the meeting to order and frames its purposes and focus.

   Gathering information: The leader opens the discussion—analyzing the situation, examining data, and looking at the issue, guided by the order of the agenda.

   Creating options: The leader asks for options, approaches, and solutions. These are listed for discussion and agreement.

   Deciding: The leader seeks consensus on the matter.

3. **Manage and focus discussion.** The leader refocuses the group when it moves off topic or offers extraneous ideas. The leader should make note of any out-of-order issues or ideas to be discussed at the end of the meeting or at a future meeting.

4. **Summarize and clarify.** Effective leaders take the issues raised and summarize the proposals so far. They offer interpretations of ideas raised if there appears to be confusion and ask for clarification and verification from the originator of the idea or issue. Examples:

   (Summarizing) "At this point in the discussion, we seem to be saying . . ."

   (Clarification) "I believe he means this. . . . Is that what you had in mind?"

5. **Seek consensus.** This is not a debate or a win/lose situation. Make sure everyone in the meeting can support the decision at a level 3 agreement or higher (refer to the Levels of Agreement handout from Activity 5.10 in this learning center, if necessary). Allow for conflicting ideas. Call on members to listen and to consider all points of view. Ask for modifications and changes that would bring everyone into agreement. See whether ideas can be combined. Using these techniques, come up with an alternative that is acceptable to all members—or move on and come back to this issue later.

6. **Use effective nonverbal communication.** Visual information is critical for effective meetings. Printing up an agenda and using it to focus the meeting by following it in order is helpful. Post the agenda so that everyone can see it during the meeting. Have a whiteboard or easel pad available for recording notes and ideas. The handout on nonverbal communication techniques (Handout 5.11.3) is useful for helping the leader use nonverbal communication during the meeting.

Nonverbal Communication Techniques

Here is a chart of nonverbal communication techniques that can be used in leading effective meetings.

	Getting Attention	Gathering Information	Creating Options	Deciding
Eye Placement	Direct: Look directly at individuals in the group.	Indirect: Scan the group.	Indirect: Scan the group.	Direct: Look directly at individuals in the group.
Body Position	Stand still with weight balanced on both feet. Hands still.	Shift weight to one leg. Smile. Use gestures and movement.	Shift weight to one leg. Smile. Use gestures and movement.	Stand still with weight balanced on both feet. Hands still.
Voice	Credible: Use flat tones that drop down at the end of phrases.	Use long, silent pauses. Speak in a friendly, melodic voice, with pitch rising at the end of phrases.	Speak in a friendly, melodic voice, with pitch rising at the end of phrases.	Credible: Use flat tones that drop down at the end of phrases. Use clear, silent pauses.
Verbal Cues	"Thank you for coming. (Pause.) Today we are here [to decide] [to discuss] [for the purpose of] . . ."	In a melodic voice, with pitch rising at the end: "Who has some good ideas/information concerning . . . ?"	In a melodic voice, with pitch rising at the end: "What would work?"	Using a credible tone of voice: "We seem agreed on . . . . Does anyone object to . . . ?"

ACTIVITY 5.12

Holding Effective Meetings: Practice

PURPOSE
To give students practice in using verbal and nonverbal strategies to lead effective meetings

MATERIALS
Whiteboard or easel pad

DIRECTIONS
1. Divide the students in groups of five. Ask each group to sit in a semicircle, either in chairs or on the floor. (Move any tables or desks out of the way.)

2. Ask the students in each group to number themselves 1 through 5.

3. Explain that each small group is a simulated meeting. Tell them they will be going through the steps for holding a meeting and learning skills for effective group leadership.

4. Ask everyone to stand up facing you. Ask them to stand with their feet approximately a foot and a half apart, toes facing forward. Ask them to balance their weight on both feet with their hands to their sides. Tell them this is their power stance. When they need to take charge and get the group's attention, they should stand this way. If they are sitting, they should sit up straight in a chair with their feet flat on the floor. Ask the students to stay in the power stance for just a few seconds to really grasp what it feels like. This stance should be used to call the meeting to order, whenever the leader needs to refocus the group, or when he or she is calling for a decision.

5. Now, ask everyone to shift their weight to one leg. Tell them that this is the approachable stance. This stance is excellent to use when they want lots of ideas to flow and discussion to happen. It should be used when gathering information or discussing options.

6. Ask everyone to sit down. Tell the students they are going to practice verbal and nonverbal strategies for getting attention. Write the following statement on the whiteboard or easel pad and tell the students it will be used to demonstrate a verbal technique:

Team *[pause silently for three beats]*, we need to get started.

7. Ask all number 1's to stand. Tell them you will use the statement to demonstrate the proper technique for using a credible tone of voice and then have them repeat it. (As you demonstrate, make sure your voice is flat and pitches down at the end of the phrase. Make sure the pause is silent. Make sure you are standing absolutely still, hands at your side.)

8. Ask the number 1's to repeat the phrase, making sure they are in the power stance and using a credible tone of voice.

9. Repeat the procedure for persons 2, 3, 4, and 5.

10. Ask the entire group to stand in the power stance using their credible tones of voice to repeat the phrase.

11. Explain that when groups are waiting for a meeting to start, most people are talking with one another. If you listen to the group, you will notice they maintain a particular noise level, with occasional lulls. To get the attention of the group, the leader needs to pitch his or her voice somewhat louder than the group but not so loud as to be shouting. If the leader does this during a lull (when the noise of the group is down), the strategy will be even more effective.

12. Explain that the leader must immediately pause following the word that gets the group's attention. This pause must be clear and silent. During the pause, the leader's body must be still. Explain to the students: What happens is the first word, "Team," gets the attention of the group. Most of them will look at the leader. If the leader is moving or looking away, they will begin to talk again. If the leader is still, looking directly at them, they will stop talking. The pause is most important. Depending on the size of the group, the pause should last two to four beats—longer for larger groups.

13. Tell the students that they will practice the strategies in three rounds.

Round 1

1. Ask each person 1 to stand in front of his or her seated group. Ask the group to talk among themselves as though they were waiting for a meeting to start, not looking at the leader.

2. Explain to the group that the leader will try to get their attention. If the leader stands still and pauses clearly, they should look at the leader when he or she says "Team" (and pauses), and then sit up and be quiet. If the leader is not still or does not pause clearly, they should look at the leader but go back to their conversations.

3. Ask person 1 to assume the power position and say: "Team (*pause*), we need to get started." Remind the leader to pitch his or her voice just above his team's conversational level but not to shout.

4. Ask the group to give feedback about the leader's stance, pitch of voice, and use of the pause.

5. Repeat this round with persons 2, 3, 4, and 5 acting as leader, until everyone has demonstrated the ability to get the attention of the group.

Round 2

1. Tell the students:

> This round we are going to add a discussion. First, the leader will get the attention of the group using the power stance, credible tone of voice, pause, and the statement: "Team (*pause*), we need to get started." When the group is at attention, the leader will say: "Thanks. (*Pause.*) Does anyone have any ideas about what we might do together for fun after school?" After the pause, the leader moves to an approachable stance by shifting his or her weight to one leg, letting his or her voice rise at the end of the phrase, and smiling.

2. Begin round 2 with person 5 acting as leader and move to persons 4, 3, 2, and 1. Ask teams to give feedback on using the steps for getting the group's attention and moving to the discussion. Were the statements clear? Were the pauses clear? Explain to the students that the pause is the most powerful technique to use for getting attention and for transitions.

Round 3

During this round, the teams are discussing ideas. One person speaks at a time. The leader realizes that it is time to make a decision (usually when there are many ideas flowing or ideas are repeated several times). The leader is going to refocus the meeting to come to a decision.

1. Ask the groups to discuss ideas, as they might at a meeting. Perhaps they could discuss an activity they might like to do after school with the other members of their team. This time the leader (standing or sitting) takes the power stance and suggests it is time to decide:

> *Thanks.* (Pause.) *Thanks for the good ideas.* (Pause.) *We need to decide.*

2. Have each person in the group practice this step.

3. Ask teams to give feedback as to how effectively each leader used stance, tone of voice, and pauses to refocus the group.

LEARNING CENTER 3

Making Presentations

Leaders are often called on to give talks and presentations to groups large and small. The activities in this learning center examine how to organize a presentation, how to "read" the audience and focus the presentation on their needs, and how to use the presentation to motivate others. Students are asked to prepare and deliver a short presentation and receive feedback from the group. (Note: Many of the skills presented in this learning center are also highly useful in running effective meetings.)

ACTIVITY 5.13

Assessing the Audience

PURPOSE To provide an understanding about audience needs during a presentation

MATERIALS Handout 5.13.1: Who's in the Audience? (one per student)

Handout 5.13.2: Audience Assessment (one per student)

DIRECTIONS
1. Distribute the Who's in the Audience? handout.

2. Explain that people in the audience might have different wants or needs—different from those of the speaker and different from other audience members. When a speaker satisfies those wants or needs, the audience will pay attention. If not, the audience might disengage and either tune out or become disruptive.

3. Review the Who's in the Audience? handout with the class. Explain and discuss the four types of audience members (Questioners, Knowledge Seekers, People People, and Explorers) and how best to engage them.

4. Distribute the Audience Assessment handout. Ask students to identify members of the group who they believe possess the characteristics of each of the types of people found in a typical audience. When finished, ask several volunteers to present their findings. See whether the group agrees with their assessments.

5. Hold a discussion using the following questions.

DISCUSSION
- Do you think these four types are present in the typical audience? Can you think of other types?

- Which of the types are likely to be polite but disappointed in the presentation—listening but feeling unsatisfied?

- Which of the types are likely to make it known to the presenter that they are not satisfied? How would they do this?

- Which types of groups (project groups, school clubs, athletic clubs, art groups, musical bands, and so forth) might have a lot of Questioners? Knowledge Seekers? People People? Explorers?

Questioners

Learning Style: Visual

The Questioner's main purpose in listening is to find out *why,* or what the reasons are behind the presentation. This person examines the *logic* of the presentation and wants to use *reasoning* with the information. When a speaker presents information logically, the Questioner will pay attention.

Techniques to use with Questioners:

- Present the material logically.
- Give examples that explain.
- Present data, logic, theories, and models.
- Be structured and organized.

Knowledge Seekers

Learning Style: Visual

The Knowledge Seeker's main purpose in listening is to find out *what* or *how much* information he or she can learn. This person wants to be able *to remember the information* presented and seeks *mastery* and *competence.* When a presenter offers data, research, facts, statistics, quotations, and citations (sources of information), the Knowledge Seeker will pay attention.

Techniques to use with Knowledge Seekers:

- Use a lecture format and a logical sequence.
- Include the latest research, statistics, and information.
- Make sure to give citations and sources.
- Be organized.

People People

Learning Style: Kinesthetic

Listeners who are People People ask *so what?* Their main purpose is to create a relationship with the presenter. They want to be *entertained.* They want to be *engaged* by the presentation of the material in unique and fun ways. Often they relate to the material in terms of personal experience or how it might impact them at a personal level. They are seeking connection with the presenter. When a presenter offers personal information and experiences and explains how the material impacts his or her life, People People become engaged and attentive.

Techniques to use with People People:

- Include personal stories.
- Include personal information.
- Use group activities and hands-on experiences.
- Use emotional stories to detail points.

Explorers

Learning Style: Auditory or Kinesthetic

The Explorer asks *what if?* He or she wants to take the information presented and examine it, reorganize it, come up with a different model or theory, and question the presenter's logic. Sometimes this person will raise questions early and often during a presentation and sometimes appears impatient, argumentative, or excited by the possibilities. When a presenter includes opportunities for questions interspersed with the presented material, the Explorer will listen—especially if there is an exploration of ideas, possible implementation, or new possibilities in dialogue with the Explorer.

Techniques to use with Explorers:

- Include opportunities for exploring the ideas presented.
- Offer a variety of views and examine several possibilities for implementation.
- When the Explorer becomes engaged, discuss with him or her the possibilities about an idea that has been presented.
- Be careful not to provoke an argument. It is better to listen and to validate an Explorer's idea than to shut him or her down or argue.

Think about some of the people in your class. Place them in one of the four categories. Give an evidence-based reason for putting them in the category you chose.

Questioners

Who in the group often asks "Why?" Who asks questions seeking to increase their understanding of the reasons for or rationale behind a topic?

Evidence for selecting these class members as Questioners:

Knowledge Seekers

Who in the group wants to have more information, data, research, statistics, or sources of information?

Evidence for selecting these class members as Knowledge Seekers:

People People

Who in the group wants to be entertained and engaged by the material and its presentation and prefers group activities?

Evidence for selecting these class members as People People:

Explorers

Who in the group likes to play with new ideas, explore new possibilities, offer other ways of looking at the topic, or suggest ways to implement ideas?

Evidence for selecting these class members as Explorers:

Yourself

Into what category would you place yourself?

Evidence for placing yourself in this category:

From *Inspiring Leadership in Teens: Group Activities to Foster Integrity, Responsibility, and Compassion,* © 2010 by Ric Stuecker, Champaign, IL: Research Press (800-519-2707, www.researchpress.com)

ACTIVITY 5.14

Identifying Audience Leaders and Barometers

PURPOSE

To provide practice in identifying audience members who are leaders and who might be useful as barometers of the entire group

MATERIALS

Handout 5.14.1: Leaders and Barometers (one per student)

Handout 5.14.2: Identifying Leaders and Barometers (one per student)

DIRECTIONS

1. Distribute copies of the Leaders and Barometers handout to each student.
2. Read the handout with the students and discuss for clarity.
3. When you feel the students have a good understanding of each type of person, hand out the Identifying Leaders and Barometers worksheet.
4. Ask students to fill out the worksheet.
5. Ask for volunteers to read their answers to each section. Discuss each.

DISCUSSION

- Why might it be important to know who the leaders in the audience are?
- Have you ever noticed a leader in the audience support the presenter? What did they do to show their support?
- Have you ever noticed a leader in the audience who did not support the presenter? What did they do? How did the presenter respond?
- How do leaders differ from barometers?
- Can a barometer also be a leader?
- Why might barometers be useful in meetings? In a presentation?

When giving a presentation, it is a good idea to identify and observe two types of people in the audience: leaders and barometers. People in an audience notice the reactions and body language of leaders and adjust their reactions accordingly. A person who is a barometer (just like barometers used in weather forecasting) can provide an "early warning" that is useful in determining when to make a change in your presentation.

It is a good idea to select several people from different sections of the audience to watch as you give your presentation. By noticing the reactions and behaviors of the leaders and barometers you have identified, you can judge whether the audience is engaged or whether it is time for an adjustment (Change the topic? Call for a break? Use a different presentation technique? Move from lecture to activity?).

Here are more details about each type of person.

Leaders

There are two types of leaders—designated and natural.

> **Designated Leaders:** When someone is elected to or selected for a leadership position—usually with a title (school principal, team captain, class president, head cheerleader)—he or she is observed by other members of the group. If this person supports and goes with the energy of the presentation (nods affirmatively, laughs at jokes, appears to agree), then the group relaxes and moves with the presenter.

> **Natural Leaders:** A natural leader might be someone who is accomplished in some valued area—an all-state football player, a student at the top of the honor roll, or some

other person who has the respect of the group. You can identify natural leaders in a group by watching the reactions of others to this person. When a natural leader asks a question or makes a comment during the session, others often look at this person while he or she talks. Like the designated leader, if this person affirms the presentation and appears to agree with the presenter, then the group relaxes and moves with the presenter.

Techniques for Interacting with Leaders

- Acknowledge the presence of designated leaders in the audience:

  "I'd like to thank Principal Smith for taking the time to attend."

  "Good to see you, Captain Jones. Our team played great last Saturday night."

- Give leaders an opportunity to express their ideas or position. If the position is contrary to yours or if the leader challenges you, validate the view expressed, thank the person giving it, and move on:

  "That's an interesting position some people take on this issue. Thanks for suggesting it."

- Ask the leader for an agreement if he or she asks a question early or states a contrary view:

  "Here are some interesting points you might consider. Can I present them to you and see whether any of them are agreeable to you?"

- If you ignore a leader, especially one who seems in conflict with the presentation, you risk splitting the group. Some audience members will connect with you, and others will support the leader. By acknowledging, validating, including, and honoring the leader and his or her ideas, you have a better chance of maintaining group unity and arriving at a win/win situation in which your ideas, as well as those of the leader, are considered and valued.

Barometers

Barometers are people who help you gauge the mood of the audience and are an early warning device that lets you know when to change the presentation, call a break, or end early. Watching the body language of several barometers in the room will help you determine how you are doing with the entire group.

Techniques for Using Barometers

- Choose people from several parts of the room.

- Choose people with different learning styles, if you know the audience well enough to do so.

- Notice body language: If a person is sitting up, nodding positively, and following you with his or her eyes, then they are engaged. If a person is looking away, sliding back in his or her chair, or otherwise not appearing interested, then he or she is not engaged and you will have to make an adjustment.

- Ask the audience: If you have trouble knowing whether the audience is with you and wanting more—just ask them:

"How are you doing? Are you interested in more information in this area?"

"Is this material useful for you?"

"Is it time for a break?"

Based on what you know about people in this class, answer the following questions:

1. If you were giving a presentation to this class, who would you identify as leaders to watch?

2. What evidence would you give for each person you selected being a leader?

3. What techniques would you use to engage this leader during your presentation?

4. Who would you select as barometers?

5. Explain as specifically as possible why you would select hem as barometers.

From *Inspiring Leadership in Teens: Group Activities to Foster Integrity, Responsibility, and Compassion,* © 2010
by Ric Stuecker, Champaign, IL: Research Press (800-519-2707, www.researchpress.com)

ACTIVITY 5.15

Organizing a Presentation

PURPOSE   To give students a simple format for a short presentation

MATERIALS   Handout 5.15.1: Organizing a Presentation (one per student)

Handout 5.15.2: Planning a Presentation (one per student)

Handout 5.15.3: Evaluating a Presentation (one per student)

A videotaped example of a presentation, if possible

PREPARATION   If possible, procure a video recording of a presentation—either an excellent student presentation or a professional presentation that would be of high interest to your students.

DIRECTIONS   *Part 1*

1. Distribute the Organizing a Presentation handout to all students.

2. Read and discuss the stages of a presentation, as explained in the handout.

3. Discuss each stage, making sure students understand it.

Part 2 (optional)

1. Show the students a video recording of an excellent student presentation or a professional presentation that would be of interest to them.

2. Use the video to demonstrate each stage of a presentation, as described on the Organizing a Presentation handout. Stop the video after each stage to discuss how the presenter accomplished each stage and evaluate its effectiveness.

3. Use the Evaluating a Presentation worksheet to assess the video presentation.

Part 3

1. Distribute the Planning a Presentation worksheet to all students.

2. Review the worksheet so students understand how to use it.

3. Explain to students that each of them will make a 3- to 5-minute presentation. Ask students to select a topic they would feel

comfortable making a presentation about, using the suggestions on the handout. (If a student requests another topic not listed, feel free to negotiate with him or her about it.)

4. You can allow PowerPoint presentations, depending on the amount of time you want students to be working on this activity. However, keep in mind that effective presentations are often best given with a minimal amount of visual aids. You might want to challenge the students to depend on their speaking skills by using only a whiteboard or chart when making their presentations.

5. Give students time to create a presentation. The amount of time depends on the size of the class. Because the suggested topics require little research, three (or so) class periods should be sufficient time for the students to prepare and create their presentations.

Part 4

1. Randomly place students in groups of two or three.

2. Ask students to read the presentation plan of their partner(s) and make suggestions.

3. Ask students to prepare a final version of their presentations. Encourage them to use a chart or other visual information during their presentation.

4. Set up a practice session in which students give their presentations to small groups of other students (three to five in a group) two or three times.

5. Schedule students to give final presentations to the entire group.

Part 5

1. Have students give their presentations to the entire group, according to the schedule you established.

2. Before the presentations, distribute copies of the Evaluating a Presentation worksheet. After each presentation, ask students in the audience to fill out the evaluation.

3. Read through the evaluations before handing them back to the presenter, making sure the remarks are positive and appropriate.

Part 6

After all students have given presentations and the evaluations have been completed and reviewed, hold a discussion using the following questions.

DISCUSSION

- What points or concepts do you want to remember about making a presentation?

- Besides the key ideas you are presenting, what are other key considerations in making an effective presentation? (How many examples to use, the order of the points being made, an engaging introduction, and a good conclusion are some possible answers.)

- What kinds of visual information are important when making an effective presentation?

A short presentation has five segments, or stages.

Stage 1: Welcome and Self-Introduction

During Stage 1, you want to make your audience feel comfortable. You want them to feel that you are both credible (knowledgeable about the subject and worth listening to) and approachable (someone who is open and engaging and whom they could ask a question or speak to after the presentation).

This is the time to give your credentials as a speaker on this topic (using a *credible* stance, tone of voice, and eye contact) and tell about yourself, briefly connecting your story to the topic you are presenting (using an *approachable* stance, tone of voice, and eye contact).

Stage 2: Overview of the Topic

During Stage 2, you offer a preview of what the audience will be hearing and an indication of the order in which you will be presenting the information. There are three major tasks of the overview:

1. **Relevance:** Explain why this material is important and why the audience should care.

2. **Outcomes:** Tell the audience what they will learn from the presentation, what skills they might gain, and what new information they will receive.

3. **Presentation Framework:** Explain the order you will use to present the information and what techniques the audience can expect (lecture? role-plays? activities?).

Stage 3: Major Content

During this stage, present the content in the order you explained. It is a good idea to begin by framing the content: "First, let's look at the history of . . ." You can use foreshadowing: "Tonight we will be looking at three aspects of . . ."

After you complete an area of content, provide a summary. You might want to stop for a moment to field questions on the topic just presented. As you move on to the next topic, link it to the previous information: "We have just examined . . . Now we will look at . . ."

Toward the end of the talk, you might want to backtrack: "Let's take a minute and look at where we've been."

Stage 4: Summary

Review the major points you want the audience to leave with.

Stage 5: Conclusion

The closing of a presentation should be inspiring, uplifting, and motivating. This is a good place to tell a brief, inspiring story that illustrates the points you have been making. Here is also a good place to encourage the audience to take the next step.

From *Inspiring Leadership in Teens: Group Activities to Foster Integrity, Responsibility, and Compassion,* © 2010 by Ric Stuecker, Champaign, IL: Research Press (800-519-2707, www.researchpress.com)

1. Pick a topic you know a lot about. For this practice presentation, pick a topic for which you don't have to do much, if any, research. Here are some topics you might consider:

   - How to Survive High School
   - Why You Should Consider Playing [name your sport]
   - Best Techniques for Getting an A
   - The Three Best Spots for Taking a Vacation
   - What Everyone Should Know Before Deciding to _____.
   - How to Survive Parents When You Are a Teenager

2. Plan your welcome and self-introduction:

   - After the welcome, make a brief statement explaining why you are a credible presenter for this topic. What life experiences can you draw on as an expert in this field? Be specific, and make sure what you say is related to the topic you have chosen.
   - Why is this a relevant topic for the audience?
   - What will the audience learn that might be helpful to them?
   - What general topics will you be presenting and in what order?

3. Consider how you will present your major points:

   Point 1

   - Will you give examples?
   - Will you give facts and/or statistics?
   - Will you tell a brief story?
   - Will you use an activity?

   Point 2

   - How will you link this point with point 1?
   - Will you give examples?
   - Will you tell a brief story?
   - Will you give facts and/or statistics?
   - Will you use an activity?

   Point 3

   - How will you link this point with point 1 and point 2?
   - Will you give examples?
   - Will you give facts and/or statistics?
   - Will you tell a brief story?
   - Will you use an activity?

4. Plan your conclusion:

   - Will you present a brief story that inspires?
   - Will you make a call to action?

From *Inspiring Leadership in Teens: Group Activities to Foster Integrity, Responsibility, and Compassion,* © 2010 by Ric Stuecker, Champaign, IL: Research Press (800-519-2707, www.researchpress.com)

Presenter's name _____

Presentation topic _____

Rate each statement using the following scale:

Excellent = 5 points   Very Good = 4 points   Good = 3 points   Fair = 2 points   Poor = 1 point

<u>Criteria</u>   <u>Points</u>

1. The presenter was knowledgeable about the topic.   _____

2. The presenter appeared prepared to give this presentation.   _____

3. The presenter used facial expressions, tones of voice, and body language   _____
   that generated audience interest and enthusiasm.

4. The presenter's volume was loud enough to be heard by all audience members   _____
   throughout the presentation.

5. The presenter stood up straight, looked relaxed, and made eye contact.   _____

6. The presenter spoke clearly and distinctly at least 95 percent of the time.   _____

7. The presenter welcomed the audience and introduced himself or herself.   _____

8. The presenter clearly spoke about three points and linked each point to the topic. _____

9. The presenter gave a conclusion that was inspiring.   _____

10. The presentation was within the specified time limit (neither too short nor too long). _____

                                                                                              Total   _____

Totals

- 41 to 50 points = Excellent
- 31 to 40 points = Very Good
- 21 to 30 points = Good
- 11 to 20 points = Fair
- 1 to 10 points = Poor

Based on the above criteria, this speaker needs to improve in the following areas:

☐ Knowledge of the topic   ☐ Clarity

☐ Preparation   ☐ Introduction

☐ Enthusiasm   ☐ Speaking Points

☐ Volume   ☐ Conclusion

☐ Posture   ☐ Time

From *Inspiring Leadership in Teens: Group Activities to Foster Integrity, Responsibility, and Compassion,* © 2010
by Ric Stuecker, Champaign, IL: Research Press (800-519-2707, www.researchpress.com)

Planning: Making Positive Changes

Inspiring leaders guide us to new possibilities and to seek positive change in the world in which we live. Positive change begins with a compelling vision. When a group defines a vision that is detailed and specific, they can create a set of goals and objectives to achieve their compelling vision. Smaller groups can examine these goals and design projects and activities that will achieve them. Once a design has been created, action groups can take the plans and create the changes. With diligence and an eye on the final outcome, the original vision can become reality.

The activities in this learning center lead step by step—from creating a vision to designing a strategy to creating action plans. They apply the concepts of consensus building and decision making based on recently developed technologies by which large groups can develop and achieve their hoped-for and ideal futures.

In small schools, entire classes can participate in planning activities for class projects. By including all parties as stakeholders, everyone is part of the decision-making process. Because the method is win/win, consensus-based decision making rather than win/lose voting, this method builds community and encourages participation.

In larger schools, representatives of stakeholder groups can be selected to participate in the process. One method for determining representatives is to ask all students in the largest possible group (say, the senior class) to identify five students they would recommend to participate in a planning workshop. Then ask all the students in that large group (that is, the senior class) whether they would be willing to serve at such a workshop. Make a list of all students identified by the large group. Make a list of those willing to serve. Invite those who are included on both lists.

Another method that works equally well is to ask all students in the largest possible group to identify five students who they think would be ideal for attending a planning workshop. Ask the students who were identified to each identify five more students they believe should take part in the workshop. Then ask those students to each name five students they believe would be ideal participants. Examine the lists of students generated by this process and invite those whose names most often appear on the suggested lists.

Service Learning

It is sometimes the complaint of students that they do not participate in the planning of service projects or that they go to planning sessions—but the plans are never implemented. Therefore, it is vitally important that students participate in a planning process for determining, as much as possible, the direction of the service learning program and the kinds of experiences that are planned.

A good visioning question that can be used is "What are the most compelling needs for service in our community?" A good question for identifying areas of service would be "What are the most compelling acts of service we could provide for our community, our neighborhood, and our school?" Identifying these areas for service would then lead to the creation of planning groups for each area. Students could suggest strategic directions and create viable action plans using the methods described in the following activities.

ACTIVITY 5.16

Developing a
Compelling Vision

PURPOSE

To show students the steps in making a compelling vision for change

MATERIALS

Newsprint or other blank paper, such as sheets from an easel pad
Markers

DIRECTIONS

1. Randomly place students in groups of five to eight.

2. Create a visualization that takes students into an ideal, successful, and compelling future. The following visualization process is designed for a group of high-school students. If you are working with students in a different context, the visualization should reflect the context in which they live.

3. Ask students to imagine themselves on graduation day. They are waiting to enter the graduation ceremony where they will receive their diplomas. Their 4 years of high school have been among the most successful in school history. Many people have remarked about how special and successful these years have been. Explain that they will walk back through the experiences they have had that made these years so great and will synthesize, or put together, the key and best elements of what they experienced.

   Pause for 15 or 20 seconds after you read each of the following items to allow students time to think. They might wish to silently jot down thoughts during this time.

   • Remember the fun activities you and your friends experienced together. What do you remember as being the outstanding activities you did together?

   • Remember how well you treated each other. What qualities of friendship do you remember about your friends?

   • Remember the social events you participated in. What were the most memorable ones?

- Remember service opportunities you participated in. What are your best memories of service?

- Remember playing sports together. What was great about playing sports?

4. Tell the students to pretend that their school has been named one of the top ten in the United States in the annual report on model high schools. It is outstanding in all aspects, and other schools come to study the success of their school. Read the following aloud to the students, pausing for 15 or 20 seconds between each. They might wish to silently jot down thoughts during this time.

  - You stand outside your school and look around the grounds. What do you notice about the grounds that make this school a model?

  - You walk into several classrooms where students are learning. What is happening that makes these classes outstanding and noteworthy? In what ideal ways are the students and teachers interacting? What makes these classes different?

  - Instruction ends and after-school activities begin. What outstanding activities do you notice?

  - You attend a game. What is it about the fans and the team that make them exemplary?

5. Ask each small group to select a recorder. Ask them to discuss and brainstorm all the things they "saw" during the visualization that would be essential to creating an ideal school year and what they want to happen at their school. Ask them to be as specific as possible about naming the elements.

6. Ask each small group to write statements describing the most desirable or ideal school year they can create by working together as a group. Statements should be specific and clear—that is, a reader of these statements from another group would understand completely what is meant. Distribute newsprint or sheets from an easel pad to each team and ask them to copy their statements onto it. Allow about half an hour for this step. The following example statements can be used as a starting point or for inspiration:

  - Students include everyone in their projects and activities; no one is excluded.

  - Students have fun together at events that are safe, drug free, and inclusive of all students.

  - Classes take field trips that are fun, enriching, and memorable.

7. Distribute additional newsprint or sheets from an easel pad to each team. Challenge them to create a picture or other visual image of what the ideal school year would look like. (For example, a diagram

of a tree—in the roots, the foundational words of students respecting each other, students including each other; on the trunk, the words "a school that creates positive memories for all students"; on the branches, the words "high-school spirit," "pride in each other's accomplishments," "winning school teams," "safe and memorable social events," etc.) Allow about half an hour for this step.

8. Give each team 5 minutes to present their visions for an ideal school year to the entire group. Ask teams to select two people to present their ideas using the picture they created and the statements they wrote.

9. Make sure to keep the drawings and statements for use in the next activity.

ACTIVITY 5.17

Moving from Vision to Plan

PURPOSE   To help students identify goals they want to plan for

MATERIALS   Large sheets of blank paper (such as newsprint or sheets from an easel pad)

Markers

Strips of paper approximately 1 × 5 inches in size (one per student)

PREPARATION   Post the pictures and charts of statements made in the previous activity by each group in the front of the room.

DIRECTIONS   1. Ask students to examine each of the pictures and the charts of statements at the front of the room.

2. Ask students to identify any statements that are similar or have the same meaning.

3. Circle the statements identified by the students as similar or having the same meaning. Ask for suggestions for combining these statements. Write the combined and modified statements for everyone to see, and cross out the statements that were circled.

4. Go through the remaining statements one by one. Ask the students: "Does this statement express an essential element for having an ideal school year?" Place a star by those statements the students believe are essential for an ideal school year.

5. Cross out any statements that did not receive stars. Ask a student (or two) who prints clearly to make a chart of the statements.

6. Suggest to the students that these statements form a set of guiding principles that will be used to evaluate the plans they generate for creating an ideal and memorable school year.

7. Ask the students to suggest areas of student life for which they need to plan specific activities in order to achieve their vision of an ideal and memorable school year. Limit the number of topics or focus areas to the number of teams you wish to create (that is, if you have 25 students, there would be five focus teams, each with five members). Here are some examples:

   • Fund-raising activities

- Raising school spirit
- Student-to-student relationships
- School-sponsored social events
- Service opportunities
- Memory items
- School pride
- Class field trips
- End-of-year trips

8. Write the name of each suggested topic or focus area on a large sheet of blank paper, followed by the numbers 1 through 5 or higher, depending on how many members you want on each focus area team. (Limiting each focus area to five or six members will help keep the teams small and manageable. Also, less popular areas will receive consideration rather than having large groups working on one or two areas.)

9. Distribute the 1 × 5-inch strips of paper (one to each student). Ask students to write their name on the strip and deposit the strip into a box or bag.

10. Draw out each strip, one at a time, and read the name aloud. As their names are called, students can select the team they want to be on by writing their name next to one of the numbers on that focus sheet. This way, students are randomly selected to choose areas they want to work on. When a focus area has all team positions filled, students will need to choose a different area.

11. Regroup students at tables according to the area they chose to work on.

12. Distribute another large sheet of blank paper to each team.

13. Ask teams to take 20 or 30 minutes to brainstorm and chart the most compelling ideas they have for that area to create an ideal school year.

14. Ask each team to present their charted ideas to the entire group. Ask the rest of the class to add any ideas they might want to consider. Examine each idea and ask, "Is this idea essential for creating an ideal school year? Is it realistic and doable?" Eliminate any that do not have the support of the entire group or are unrealistic or undoable.

15. Ask a team member to make a list of all remaining compelling ideas. These will be used during an action planning activity later in this learning center.

DISCUSSION

- Are these the most compelling ideas we have for creating an ideal school year?
- Are there any others?
- Are all these ideas realistic and doable?
- Does everyone feel as though his or her ideas have been heard and considered?

ACTIVITY 5.18

Identifying and Solving Constraints

PURPOSE

To help students identify possible constraints to fulfilling their plans and to find solutions for overcoming them

MATERIALS

Large sheets of blank paper (such as newsprint or sheets from an easel pad)

Markers

DIRECTIONS

1. Ask students to return to the groups they were in during the previous activity, Moving from Vision to Plan.

2. Explain to students that they are going to consider constraints to their projects and solutions to those constraints. Explain that a constraint is anything that might pose a problem to completing a project.

3. Ask students to brainstorm all possible constraints to their projects. Ask them to list each constraint on a large sheet of blank paper. Allow about 15 minutes.

4. Ask students to consider each of the constraints. Ask them to identify those that are out of their control by placing an X next to the constraints. Ask them to use a star to identify any constraints that might have a doable solution.

5. Ask students to divide a large, blank sheet of paper in half by drawing a vertical line down the middle. On the left half, they should list constraints that they can manage or find solutions for. On the right half, they should list possible solutions to each constraint.

6. When students are finished, ask each small group to present their constraints and solutions to the larger group. When each group is finished, ask the larger group whether they have any additional solutions for each constraint.

7. Ask one person in each group to make a final list of constraints and solutions. This list will be useful in the next activity, Creating Action Plans.

DISCUSSION

- Do you believe the solutions presented will negate the constraints that have been identified?
- How do we handle constraints that are out of our control?
- Why do you believe it is a good idea to identify constraints and solutions for constraints *before* making action plans?

Creating Action Plans

PURPOSE To create compelling and doable action plans to fulfill the identified strategic directions and areas of concern

MATERIALS Handout 5.19.1: Action Plan (approximately 10 per work group)

File folders for storing completed Action Plans (one folder per team)

PREPARATION Post the list of compelling ideas developed in Activity 5.17, Moving from Vision to Plan.

DIRECTIONS 1. Ask students to return to the group they were working with during the previous activity, Identifying and Solving Constraints.

2. Have students look at the list of compelling ideas from Activity 5.17, Moving from Vision to Plan. Ask them to think about all the ideas and create a project to fulfill each one.

3. Distribute 10 or so action plan forms to each group. Ask groups to complete an action plan for each project:

Project Description: This should be as detailed as possible. For example:

> The senior class will hold a car wash at Sullivan's Service Station on Saturday, October 1, from 10 A.M. to 2 P.M. Student volunteers will wash cars with soap and water, clean windows using window cleaner, vacuum interiors, and wipe all interior surfaces with clean cloths.

Completion Date: Each activity should take no more than 90 days to prepare and complete.

Team Members: Any member of the larger group may volunteer to be part of the action team. The team should elect or otherwise choose a captain.

Steps: Describe every step necessary to complete the project. For each step, complete the following:

> **Who:** Name the person responsible for performing and/or overseeing this step.

When: Set the date by which that step must be completed.

Approval: List the name of anyone who most give approval, if approval is necessary for this step.

Support from: List the name of anyone whose help and support you might need to complete the project.

Approved: This line is signed by the teacher or principal to indicate approval of the entire proposal.

4. Distribute a file folder to each group. Ask the groups to put their completed action plan forms in the folder. Be sure that each group writes the name of its focus area on the file folder.

DISCUSSION

- Is the project description detailed and complete?
- Have you anticipated all the steps necessary to complete the project?
- Do you have a person responsible for each step?
- Are the due dates reasonable and clear?
- Do you need someone's help to complete the project? Is that person's name listed on the form?
- For each step, from whom do you need approval?
- When will the action group meet again?

Westlake High School Media Center

Project Description

Completion Date

Captain

Team Members

Steps	Who	When	Approval
1.			
2.			
3.			
4.			
5.			
6.			

Support from

Approved

From *Inspiring Leadership in Teens: Group Activities to Foster Integrity, Responsibility, and Compassion,* © 2010 by Ric Stuecker, Champaign, IL: Research Press (800-519-2707, www.researchpress.com)

ACTIVITY 5.20

Scheduling Activities

PURPOSE   To create a year's calendar of activities without conflicts

MATERIALS   Handout 5.20.1: Calendar (one per student)

PREPARATION On a whiteboard or easel pad, create a large version of the calendar. Place it where everyone in the room can see it.

DIRECTIONS
1. Distribute copies of the calendar to all students. The first page is a blank calendar; the second is a calendar completed as an example.

2. Ask teams to select one person to hold their file folder of action plans (from Activity 5.19, Creating Action Plans).

3. Ask the students with the action plans to list each project and its tentative completion date on the large calendar you created on a whiteboard or easel pad. If there are conflicts, do not worry about them at this point.

4. Examine the calendar to see whether events are spread out throughout the year and whether there are any conflicts.

5. Suggest changes of completion dates for any conflicting projects.

6. Take a final look at the calendar to make sure all deadline conflicts have been resolved.

7. Ask students to refer to this calendar as a model for filling out their own calendars.

8. It is a good idea to keep the large calendar displayed for future reference and to make changes in case other conflicts occur.

DISCUSSION
- Are there any conflicting dates? If so, can we negotiate a change?
- Would any of the projects be better suited for a different time of year?
- Do we have too many projects in any one quarter?
- Will these projects create a compelling and ideal year?

Leadership Project Areas	Quarter 1 Projects	Quarter 2 Projects	Quarter 3 Projects	Quarter 4 Projects
Area 1				
Area 2				
Area 3				
Area 4				
Area 5				
Area 6				
Area 7				

From *Inspiring Leadership in Teens: Group Activities to Foster Integrity, Responsibility, and Compassion,* © 2010
by Ric Stuecker, Champaign, IL: Research Press (800-519-2707, www.researchpress.com)

Calendar: Example

Leadership Project Areas	Quarter 1 Projects	Quarter 2 Projects	Quarter 3 Projects	Quarter 4 Projects
Area 1 Fund-Raising	Fall Yard Sale (September)	Poinsettia Sale (December)	Valentines (February)	Raffle (May)
Area 2 School Service	Hall Murals (October)	Turkey Dinner (November) Peer Tutoring (December)	Peer Tutoring (February)	Peer Tutoring (May)
Area 3 Community Service	Elderly Projects (September/October)	Christmas Collections (November)	Elderly Projects (February/March)	Zoo Trips (May)
Area 4 School Spirit	Pep Store (September/October) Fall Bonfire (October)	Pep Rally (November) Pep Store (November/December)	Pep Rally (March) Pep Store (January/March)	Field Day (May)
Area 5 Social	Fall Meet and Greet (October)	Winter Dance (December)	Spring Fling (March)	Prom (May)
Area 6 Peer Programs	Peer Mediation Training (September/October)	Peer Mediation Center (November/December)	Peer Mediation Center (January/March)	Peer Mediation Center (April/May)
Area 7 Memories	Candid Photos (September/October) Sweatshirt Design Contest (September/October)	Individual and Team Pictures (November/December) Candid Photos (November/December)	Team Photos, Activity Photos, Design Pages (January/March)	Edit Memory Book and Publish (April/May)

Unit Resources

Emery, M., & Purser, R. E. (1996). *The Search Conference: A powerful method for planning organizational change and community action.* San Francisco: Jossey-Bass.

Garmston, R. (1997). *The presenter's fieldbook: A practical guide.* Norwood, MA: Christopher-Gordon.

Garmston has written an exemplary guidebook for presentation skills.

Gelb, M. J. (1988). *Present yourself!* Torrance, CA: Jalmar Press.

This is an excellent quick study for developing presentation skills.

O'Connor, J., & Seymour, J. (1994). *Training with NLP: Skills for managers, trainers and communicators.* London: Thorsons.

O'Connor and Seymour write clearly about NLP techniques for communicating.

Weisbord, M. R., & Janoff, S. (1995). *Future Search: An action guide to finding common ground in organizations and communities.* San Francisco: Berrett-Koehler.

Zuieback, S. L. (n.d.). *Facilitating community partnerships.* Sebastopol, CA: National Training Associates.

Introduction   319

Activities

6.1   Wellness Wheel: Personal Health Assessment   321

        Handout 6.1.1: Personal Health Self-Assessment   323

6.2   When Am I in My Power?   325

6.3   Touching My Spirit: What Is Greater Than I Am?   328

6.4   Personal Transformation   330

6.5   Affirmations   334

6.6   Setting Boundaries   336

        Handout 6.6.1: Six-Step Process for Setting Boundaries   338

        Handout 6.6.2: Setting Boundaries Script   339

6.7   Asking for Forgiveness   340

        Handout 6.7.1: Six-Step Process for Asking for Forgiveness   342

        Handout 6.7.2: Asking for Forgiveness Script   343

6.8   Personal Dilemmas   344

        Handout 6.8.1: Steve's Dilemma   345

        Handout 6.8.2: Tomasina's Dilemma   346

        Handout 6.8.3: Mario's Dilemma   347

        Handout 6.8.4: Mack's Dilemma   348

        Handout 6.8.5: Robert's Dilemma   349

        Handout 6.8.6: Celeste's Dilemma   350

        Handout 6.8.7: Beverly's Dilemma   351

        Handout 6.8.8: Lamar's Dilemma   352

        Handout 6.8.9: Jennifer's Dilemma   353

        Handout 6.8.10: Bob's Dilemma   354

6.9   My Spiritual Journey   355

        Handout 6.9.1: My Spiritual Journey Map   357

6.10   This I Believe   358

Unit Resources   361

UNIT 6 INTRODUCTION

Living Peace

This book rests on the premise that the leaders who most inspire us are able to encourage us to become the best that we can be. They inspire us to look within ourselves and find our personal power, beliefs, and convictions. Upon this personal power, we build ourselves into inspiring leadership in the roles we play in our lives. This unit asks participants to look deeply into themselves and find the internal foundation of their character and leadership. Some might call this "soul." Others might call it "spirit." In this sense, it is a spiritual journey toward personal peace.

OVERVIEW OF ACTIVITIES

The activities in this unit lead students on a journey of self-discovery and are designed to help them identify the internal qualities and strengths that are the basis of inspiring leadership.

- In Activity 6.1, students assess their personal well-being. The assessment tool looks at social, intellectual, emotional, physical, and spiritual health.

- Activities 6.2 and 6.3 give students the opportunity to examine their inner power and connection to something greater than themselves.

- The theme of Activity 6.4 is transformation: letting go of the past and moving toward one's hoped-for future. Activity 6.5 builds on that theme and asks students to develop personal affirmations to promote their growth.

- Activity 6.6 teaches students the six steps for safely and effectively setting boundaries. Students are given the opportunity to practice this skill in a role-play. In Activity 6.7, students learn a simple process for asking for forgiveness when they have crossed a boundary or not honored an agreement.

- Making moral decisions is the focus of Activity 6.8. The activity presents hypothetical dilemmas about situations often faced by young people and gives students the opportunity to propose and discuss solutions from a moral standpoint.

- Activity 6.9 allows students to examine their personal journeys and map out their beliefs, purposes, hopes, dreams, and destinations in life. Activity 6.10 reinforces that theme and encourages them to identify and write about their core beliefs.

ACTIVITY 6.1

Wellness Wheel: Personal Health Self-Assessment

In this activity, students should be given the time and space to write and to take the Personal Health Self-Assessment privately.

PURPOSE

To help students assess their personal health as a basis for personal peace

MATERIALS

Handout 6.1.1: Personal Health Self-Assessment (one per student)

Large, dinner-size paper plates to serve as "wellness wheels" (one per student)

DIRECTIONS

1. Distribute the paper plates. Ask students to place their hand on the back of the paper plate and to draw an outline with their fingers outstretched. Ask students to write the following words, one per finger or thumb: *social, intellectual, emotional, physical,* and *spiritual.*

2. Hold a discussion, using the following questions:

   • What does it mean to be healthy?

   • Look at each of the words on your hand drawing. What would it mean to be healthy in each of these areas? (Ask students to be specific in describing health in each area.)

   • What might a person do to be healthy in each specific area?

3. Suggest to students that you have used the hand as a *symbol* and ask what a hand might symbolize to them concerning health. Point out that each of them has a "hand" in their personal health in each of these important areas of well-being.

4. Suggest to students that peace begins inside each of them and that one's personal peace rests on one's personal health and balance.

5. Distribute copies of the Personal Health Self-Assessment. Ask students to answer the questions and then score the inventory according to the directions. Provide help as needed in scoring.

6. Hold a discussion, asking the following questions:

   - Raise your hand if your strongest area of health is physical. Emotional? Intellectual? Spiritual? Social?

   - What are some ways someone could improve his or her personal health in each of these areas?

7. Ask students to turn their paper plates to the front side. On that side, which is blank, ask them to divide their plate into five separate, approximately equal, segments (like a pie). Ask students to label the sections *social, intellectual, emotional, physical,* and *spiritual.*

8. Ask students to write down one activity they could do each week to improve their personal health in each area. Ask them to make specific and doable suggestions.

9. When students are finished, place them in groups of three. Ask students to discuss the activities they selected and which activities they are most likely to do.

DISCUSSION

- If you were healthy in each section of your "wellness wheel," you would have balanced health. Why do you suppose balanced health is good?

- Why do you suppose it is difficult for each of us to maintain balance in our health?

- How does being balanced and healthy contribute to personal peace? Peace in general?

Read each of the following statements carefully and decide whether it is always true, often true, sometimes true, or never true. Allocate points as shown on the scoring scale below. Be as honest as you can. Think about how you actually behave, not how you would like to behave. Respond to each item. When you have completed the inventory, you will be able to score it to determine your personal health.

Scoring Scale

The statement is always true = 3 points

The statement is often true = 2 points

The statement is sometimes true = 1 point

The statement is never true = 0 points

Statement	*Points*
1. I like to do things with my friends, especially on the weekends.	_____
2. I discuss my ideas and thoughts with my friends, teachers, and others.	_____
3. I feel good about myself.	_____
4. I like to engage in sweat-producing activities at least three times a week.	_____
5. I believe there is a power that is greater than I am.	_____
6. I participate in school activities.	_____
7. I enjoy learning new things.	_____
8. I enjoy my life.	_____
9. I take care of my body by eating right.	_____
10. I trust that things will turn out all right.	_____
11. I have at least one very good friend.	_____
12. I challenge myself by reading and thinking.	_____
13. When I make mistakes, I change how I do things.	_____
14. I work out and take care of my body.	_____
15. I believe I am a good person.	_____
16. I think of myself as a good friend to have.	_____
17. I like to study topics I enjoy learning about.	_____
18. I set realistic goals for myself.	_____
19. I take care of myself by getting good sleep and taking care of personal hygiene.	_____
20. I believe most people are good at heart.	_____
21. Given a choice of being alone or being with others, I choose to be with others.	_____

From *Inspiring Leadership in Teens: Group Activities to Foster Integrity, Responsibility, and Compassion,* © 2010 by Ric Stuecker, Champaign, IL: Research Press (800-519-2707, www.researchpress.com)

Statements	Points
22. I think deeply about certain topics.	_____
23. When I am wrong, I accept responsibility.	_____
24. I avoid alcohol and other harmful drugs.	_____
25. I love being alive.	_____
26. I try to help others when I can.	_____
27. I like to debate ideas with others.	_____
28. I feel good about who I am.	_____
29. I take care of my body.	_____
30. I feel connected to my personal power and the wonder of the universe.	_____

Transferring and Interpreting Scores

Use the following chart to record your scores. The small number in each block corresponds to the 30 individual items for which you recorded values of 0, 1, 2, or 3 on the preceding statements. Transfer your 30 individual item scores to the Score Transfer chart. Next, add the values in each column (columns I through V) and place the totals at the bottom. When you have the columns totaled, transfer their values to the Score Interpretation chart that follows.

Score Transfer

I	II	III	IV	V
1	2	3	4	5
6	7	8	9	10
11	12	13	14	15
16	17	18	19	20
21	22	23	24	25
26	27	28	29	30

Totals

I	II	III	IV	V

Score Interpretation

Transfer the values from each column on the Score Transfer chart to the Column Score lines below.

Column	Column Score	Personal Health Area
I	_____	Social
II	_____	Intellectual
III	_____	Emotional
IV	_____	Physical
V	_____	Spiritual

The range of scores is 0 to 18 for each personal health area. Identify your highest scores and celebrate your accomplishments. Take a good look at your lower scores and identify areas you might want to work on for improving your personal health.

When Am I in My Power?

PURPOSE   To give students the opportunity to describe the times in their lives when they touch the core of their inner power

MATERIALS   Drawing paper or newsprint (one sheet per student)

Colored markers, crayons, or chalk

Optional: Soft music to play while the students draw

DIRECTIONS   1. Introduce the concept of being "in power"—the feelings people get when they feel good about themselves, "in the flow," centered, and powerful.

2. Explain that power does not mean power over another person. You might want to discuss these questions:

   • What do you think the word "power" means?

   • How do we usually use this word?

   • What might we mean by the phrase "personal power"?

   • Have you ever met someone who was personally powerful but not necessarily physically strong?

   • What characteristics did this person have that made him or her powerful?

   • Who is more powerful—a physically strong person or someone with interior strength? Why?

3. Hand out the art materials and ask students to put them aside temporarily while you conduct a guided relaxation exercise.

4. Give students the following instructions, pausing at least 10 seconds between each direction:

   • I'd like you to place yourself into a comfortable position.

   • Close your eyes. If you are uncomfortable closing your eyes, look in front of you at the floor. Make no eye contact with anyone until we are finished.

   • Relax. Take a deep breath. Inhale until your lungs are full, hold your breath a moment, and then let your breath go.

- Relax. Take another deep breath. *(Pause 5 seconds.)* Hold it. *(Pause 5 seconds.)* Let it go.
- Relax. Let go of any tension in your feet. Uncurl your toes. Allow any tension in your feet to loosen.
- Relax. Let any tension or tightness in your legs loosen and flow out of you.
- Relax. Let any tension in your trunk or your belly loosen and relax.
- Let any tension or tightness in your shoulders flow out. Relax your shoulders.
- Let any tension or tightness in your arms flow out. Relax your arms.
- Let your fingers fall loose. Relax your hands.
- Let go of any tension in your head. Loosen your jaw. Relax.
- Imagine you are in a boat floating. Let yourself go.
- As you float, you become totally relaxed, more and more relaxed.
- You are floating back into your life, back to a time and a place where you felt totally centered, totally energized, and totally powerful.
- Where were you? What could you see? What could you hear?
- How is the weather? Who are you with?
- What are you doing?
- Enjoy this feeling of being centered and powerful. Relax and breathe into it.
- Take several deep breaths.
- Stay relaxed. Gradually open your eyes.
- Come back fully into the room. Do not talk.
- Slowly pick up your markers, crayons, or chalk and draw a representation of this time you were "in your power."

5. If you chose some soft music for this exercise, play it now. Allow students to draw for 5 or 10 minutes or until everyone is finished. Ask students to put away their markers, crayons, or chalk.

6. Ask students to sit in circles of six to eight.

7. Ask students to hold their drawings in front of themselves and ask them to look at all the other drawings in their circle, without speaking.

8. After students have examined each of the drawings, ask one student in each group to volunteer to speak first, describing to the group as fully as possible the time he or she felt inner power. The other students share their drawings in the same fashion.

9. When all students have described their experiences within their small groups, ask for volunteers to present their drawings and explain their personal power for the entire group.

DISCUSSION

• Were there any similarities in where you experienced personal power and where others experienced personal power?

• Were there any surprising differences—were you surprised by where someone else felt personal power?

• In general, did most people feel personal power alone? With others? In nature? In some special place?

• Why is it important to know where you find your personal power?

• What is the relationship between personal power and leadership?

ADDITIONAL IDEAS

• Collect stories from other sources describing times people have experienced being "in their power." (If you have the opportunity, conduct this activity with a group of adults from your community and then share their experiences with the students.)

• Review the *Chicken Soup for the Soul* books for stories to share. Another source is *My Spirit Flies: Portraits and Prose of Women in Their Power,* by M. Cathy Angell (Bay City Press, 1997).

• Invite a group from the community to sit on a panel and discuss times when they have felt they have been individually "in their power."

ACTIVITY 6.3

Touching My Spirit: What Is Greater Than I Am?

PURPOSE   To permit students to examine their connection to something greater than themselves

MATERIALS   Drawing paper or newsprint (one sheet per student)

Colored markers, crayons, or chalk

Optional: Soft music to play while the students draw

DIRECTIONS 1. Hand out the art materials and ask students to have them available to use after a brief discussion.

2. Hold a discussion, using the following questions:

   • What does the word "spiritual" mean to you?

   • What might it mean to other people?

   • Have you ever been somewhere or done something that made you feel deeply spiritual?

   • If so, what was that like for you? Where were you? What were you doing?

   • What do you think "something greater than you" might mean? What is greater than you?

   • Have you ever felt connected to or close to something that made you feel deeply spiritual?

   • When was the last time you felt spiritual in your life? What was it like for you?

   • If you wanted to feel deeply spiritual and connected to something greater than you, where would you go? What would you do?

3. If you chose some soft music for this exercise, play it now. Explain to the students that they do not have to draw a specific picture but can use colors and shapes to express their spiritual feelings. Allow students to draw for 5 or 10 minutes or until everyone is finished drawing.

4. When students have finished drawing, ask them to put away their art materials and sit in circles of five or six. Ask them to hold their drawings in front of themselves so other students can examine the drawings in silence.

5. Ask students to take turns describing their drawings and their spiritual feelings to each other within the small group.

6. When the students have shared in their small groups, ask for volunteers to describe their drawings and spiritual feelings to the class.

DISCUSSION

- Is there a difference between feeling spiritual and feeling personal power? If so, what are the differences?

- How many of the people in the class felt connected to something "greater than themselves?"

- How would you describe "greater then you?" A spiritual being? The universe? An energy that is greater than you? Your connection to others?

- Do you think it is necessary for a leader to feel a spiritual connection to something greater than himself or herself?

A C T I V I T Y 6 . 4

Personal Transformation

PURPOSE

To give students the opportunity to experience a transformation, letting go of the past and moving into a hoped-for future

MATERIALS

Drawing paper or newsprint (one sheet per student)

Colored markers, crayons, or chalk

A small charcoal grill (if permitted)

Long matches or a candle lighter (if permitted)

Modeling clay or Play-Doh

Optional: Soft music to play as students draw

NOTE

If your situation does not permit a grill, you can ask the students to tear up their drawings into miniscule pieces and place the pieces in a black plastic bag. For a high-tech version, use a paper shredder.

DIRECTIONS

1. Distribute the art supplies and ask students to put them aside temporarily.

2. Ask students to assume a relaxed position, either seated or lying on the floor. Tell them to listen and follow these instructions:

   - Relax. Take a deep breath. Hold the breath a moment and breathe out.

   - Breathe deeply again. Breathe in. *(Pause.)* Hold the breath a moment. *(Pause.)* Breathe out.

   - Relax. Close your eyes if you wish. If you do not like closing your eyes, look in front of you at the floor. Do not make eye contact with anyone until this exercise is finished.

   - Relax. Let the chair or the floor hold your body. Let all of your body relax.

   - As you relax, imagine you are floating in a boat. You can hear the water surrounding you as you float. You are at peace and totally relaxed.

   - You are drifting back in time. Let yourself go backward in time.

- You are drifting back to your earliest memories. How far back can you remember? Let yourself relax. Be at peace and let yourself drift back to your earliest memories.

- Drift back to the earliest age you can remember. How old do you think you are?

- Imagine your happiest memories. Imagine playing.

- What is your earliest memory playing? How old are you? Where are you?

- Are you with anyone? What do you see? What do you hear?

- Relax and just drift in your memories—happy memories.

- Of all the toys and objects you have and can remember having, which objects most represent you as a child?

- Which of your possessions belong in your childhood?

- Which of those would you be willing to give up—to let go of—to represent your transformation from childhood to adulthood?

- Select something from your childhood that you would be willing to give up, then gradually open your eyes.

3. Instruct students to stay quiet and not talk. Have them use their art supplies to draw the object from their childhood that they would be willing to let go.

4. If you chose some soft music for this exercise, play it now. Allow students to draw for 5 or 10 minutes or until everyone is finished. Ask students to put away their markers, crayons, or chalk.

5. Have the students form circles of three or four. Ask students to discuss the object they drew and to explain to their small group why it represents them as a child.

6. When the groups have finished their discussions, ask students to return to the place where they drew their objects.

7. Ask students to turn over their drawings and remain quiet as you read a number of items. Ask students to draw a letter, symbol, or sign that represents a larger thought or idea about each of the following items (pause for at least 10 seconds between each item):

- A time in your life you'd like to forget

- A person in your life you'd like to forget

- A person you need to forgive

- A person you need to receive forgiveness from

- A personal loss

- A sadness

- A dream of your childhood

- Something someone said to you that made you feel sad or angry
- Something you did or said that hurt someone
- Something you feel guilty about
- Rumors or gossip about you
- Gossip or rumors you spread
- A time you cried

8. Ask students to fold up their papers as small as they'd like so that no one can read anything drawn or written there.

9. Take students outside to the charcoal grill. Ask them to stand at least 5 feet away from it.

10. Collect the folded up sheets and place them in the grill. Light them on fire with a long match or a candle lighter. Let the papers burn until they are ashes.

11. Return to the teaching area and pass out the clay. Let the students mold the clay as you say this to them:

    - You are the inventor and the molder of your life.
    - Think about where you are in your life's journey.
    - Think about your hopes, dreams, and aspirations for your future.
    - Think about the man or woman you hope to become.
    - As you think about these things, use your clay to make a symbol of yourself and your transformation from where you are now to where you want to go on your journey.

12. Give students about 10 minutes to create their clay figures. When they are finished, ask them to form circles of three or four.

13. Ask each person to tell their small group about the figure they made and why it represents the future they hope to make or the transformation they hope will occur in their lives.

14. When the groups have finished their discussion, let them destroy their figures and put the clay back into its container. Suggest to the students that they are now free to mold and create their experience in different ways throughout their lives.

DISCUSSION

- How did it feel to destroy something that represented your childhood?
- How did it feel to destroy and let go of difficult times from your past?
- What might we need to do to let go of hurts we have received in the past?

- What was it like for you to create a symbol of a new direction in your life?

- Do you believe you can let go of things that happened in your past and create a new direction or new future for yourself? Why or why not?

ACTIVITY 6.5

Affirmations

PURPOSE To assist students in creating personal affirmations to promote their personal growth

PREPARATION For this activity, students will need space where they can work privately.

DIRECTIONS 1. Explain that what we tell our unconscious mind often becomes true for us and helps us make positive changes in how we feel about ourselves and makes what we want for ourselves come true.

2. Define "affirmation" for the students: a short positive statement about yourself that describes a desired change as already accomplished. Explain that effective affirmations usually have four characteristics:

- The affirmation is phrased in the present tense ("I am . . ." "I have . . .").
- The affirmation is phrased as though it is already accomplished.
- The affirmation is positive ("I am organized," rather than "I am not disorganized").
- The affirmation is short and direct: "I am energetic."

3. Explain that affirmations are useful in the following ways:

- To foster positive self-feelings: "I am enjoying myself."
- To counteract negative thinking that leads to failure: "I am agile and play well" instead of "I'm not a good player."
- To promote a better life: "I am prosperous and successful" or "I attract good and loving people into my life."
- To foster health: "I am strong and healthy."

4. Ask the group for some examples of affirmations that have the four characteristics. For example:

- "Other people like me."
- "I am athletic and graceful."

- "I am confident."
- "I am an excellent and diligent student."

5. Ask them to think about what positive changes they would you like to make in themselves.

6. Distribute the paper and pens or pencils and have students write down their own affirmations relating to these goals.

DISCUSSION

- Why might affirmations be helpful?
- Why do you think affirmations are written in positive language rather than negative (for example, "I will come to class on time" rather than "I will stop being lazy" or "I will not come late to class")?
- Where in your life might you find affirmations useful?
- What relationship do you think affirmations have with leadership?

ACTIVITY 6.6

Setting Boundaries

PURPOSE To help students learn a safe and clear method to set boundaries with someone when they feel a boundary has been crossed

MATERIALS Handout 6.6.1: Six-Step Process for Setting Boundaries (one per student)

Handout 6.6.2: Setting Boundaries Script (one for each role-player)

DIRECTIONS 1. Tell the group that all of us find ourselves in situations where we believe our boundaries have been crossed or agreements have been broken by another person.

2. Suggest that often we try to deal with such situations in inappropriate ways, or in ways that lead to further conflicts. For example, sometimes the party who feels offended gathers a group of supporters or spreads gossip or rumors. Explain that there is a better way to deal with these situations: the Six-Step Process for Setting Boundaries.

3. Ask students whether they know of any times when someone's boundaries were not honored or agreements were broken. Ask them to share such situations with the group. Ask students to describe what happened and how the situation was resolved, if it was.

4. Give each student a copy of the six-step process. Discuss each step using the following example:

   Tom and Bill had an agreement to get together after school, but Bill never showed up.

   a. Ask *permission.* Tom asks Bill, "Can I see you for a moment? Will you listen to what I have to say?"

   b. What are the *data?* Tom says, "Yesterday, we had plans to meet at my house and hang out. I waited for an hour for you to come, and you didn't show up."

   c. What's the *feeling?* Tom says, "I felt sad and angry."

d. What are the *judgments?* Tom says, "This isn't the first time this has happened. I think I can't trust you. I don't think you're trustworthy."

e. What do you *want?* Tom says, "I want to be able to believe you, Bill."

f. What do you *choose* for yourself? Tom says, "I am choosing to be trustworthy and to do what I say I am going to do."

5. Ask for two volunteers to role-play a situation. Give each role-player a copy of the script and ask them to perform the short demonstration. After each step, ask them to stop. Hold a discussion about each step.

6. When you have discussed the scripted situation, arrange students in groups of three. Ask students to identify themselves as A, B, or C.

7. Run three rounds of role-plays, with two students playing the roles in a situation and the third observing the process and giving feedback. Students should take a turn at each role and as observer. You can ask students to come up with their own situations or use the following ideas:

   • When you aren't at school, you hang out all the time with a friend who lives next door. At school, she hangs out with another set of friends and ignores you when you say hello or walk up to talk.

   • You tell a close friend that your dad just lost his job. You ask the person to keep it confidential. Next day at school, three people ask you if it's true that your dad was fired.

   • When you walk by, a classmate makes a negative remark about your body shape.

   • Without your knowledge or consent, a friend copies your homework. The teacher thinks you let this person do it.

   • A friend tells you that another friend said you were having sex with your girlfriend/boyfriend.

DISCUSSION

• Do you think this boundary-setting process works?

• Is it difficult or easy to use? Why?

• When in your life might you use this technique?

• What are the key elements to remember about using this strategy?

It is often helpful to have a clear way of resolving a situation in which a boundary has not been honored or an agreement has been broken. Here are the steps.

Step 1: Get permission

Ask the person you want to confront whether he or she will listen to you.

Step 2: Present the data

Describe with details what happened.

Step 3: Describe your feelings

Explain what feelings were evoked because of this situation. Were you angry? Sad? Afraid?

Step 4: Present your judgments

State what you believe to be true about this person and his or her actions.

Step 5: State what you want

Tell the other person what you want from him or her.

Step 6: State what you choose

Decide what you choose for yourself and explain it to the other person.

From *Inspiring Leadership in Teens: Group Activities to Foster Integrity, Responsibility, and Compassion*, © 2010 by Ric Stuecker, Champaign, IL: Research Press (800-519-2707, www.researchpress.com)

Step 1: Get permission

Juanita: Maria, could I talk with you a minute?

Maria: Sure.

Step 2: Present the data

Juanita: Maria, I thought you were my friend. But yesterday when we were taking the math test you looked at my paper, and now the teacher thinks I was cheating. She just showed me both of our papers, and we had exactly the same problems correct and wrong.

Step 3: Describe your feelings

Juanita: Now I am angry because I am in trouble, and I am scared the teacher won't believe me and I'll get in trouble at home with my parents.

Maria: I am sorry, Juanita, but I have to pass that test. My parents will ground me if I don't.

Step 4: Present your judgments

Juanita: I think you don't care whether I get into trouble, and I think you should study and not copy my answers.

Step 5: State what you want

Juanita: I want you to respect me, and I want the teacher to believe I am honest.

Maria: I'm sorry, Juanita. I shouldn't have copied your answers.

Step 6: State what you choose

Juanita: I am choosing to be honest. I'm going to tell the teacher that I didn't know you were copying my answers.

Maria: I'll go with you and tell the teacher it was all my fault.

From *Inspiring Leadership in Teens: Group Activities to Foster Integrity, Responsibility, and Compassion,* © 2010 by Ric Stuecker, Champaign, IL: Research Press (800-519-2707, www.researchpress.com)

A CTIVITY 6.7

Asking for Forgiveness

PURPOSE   To assist students in learning a simple process for asking for forgiveness when they have crossed a boundary or not honored an agreement

MATERIALS   Handout 6.7.1: Six-Step Process for Asking for Forgiveness (one per student)

Handout 6.7.2: Asking for Forgiveness Script (one per role-player)

DIRECTIONS   1. Tell the students that they may sometimes find themselves in a situation where they would want to ask forgiveness from someone for crossing a boundary or failing to honor an agreement.

2. Explain that sometimes when we need to ask for forgiveness, we fear what others might think of us. We sometimes make matters worse by trying to ignore the fact that we have crossed someone's boundary or by telling ourselves "It's no big deal." Some people even accuse the offended party of causing them to cross the boundary!

3. Suggest that there is a way of dealing with these situations. It's called the Six-Step Process for Asking for Forgiveness.

4. Ask students whether they know of any times when they crossed someone's boundaries or did not honor an agreement they had made. Ask them to share such situations with the group. Ask students to describe what happened and how the situation was resolved, if it was.

5. Give each student a copy of the handout. Go through each step, using the following example:

   Two boys had an agreement to get together after school.

   a. Ask *permission.* Bill asks Tom, "Can I see you for a moment? Will you listen to what I have to say?"

   b. What are the *data?* Bill says, "Yesterday, we had plans to meet at your house and hang out. I didn't show up."

   c. What's the *feeling?* Bill says, "I felt sad and guilty."

   d. What are the *judgments?* Bill says, "This isn't the first time this has happened. I don't blame you if you can't trust me."

340

    e. What do you *want?* Bill says, "I want you to be able to trust me."

    f. What do you *choose* for yourself? Bill says, "I am choosing to be trustworthy and to do what I say I am going to do."

6. Ask for volunteers to role-play a situation. Give each role-player a copy of the script and ask them to perform the short demonstration, stopping after each step for group discussion.

7. When you have discussed the role-play, arrange students in groups of three. Ask students to identify themselves as A, B, or C.

8. Run three rounds of role-plays, with two students playing roles and a third observing the process and giving feedback. Students should take a turn at each role and as observer. You can ask students to come up with their own situations or use the following ideas:

- You are standing with some of your friends when another one of your friends walks by. One person in the group says something insulting about the friend who walks by loud enough for him or her to hear. Several people laugh. You say nothing. Your friend who walked by looks back and sees you.

- A friend has confided in you that his mom and dad are getting a divorce. He asks you not to say anything to anyone, but you do. On the bus to school, another friend asks him whether it is true—in front of both of you.

- You promise a friend to come over to her house to hang out one weekend. Another friend asks you to go to the movies. You go to the movies without telling the friend who invited you to hang out.

- During class, you and a friend are talking while the teacher is presenting a lesson. The teacher notices your friend talking but doesn't notice you. The teacher gives your friend a detention. You say nothing and let your friend be punished.

DISCUSSION

- Do you think this process works?
- Is it difficult or easy to use? Why?
- When in your life might you use this technique?
- What are the key elements to remember about using this strategy?

It is often helpful to have a clear way of resolving a situation when you have crossed a boundary or not honored an agreement. Here are the steps:

Step 1: Get permission

Ask the person you want to ask forgiveness from whether he or she will listen to you.

Step 2: Present the data

Describe with details what happened.

Step 3: Describe your feelings

Describe what feelings were evoked because of this situation. Were you angry? Sad? Afraid?

Step 4: Present your judgments

State what you believe to be true about yourself and your actions.

Step 5: State what you want

Tell the other person what you want from him or her.

Step 6: State what you choose

Decide what you choose for yourself and explain it to the other person.

From *Inspiring Leadership in Teens: Group Activities to Foster Integrity, Responsibility, and Compassion,* © 2010 by Ric Stuecker, Champaign, IL: Research Press (800-519-2707, www.researchpress.com)

Step 1: Get permission

Jessie: Hey, Francine, could I talk with you?

Francine: Sure.

Step 2: Present the data

Jessie: The other day, you told me you had a crush on Jake. You told me you hoped he'd ask you out soon. You asked me not to tell anyone, but I did. I told Mandy. Mandy spread it around, and I heard Jake found out.

Step 3: Describe your feelings

Francine: I can't believe it!

Jessie: I am so sorry. I'm angry at Mandy for telling, but I feel really guilty for telling her.

Step 4: Present your judgments

Jessie: I was stupid to trust Mandy. I wanted her to like me. If you had done this to me, I would be furious.

Francine: I'm pretty mad—and I'm embarrassed.

Jessie: I know, and I'm sorry.

Step 5: State what you want

Jessie: I hope you can forgive me. I want us to be friends.

Francine: I don't know. Maybe. Now Jake and his buddies all know. I'm not sure I can trust you.

Step 6: State what you choose

Jessie: I understand. I am choosing to watch what I say and to remain friends with you. I hope you can forgive me.

Francine: I can respect you for telling me, but I'm not sure.

From *Inspiring Leadership in Teens: Group Activities to Foster Integrity, Responsibility, and Compassion,* © 2010 by Ric Stuecker, Champaign, IL: Research Press (800-519-2707, www.researchpress.com)

ACTIVITY 6.8

Personal Dilemmas

PURPOSE   To give students the chance to consider perplexing real-life situations in which a moral decision needs to be made

MATERIALS   Any of the 10 Personal Dilemma handouts chosen for discussion (Handouts 6.8.1 through 6.8.10; one per student)

DIRECTIONS

1. Distribute to each student a copy of the first dilemma being discussed.

2. Ask students to read the dilemma silently and write the answers to the questions specifically relating to the story.

3. As a group, go over each question separately. When there are definite differences of opinion, create a debate with a spokesperson for each side of the argument.

4. Discuss as many dilemmas as time permits. Ask the following questions for each dilemma.

DISCUSSION

- Was the dilemma or difficult situation realistic?
- Have you ever had to make a decision in a similar situation?
- Could you share the situation and what you did?
- What decision would a mature leader make?
- Is making the mature decision difficult? If so, why?

Steve is a member of his high school's STAR leadership program. Members are asked to sign a pledge saying they will not use drugs or alcohol for the entire school year. Steve has signed this pledge.

After a Friday night football game, several of Steve's friends invite him to a keg party. It is at the home of a football player who is one of Steve's good friends, Jason. Mark, who is also a member of the STAR program, lives down the street from Jason but has not been invited to the party.

It is hot inside the house, so Steve and some buddies go outside to the front lawn. Mark is driving home from a date, looks over, and sees Steve at the party. He sees Steve standing with several persons who are drinking beer.

Questions

1. What should Mark say to Steve when he meets him at school on Monday?

2. Should Mark talk with the STAR program monitor about seeing Steve at the keg party?

3. Is it okay for someone who has pledged not to drink to attend a keg party, even if he chooses not to drink?

4. Does attending a keg party even if you choose not to drink encourage others to drink? Is that okay?

5. If Steve was drinking at the party, what should he do about staying in the STAR program?

6. What should the consequences be for someone who makes a pledge to a group and then breaks that pledge?

From *Inspiring Leadership in Teens: Group Activities to Foster Integrity, Responsibility, and Compassion,* © 2010 by Ric Stuecker, Champaign, IL: Research Press (800-519-2707, www.researchpress.com)

Tomasina is a member of a student support group at her high school. The support group is a place where students can discuss their life situations and receive support from peers. An adult leader runs the group each week.

Tomasina is very good friends with Rosa, who does not attend the support group, even though several of her friends do. Rosa is very inquisitive about what goes on at the support group and who says what about whom. Everyone in the group has pledged confidentiality—nothing that is said in the group and no information about the group, including who attends, is to be revealed by any of the members.

Tomasina spends a night at Rosa's house. Late in the evening, Tomasina and Rosa help themselves to some of Rosa's father's beer. Tomasina gets very talky and begins revealing what she has heard in the support group concerning friends of Rosa's who attend. The next morning, when Tomasina is leaving, Rosa thanks her for the information Tomasina let her in on.

Questions

1. What should Tomasina say to Rosa?

2. Because she is not in the support group and has not pledged confidentiality, can Rosa use this information?

3. What should Tomasina say to the friends whose confidences she revealed?

4. Does it matter what the confidences were?

5. If someone in the support group discovers from Rosa that Tomasina has been revealing confidences, what should that person do?

6. If Tomasina tells the support group about her indiscretions, what should the consequences for Tomasina be? Who should decide?

7. If Tomasina does not tell the support group but someone in the group finds out and tells, what should the consequences be? Who should decide?

From *Inspiring Leadership in Teens: Group Activities to Foster Integrity, Responsibility, and Compassion,* © 2010 by Ric Stuecker, Champaign, IL: Research Press (800-519-2707, www.researchpress.com)

Mario and his friends are out one evening having pizza for dinner. His sister Teresa is 16 and is sitting with her boyfriend, Raphael, at a nearby table. They have been going out for nearly 2 years, and everyone predicts that Teresa and Raphael will get married after high school. The conversation among Mario and his friends turns to sex—who people think are having sex with whom, birth control, and abortion. Teresa is sitting where Mario can see her. As the conversation continues, Mario sees Teresa becoming more and more upset. In fact, she and Raphael leave the table abruptly.

Questions

1. Should Mario ask Teresa why she became so upset?

2. Should Mario talk to Raphael about why they left quickly?

3. If Mario discovers that Teresa is having sex with Raphael, what should he do or say?

4. If Mario discovers that Teresa thinks she might be pregnant, what should he do or say?

5. Should Mario talk to his parents about what happened in the restaurant? If he finds out that Teresa is having sex, should he talk to his parents? If he discovers Teresa thinks she might be pregnant, should he talk with his parents?

From *Inspiring Leadership in Teens: Group Activities to Foster Integrity, Responsibility, and Compassion*, © 2010 by Ric Stuecker, Champaign, IL: Research Press (800-519-2707, www.researchpress.com)

Mack and his dad have always been close. Mack's dad and mom divorced when Mack was five. His dad was his coach in grade school. They still work out together in the off season and run together several times a week. Mack's dad is very involved with the Youth Soccer League, where he coaches. He is a very popular coach.

One afternoon when Mack is staying with his dad, Mack goes into his dad's closet to borrow a pair of workout shorts. They are high up in the closet. When he pulls down the shorts, some magazines fall off a shelf. The magazines are filled with pornographic photographs of nude men.

Questions

1. What should Mack think about his dad?

2. Should Mack tell his dad that he found the magazines?

3. Should Mack talk to anyone else about finding the magazines? His mom? Someone at school? His friends?

4. What should Mack's dad do or say if Mack tells him what happened?

5. Should Mack's dad continue to coach boys?

From *Inspiring Leadership in Teens: Group Activities to Foster Integrity, Responsibility, and Compassion*, © 2010 by Ric Stuecker, Champaign, IL: Research Press (800-519-2707, www.researchpress.com)

Sebastian is a great athlete. He is the key player on the basketball team. When Sebastian is not playing, the team has a hard time winning. The next game is the regional final against a really tough team, and the whole school is excited.

Sebastian might fail math. If he doesn't do well on the next test, the teacher might ask the coach to bench Sebastian. It is school policy that if a player's grade goes lower than a C during the semester, that person can't participate in extracurricular activities.

Robert is smart, on the team, and a good friend of Sebastian. Sebastian says to him the morning before the test, "I've studied all night, and I just can't get it."

Robert says, "What do you want me to do?"

Sebastian says, "Just let me see your paper during the test so I can check my work. I'll only check to see I've done it right."

The coach sees the two boys in the hall and says, "I'm counting on you guys to pass that test. Don't let me or the team down, guys."

Questions

1. What should Robert do?

2. Is what Sebastian wants to do really cheating?

3. What if Sebastian tells the other guys on the team that Robert is going to make sure he passes the test? Should Robert then let him see his paper?

4. Should Robert remain friends with a guy who asks him to do something dishonest?

5. Should the math teacher take Sebastian off the team if he fails the test?

6. How come cheating on the test is a big deal if no one gets hurt and Sebastian gets to play?

7. If Sebastian and Robert don't get caught, is it okay?

From *Inspiring Leadership in Teens: Group Activities to Foster Integrity, Responsibility, and Compassion,* © 2010 by Ric Stuecker, Champaign, IL: Research Press (800-519-2707, www.researchpress.com)

Celeste has noticed that Alicia has occasional bruises. Alicia has been dating Jared for nearly a year. Celeste goes out with Raymond, one of Jared's teammates.

One weekend, Alicia calls Celeste and asks her to bring over her makeup kit. "You are really good with makeup," Alicia says, "and I need your help."

When Celeste arrives, Alicia is wearing sunglasses. When she takes them off, Celeste sees how swollen and bruised one of her eyes is.

"I am so stupid," Alicia says. "I fell down and hit my eye."

Celeste replies, "Girl, you must think I'm dumb. You didn't fall. Jared did this to you."

Alicia starts to cry. "It was my fault. I made Jared mad."

Questions

1. What should Celeste tell Alicia?

2. Should Celeste tell her boyfriend, Raymond, what happened to Alicia?

3. What kind of help might Celeste offer?

4. What should happen to Jared?

5. If Raymond finds out, what should he do?

From *Inspiring Leadership in Teens: Group Activities to Foster Integrity, Responsibility, and Compassion,* © 2010 by Ric Stuecker, Champaign, IL: Research Press (800-519-2707, www.researchpress.com)

Beverly works with Marcella after school and weekends. Beverly knows that Marcella's family is poor and that Marcella needs her job to help out her family. Beverly is working so she has extra spending money.

Several times, Beverly has noticed Marcella taking money from the cash register. When Beverly arrives at work, her boss asks her and Marcella to join her in the office. The boss closes the door and says to the two girls, "One of you is a thief. One of you has been taking money from the cash register. One of you will no longer be working here."

Beverly looks at Marcella, who starts to cry.

Questions

1. What should Beverly say or do?

2. What if Marcella insists she is innocent?

3. What steps should the boss take?

4. Should Beverly take the blame so Marcella won't lose a job she needs?

5. Should Beverly have informed on Marcella when Beverly first saw her taking the money from the register?

Lamar and Ben hang out when they are in their neighborhood, but at school Lamar hangs out with his friends on the basketball team. Lamar likes Ben when he is at home. He often goes over to Ben's house and Ben comes over to his. Ben is not as good at sports as Lamar is.

Lamar is standing in the school hallway with his teammates. Ben comes out of the restroom. One of Lamar's teammates makes a joke about Ben. All the boys laugh, then one of them says, "What a goof." Another says, "Yeah, what a geek."

Lamar sees that Ben is looking at him. Someone from the team says, "Come on, Lamar, let's get outta here."

Questions

1. What should Lamar do?

2. Should Lamar continue to be friends with the team?

3. Should Lamar do anything when the team makes fun of his friend? Say anything later?

4. What should Lamar say to Ben?

5. Should Ben continue to hang out with Lamar?

From *Inspiring Leadership in Teens: Group Activities to Foster Integrity, Responsibility, and Compassion,* © 2010 by Ric Stuecker, Champaign, IL: Research Press (800-519-2707, www.researchpress.com)

Jordan is very popular. He makes good grades and gives great parties. Everyone was surprised when he asked Jennifer to prom. Jennifer is also very smart, but she is a little overweight and does not hang out with Jordan's crowd very often. But because Jordan sometimes does weird things, everyone laughed and thought it was fun that he asked Jennifer to prom.

Jennifer got very excited about being asked to the prom by Jordan. She told everyone she saw about it. She bought a great dress. She borrowed money from her mom and made an appointment to have her hair done at a very expensive salon.

On Wednesday afternoon before the prom, Jordan was sitting with his group of friends when Jennifer arrived. He looked at her and laughed. "You didn't really believe I'd take *you* to the prom, did you?" he said. Then everyone else around him laughed.

Questions

1. What should Jennifer do?

2. What do you think Jordan's friends might think of Jordan?

3. Should Jennifer go to the prom with someone else?

4. What should Jennifer do or say when she comes back to school?

5. What should Jordan's friends say or do?

6. What should Jennifer's friends say or do?

From *Inspiring Leadership in Teens: Group Activities to Foster Integrity, Responsibility, and Compassion,* © 2010 by Ric Stuecker, Champaign, IL: Research Press (800-519-2707, www.researchpress.com)

Bob has been dating Wendy for nearly 6 months. They have a great time together. In fact, they have had some serious discussions about going to the same college so they can be together. Everyone says they are a perfect couple and look great together. Bob and Wendy go to the same church, and each has taken a pledge to wait to have sex until they are married. They made this pledge in front of the congregation.

It's Bob's birthday. After Bob's birthday party, Bob and Wendy are alone. They are kissing and making out. Wendy slides a condom into Bob's hand. She whispers, "I love you, Bob. I want to take our love to the next level."

Questions

1. How should Bob respond?

2. What do you think Bob's opinion of Wendy is now?

3. Should Bob and Wendy continue to date?

4. What should Bob tell people at church, especially the youth pastor who had the youth group take the pledge?

5. Should Bob and Wendy continue to plan to go to the same college?

From *Inspiring Leadership in Teens: Group Activities to Foster Integrity, Responsibility, and Compassion,* © 2010 by Ric Stuecker, Champaign, IL: Research Press (800-519-2707, www.researchpress.com)

ACTIVITY 6.9

My Spiritual Journey

PURPOSE
To encourage students to examine their personal journeys so far and to map out their beliefs, purposes, hopes, dreams, and destinations

MATERIALS
Large sheets of drawing paper or newsprint (one sheet per student)

Colored markers, crayons, or chalk

Handout 6.9.1: My Spiritual Journey Map (one per student)

Optional: Soft music to play while students draw

DIRECTIONS
1. Discuss the following questions:

   - Why do we need and use road maps?

   - Why might a personal road map of and for our lives be a good thing?

2. Suggest that the students will now have an opportunity to draw a personal road map. Tell them this road map is made up of places they have been in the past and destinations they want to reach in the future.

3. Distribute copies of the My Spiritual Journey map. Explain that this map is a guide they can choose to use if they wish, or they can make up their own version. However, they must have these elements on their personal map:

   - Where I come from

   - Some memories I have

   - A time I'd do over

   - Three things I absolutely believe to be true

   - Several highs and lows in my life

   - Something I've had to overcome

   - My personal strengths

   - Where I am heading

4. If you chose some soft music for this exercise, play it now. Give students 15 to 20 minutes to draw their map. Set the requirement that they draw privately in silence and not show their maps to anyone else.

5. Arrange students in circles of six to eight. Ask each group to select a leader to keep time and to make sure each person gets the opportunity to present his or her map.

6. Ask each person to take 3 to 5 minutes to present his or her spiritual journey map to the small group.

DISCUSSION

• Do you find it hard or easy to talk about yourself? Are some things harder than others to talk about? Easier? What makes it hard or easy to talk about yourself?

• Were other people's journeys similar or different from yours? In what ways?

• What are some things you admired about other people's maps in your group?

• What is spiritual about this journey?

Where I come from:

_____

_____

GROWING UP

My strengths:

_____

_____

Memories:

_____

_____

_____

Three things I believe:

_____

_____

_____

Something I've had
to overcome:

_____

_____

A time I'd do over:

_____

Some ups and downs in my life:

Ups and downs

Ups and downs

Where I'm heading:

_____

_____

From Inspiring Leadership in Teens: Group Activities to Foster Integrity, Responsibility, and Compassion, © 2010
by Ric Stuecker, Champaign, IL: Research Press (800-519-2707, www.researchpress.com)

ACTIVITY 6.10

This I Believe

This activity can be an in-class or at-home essay assignment. If done in class, give students plenty of time to think and write, possibly an entire class period, depending on your class and their ability to write.

PURPOSE

To encourage students to identify and write about their core beliefs, using the essays and essay format from the "This I Believe" program on National Public Radio

MATERIALS

Copies of several "This I Believe" essays (or students may review them online)

Equipment to present a radio broadcast (real or simulated)

PREPARATION

Visit the "This I Believe" section of National Public Radio's website (www.npr.org/templates/story/story.php?storyId=4538138) and review the essays presented there. Written by Americans from all walks of life, these essays describe the core beliefs of a variety of people. There are essays written by contemporary citizens as well as those first broadcast by Edward R. Murrow in the 1950s by famous Americans such as Helen Keller, Harry Truman, and Albert Einstein. Some of the essays have been written by teenagers.

Here are some possibilities for broadcasting your essays:

- Set up a simulated radio station in your teaching area using a microphone and speakers.
- Set up a screen with a table and chair behind it so you cannot see the reader. Have students "broadcast" their essays to the listening audience of their classmates.
- Using your school's public address system, have students broadcast their essays to the classroom.

DIRECTIONS

1. If you have access to a computer lab, it is a good idea for students to preselect several essays to read from the "This I Believe" website. Or, if you wish, you can give students specific criteria for selecting essays (for example, two historical essays, one or two essays from teenagers, an essay from someone who inspires you).

2. Ask students to copy and paste two essays that particularly inspire them. Invite volunteers to read the essays they chose to the entire class.

3. After each reading, discuss the following questions:

- What was it about this essay that inspired you to choose it? The writer? The message?

- In a few sentences, describe the core belief expressed by the writer.

- Which for you were more powerful—essays from historical figures or essays from regular Americans?

4. Discuss with the students the format of the essays (fully described at www.npr.org/thisibelieve/guide.html). Guidelines are as follows:

- *Tell a story.* Examine the events of your life and ground your descriptions of beliefs in those events. This story should be real and tie into your personal philosophy.

- *Be brief.* Essays should be 350 to 500 words.

- *Name your belief.* Your belief should be stated in a sentence or two.

- *Be positive.* State your belief and philosophy in terms of what you believe, not what you don't believe. Use "I" instead of "you" or "we." Avoid preaching—telling others what they should or should not do.

- *Be personal.* Write in words and phrases that you are comfortable speaking.

5. Ask students to write a draft of their own "This I Believe" essay.

6. When students have completed a draft, pair them or ask them to form groups of three or four. Have the students read their essays aloud, receive feedback, and revise. Encourage them to keep editing and simplifying until their essays read smoothly and reflect the core values of the writer in words he or she is comfortable reading.

7. Ask students to read their essays to their partners or small groups as though they were reading them over the radio. Have them practice at least five times before they present their essays to the class.

   This may also be a good time for students to listen to several samples from the NPR website to hear how a radio essay should sound.

8. Have students broadcast their essays, using one of the formats suggested or one of your own design.

9. Ask students to give each other feedback using the following questions:

   • What did you like about the essay?

   • Did anything in particular move you? Surprise you? Entertain you? Touch you?

10. If you wish, you can suggest that students submit their essays to NPR, following the guidelines found on the "This I Believe" website.

DISCUSSION

• Edward R. Murrow, a famous broadcaster during World War II and in the years thereafter, said, "Never has the need for personal philosophies of this kind been so urgent." The producers of "This I Believe" at NPR think we are living at a time when personal philosophies are also urgent. Do you believe this is true for our day and time?

• What recent events might make this need urgent today?

• Why do you believe that the producers at NPR chose a wide range of Americans to submit essays rather than just famous Americans?

• Why do you believe having a personal philosophy is urgent and necessary?

• Can personal philosophies be funny? Are they just as real and important as those with a serious tone? In what ways?

Unit Resources

Angell, M. C. (1997). *My spirit flies: Portraits and prose of women in their power.* Bellingham, WA: Bay City Press.

DiLallo, F. A. (2001). *The Peace Project: A relaxation meditation for young adults* (audio CD). Sylvania, OH: The Peace Project.

This CD, with music by Grammy-nominated Tim Story, includes teachings on developing personal strategies for peaceful living, two guided meditations, and a set of positive affirmations, all easily adapted to classroom use. A teacher's guide is available.

Goldstein, A. P. (2000). *The PREPARE® Curriculum: Teaching prosocial competencies.* Champaign, IL: Research Press.

Goldstein's work in the area of prosocial skill building for all students, including antisocial youth, is legendary. Especially good is his approach to role-plays.

Stuecker, R., with Rutherford, S. (2001). *Reviving the wonder: 76 activities that touch the inner spirit of youth.* Champaign, IL: Research Press.

Stuecker, R. (2004). *Cultivating kindness: Activities that promote integrity, respect, and compassion in elementary and middle-school students.* Champaign, IL: Research Press.

Girls Circle Association
A Project of the Tides Center
458 Christensen Lane
Cotati, CA 94931
www.girlscircle.com

The Peace Project
http://peace2usolutions.com/

Centerville–Washington Park District Wellness Wheel
www.cwpd.org/wellness_wheel.htmlwww.cwpd.org/wellness.htm

Boys to Men Mentoring Network
9587 Tropico Drive
La Mesa, CA 91941
(619) 469–9599
www.boystomen.org

APPENDIX

Using *Inspiring Leadership in Teens* in Schools and in Workshop Formats

More and more high schools and middle schools are developing student leadership classes and programs that teach concepts in leadership, examine the leadership styles of historical and modern leaders, foster communication skills, improve skills in making presentations and running meetings, and offer opportunities for self-examination of one's skills, attitudes, and behaviors. Often these approaches are linked to service learning activities in which students volunteer for projects in their communities or offer individual services to schools, hospitals, missions, local organizations, and other community service agencies. Many schools also teach skills to students who assume leadership positions in the school, such as student council, clubs, and teams, and to students who show leadership potential in the classroom.

A number of schools have created opportunities for students to work with adult moderators to identify or create projects within their areas of interest. This form of developing student leadership is based on community development models such as Future Search, Search Conferences, Open Space, and other programs in which large groups of motivated people find common ground and common energy to create change through consensus building and positive energy. *Inspiring Leadership in Teens* favors these models over more traditional student government models in which representatives are elected. Under these models, all students have an opportunity to participate where their hearts and heads lead them.

The *Inspiring Leadership in Teens* curriculum is based on the belief that direct teaching of leadership skills and understanding the work of other inspiring leaders is essential to developing leadership in young people. Furthermore, it is a curriculum that is based on positive values, personal integrity, and compassion.

If you use the entire approach in *Inspiring Leadership in Teens,* you can create a course of approximately 21 weeks. Depending on your teaching style, the number of students in your classroom, the length of class periods, and your school calendar, the program might take less time or more time.

As an alternative, all or part of the material in the *Inspiring Leadership in Teens* program can be presented as workshops. For example, you might set aside 2 days to do the first unit on creating a learning community instead of using 2 weeks.

TRADITIONAL, SCHOOL-BASED FORMAT

Weeks 1–2: Creating a Learning Community (Unit 1)

During this 2-week unit, students create a community by learning each other's names and backgrounds. They set rules for learning and for the community to operate under for the entire course, and they identify learning goals and begin to discover their leadership skills.

Week 1

Day 1
- Activity 1.1—Forming Groups: Group Puzzles
- Activity 1.2—Forming Groups: Name Tags
- Activity 1.3—Learning Names

Day 2
- Activity 1.4—Learning Some Facts About Each Other
- Activity 1.5—What We Think About
- Activity 1.6—Rules We Can Live By

Day 3
- Activity 1.7—Rules: What Happens When . . .? What Happens If . . .?
- Activity 1.8—Taking Personal Responsibility
- Activity 1.9—Working Together: A Ball Game

Day 4
- Activity 1.10—Interviews: Presenting . . .

Day 5
- Evaluation Meeting

Week 2

Day 1
- Activity 1.11—Distinguishing Types of Intelligence

Day 2
- Activity 1.12—Seven Ways to Be Smart

Day 3
- Activity 1.13—The Tree of Me

Day 4
- Activity 1.14—What I Need to Succeed

Day 5
- Evaluation Meeting

Weeks 3–9: Studying Leadership: Researching Inspiring Leaders (Unit 2)

During this 7-week unit, student teams form publishing companies and select inspiring leaders to research. They create a book of biographies, give PowerPoint presentations, and create a hall of fame exhibit about the leaders they chose.

Week 1

Day 1
- Activity 2.1—Defining Inspiring Leadership

Days 2–3
- Activity 2.2—Publishing Company Kickoff

Days 4–5
- Activity 2.3—Completing a Job Application

Week 2

Days 1–2
- Activity 2.4—Obtaining Effective Letters of Reference

Day 3
- Activity 2.5—Creating a Strong Résumé (Introduction)

Day 4
- Activity 2.5—Creating a Strong Résumé (Drafts)

Day 5
- Activity 2.5—Creating a Strong Résumé (Final)

Week 3

Day 1
- Activity 2.6—Interviewing for a Job Position (Introduction)

Day 2
- Activity 2.6—Interviewing for a Job Position (Hold Interviews)

Day 3
- Activity 2.6—Interviewing for a Job Position (Finish Interviews)

Days 4–5
- Activity 2.7—Creating Publishing Companies

Week 4

Day 1
- Activity 2.8—Finding an Inspiring Leader to Study

Days 2–4

- Activity 2.9—Refining Research and Writing Skills

Day 5

- Evaluation Meeting (beginning on page 55)

Week 5

Days 1–4

- Activity 2.10—Creating a PowerPoint Presentation

Day 5

- Evaluation Meeting (beginning on page 55)

Week 6

Days 1–4

- Activity 2.11—Creating a Publishing Company Display

Day 5

- Evaluation Meeting (beginning on page 55)

Week 7

Day 1

- Activity 2.12—Evaluating Individual and Team Performances: Book Exchange (teams exchange books and evaluate each chapter according to the rubric and book critique form; see Handouts 2.9.2 and 2.9.3)

Days 2–3

- Activity 2.12—Evaluating Individual and Team Performances: PowerPoint Presentations (teams evaluate each other's presentations using the rubric; see Handout 2.10.1)

Day 4

- Activity 2.12—Evaluating Individual and Team Performances: Publishing Company Displays (teams evaluate each other's displays using the rubric; see Handout 2.11.1)

Day 5

- Activity 2.13 —Holding the BlueBerry Awards Ceremony

Weeks 10–12: Creating Leadership Portfolios (Unit 3)

This 3-week unit focuses on identifying the 10 critical characteristics of leaders, taking a self-inventory for these characteristics, developing a personal mission statement, and creating a personal brochure. These elements result in a leadership portfolio for each student.

Week 1

Day 1

- Activity 3.1—Taking a Leadership Self-Inventory

Days 2–4
- Activity 3.2—Acquiring Characteristics of Inspiring Leaders

Day 5
- Activity 3.3-Exploring Personal Integrity and Responsibility

Week 2

Day 1
- Activity 3.4—Making Personal Agreements

Day 2
- Activity 3.5—Exploring Personal Dreams

Day 3
- Activity 3.6—Discerning What I Value in Life

Day 4
- Activity 3.7—Identifying Characteristics I Admire

Day 5
- Activity 3.8—Understanding Strengths and Roadblocks

Week 3

Day 1
- Activity 3.9—Identifying Contributions I Hope to Make

Day 2
- Activity 3.10—Creating a Personal Mission Statement

Day 3
- Activity 3.11—Simplifying My Personal Mission Statement

Days 4–5
- Activity 3.12—Making a Personal Brochure

Weeks 13–14: Understanding Communication (Unit 4)

In this 2-week unit, students focus on understanding learning styles, communicating one to one, and using nonverbal communication strategies. They also learn about the art of negotiation and practice their negotiation skills.

Week 1

Day 1
- Activity 4.1—Understanding Learning Styles

Day 2
- Activity 4.2—Discovering the Learning Styles of Others
- Activity 4.3—Negotiating One to One
- Activity 4.4—Shutting Down Communication

Day 3
- Activity 4.5—Communicating with Head and Heart

Day 4
- Activity 4.6—Understanding Power and Influence
- Activity 4.7—Face to Face: Using Eye Placement and Body Position

Day 5
- Activity 4.8—Using Your Voice

Week 2

Day 1
- Activity 4.9—Using "I" Messages

Day 2
- Activity 4.10—Negotiating Agreement (Skit)

Days 3–5
- Activity 4.11—Negotiating Agreement (Role-Plays)

Weeks 15–18: Leading Groups (Unit 5)

This 4-week unit takes the skills developed in Unit 4 and expands on them. It teaches young leaders how groups function, how to understand group dynamics and the roles people play in groups, how to lead a meeting, how to make effective presentations, and how groups can develop plans and strategies for community projects. Unit 5 is divided into four "learning centers."

Week 1

Learning Center 1: Understanding the Stages of Team Formation
Day 1
- Activity 5.1—Understanding the Team-Building Process

Day 2
- Activity 5.2—Guiding the Team Through Stages: Strategies

Day 3
- Activity 5.3—Understanding Leadership Roles

Day 4
- Activity 5.4—Card Towers

Day 5
- Activity 5.5—Silent Puzzles
  and/or
- Activity 5.6—Great Escape

Week 2

Learning Center 2: Understanding Leadership Styles
Day 1
- Activity 5.7—Identifying Leadership Styles
- Activity 5.8—Experiencing Types of Leadership Styles

Day 2
- Activity 5.9—Making Team Agreements
- Activity 5.10—Understanding Levels of Agreement

Day 3
- Activity 5.11—Holding Effective Meetings
- Activity 5.12—Holding Effective Meetings: Practice

Learning Center 3: Making Presentations
Day 4
- Activity 5.13—Assessing the Audience

Day 5
- Activity 5.14—Identifying Audience Leaders and Barometers

Week 3

Learning Center 3: Making Presentations (continued)
Days 1–2
- Activity 5.15—Organizing a Presentation

Days 3–5
- Activity 5.15—Student Presentations and Evaluations

Week 4

Learning Center 4: Planning—Making Positive Changes
Days 1–2
- Activity 5.16—Developing a Compelling Vision

Day 3
- Activity 5.17—Moving from Vision to Plan
- Activity 5.18—Identifying and Solving Constraints

Day 4
- Activity 5.19—Creating Action Plans

Day 5
- Activity 5.20—Scheduling Activities

Weeks 19–21: Living Peace (Unit 6)

This culminating 3-week unit asks students to look at their personal lifestyles, to base their leadership skills on personal health and wellness, to set personal boundaries, to ask for forgiveness when needed, and to make decisions that are based on integrity and compassion.

Week 1

Day 1
- Activity 6.1—Wellness Wheel: Personal Health Assessment

Day 2
- Activity 6.2—When Am I in My Power?

Day 3
- Activity 6.3—Touching My Spirit: What Is Greater Than I Am?

Day 4
- Activity 6.4—Personal Transformation

Day 5
- Activity 6.5—Affirmations

Week 2

Day 1
- Activity 6.6—Setting Boundaries

Day 2
- Activity 6.7—Asking for Forgiveness

Days 3–5
- Activity 6.8—Personal Dilemmas

Week 3

Days 1–2
- Activity 6.9—My Spiritual Journey

Days 3–5
- Activity 6.10—This I Believe

FIVE-DAY LEADERSHIP RETREAT

Many schools like to use a retreat setting away from school, which provides a more intensive learning experience and allows for concentrated learning and evening sessions over a 5-day period.

Many communities have facilities with kitchens and sleeping quarters. It is possible to run a retreat on the school campus if you can use an isolated area and bring in lunch and dinner. In that case, students go home to sleep. In either case, you will need some adults to help monitor students during daily activities and, for overnight retreats, at night. Two trainers—or a team of trainers, each taking a different section of the experience—are recommended for the retreat format.

Daily Schedule

Before the retreat begins, the teachers/trainers should set up the space (see "Arranging the Learning Space" in Unit 1 beginning on page 14).

Because this is a retreat format rather than a classroom format, Unit 2—which asks students to research a leader who inspires them—is not included. Unit 2 relies on computers for research and writing, which are usually not available at retreat settings. (Unit 2 might be done in the classroom before a retreat, however.) Also, only selected activities from Unit 3 and Unit 6 are included.

Day 1

8 to 9 A.M.
- Breakfast

9 A.M. to 12 noon
- Welcome and Orientation

Unit 1—Creating a Learning Community
- Activity 1.1—Forming Groups: Group Puzzles
- Activity 1.2—Forming Groups: Name Tags
- Activity 1.3—Learning Names
- Activity 1.4—Learning Some Facts About Each Other
- Activity 1.5—What We Think About
- Activity 1.6—Rules We Can Live By
- Activity 1.7—Rules: What Happens When . . .? What Happens If . . .?

12 noon to 1 P.M.
- Lunch

1 to 5 P.M.
- Activity 1.8—Taking Personal Responsibility
- Activity 1.9—Working Together: A Ball Game
- Activity 1.10—Interviews: Presenting . . .
- Activity 1.11—Distinguishing Types of Intelligence
- Activity 1.12—Seven Ways to Be Smart
- Activity 1.13—The Tree of Me
- Activity 1.14—What I Need to Succeed

5 to 6 P.M.
- Free Time

6 to 7 P.M.
- Dinner

7 to 11 P.M.

Unit 3—Creating Leadership Portfolios
Phase 1: Inspiring Leadership Self-Assessment Workshop
- Activity 3.1—Taking a Leadership Self-Inventory
  - Integrity
  - Compassion
  - Belonging
  - Aspiring

- □ Self-Reflection
- □ Decisiveness

Day 2

8 to 9 A.M.
- Breakfast

9 A.M. to 12 noon
- Activity 3.1—Taking a Leadership Self-Inventory (continued)
  - □ Curiosity and Creativity
  - □ Fun and Humor
  - □ Role Model
  - □ Confidence
  - □ Goal-Setting Worksheet
  - □ My Goals

12 noon to 1 P.M.
- Lunch

1 to 5 P.M.
Unit 3—Creating Leadership Portfolios (continued)
Phase 2: Creating a Personal Mission Statement
- Activity 3.5—Exploring Personal Dreams
- Activity 3.6—Discerning What I Value in Life
- Activity 3.7—Identifying Characteristics I Admire
- Activity 3.8—Understanding Strengths and Roadblocks
- Activity 3.9—Identifying Contributions I Hope to Make
- Activity 3.10—Creating a Personal Mission Statement
- Activity 3.11—Simplifying My Personal Mission Statement

5 to 6 P.M.
- Free Time

6 to 7 P.M.
- Dinner

7 to 11 P.M.
Unit 4—Understanding Communication
- Activity 4.1—Understanding Learning Styles
- Activity 4.2—Discovering the Learning Styles of Others
- Activity 4.3—Negotiating One to One
- Activity 4.4—Shutting Down Communication
- Activity 4.5—Communicating with Head and Heart

Day 3

8 to 9 A.M.
- Breakfast

9 A.M. to 12 noon
Unit 4—Understanding Communication (continued)
- Activity 4.6—Understanding Power and Influence
- Activity 4.7—Face to Face: Using Eye Placement and Body Position
- Activity 4.8—Using Your Voice

12 noon to 1 P.M.
- Lunch

1 to 5 P.M.
- Activity 4.9—Using "I" Messages
- Activity 4.10—Negotiating Agreement (Skit)
- Activity 4.11— Negotiating Agreement (Role-Plays)

5 to 6 P.M.
- Free Time

6 to 7 P.M.
- Dinner

7 to 11 P.M.
Unit 5—Leading Groups
Learning Center 1: Understanding the Stages of Team Formation
- Activity 5.1—Understanding the Team-Building Process
- Activity 5.2—Guiding the Team Through Stages: Strategies
- Activity 5.3—Understanding Leadership Roles
- Team Challenges:
  - Activity 5.4—Card Towers
  - Activity 5.5—Silent Puzzles
  - Activity 5.6—Great Escape

Day 4

8 to 9 A.M.
- Breakfast

9 A.M. to 12 noon
Unit 5—Leading Groups (continued)
Learning Center 2: Understanding Leadership Styles
- Activity 5.7—Indentifying Leadership Styles
- Activity 5.8—Experiencing Types of Leadership Styles
- Activity 5.9—Making Team Agreements
- Activity 5.10—Understanding Levels of Agreement

- Activity 5.11—Holding Effective Meetings
- Activity 5.12—Holding Effective Meetings: Practice

12 noon to 1 P.M.
- Lunch

1 to 5 P.M.
Unit 5—Leading Groups (continued)
Learning Center 3: Making Presentations
- Activity 5.13—Assessing the Audience
- Activity 5.14—Identifying Audience Leaders and Barometers
- Activity 5.15—Organizing a Presentation

5 to 6 P.M.
- Free Time

6 to 7 P.M.
- Dinner

7 to 11 P.M.
Unit 5—Leading Groups (continued)
Learning Center 4: Planning—Making Positive Changes
- Activity 5.16—Developing a Compelling Vision
- Activity 5.17—Moving from Vision to Plan
- Activity 5.18—Identifying and Solving Constraints

Day 5

8 to 9 A.M.
- Breakfast

9 to 11 A.M.
Unit 5—Leading Groups (continued)
Learning Center 4: Planning—Making Positive Changes (continued)
- Activity 5.19—Creating Action Plans
- Activity 5.20—Scheduling Activities

11 A.M. to 12 noon
- Lunch

12 noon to 4 P.M.
Unit 6—Living Peace
- Activity 6.1—Wellness Wheel: Personal Health Self-Assessment
- Activity 6.2—When Am I in My Power?
- Activity 6.4—Personal Transformation
- Activity 6.5—Affirmations

4 to 5 P.M.
- Closure

ONE-, TWO-, AND THREE-DAY WORKSHOPS

These workshops are designed to be held on school sites, usually in a small gym or large multipurpose room. Unlike the 5-day retreat, these workshops focus on one area of leadership and can be conducted at various times throughout the year. Two teachers or trainers are recommended. Lunch can be brought in. It is a good idea for students in these workshops to be isolated from peers who are not in the workshops.

Some schools offer these workshops at retreat settings, where additional learning and activities can be included. As with the 5-day retreat, sites with food service and lodging accommodations work well.

Workshop 1: Communication Skills (1 Day)

This workshop focuses on individual communication skills, how individuals learn and process information, speaking from the heart, and using "I" messages.

8 to 11 A.M.

- Introduction and Overview
- Activity 1.6—Rules We Can Live By
- Activity 4.1—Understanding Learning Styles
- Activity 4.2—Discovering the Learning Styles of Others
- Activity 4.3– Negotiating One to One

11 to 11: 30 A.M.

- Lunch

11:30 A.M. to 2 P.M.

- Activity 4.4—Shutting Down Communication
- Activity 4.5—Communicating with Head and Heart

2 to 2:15 P.M.

- Break

2:15 to 3:30 P.M.

- Activity 4.9—Using "I" Messages
- Closure

Workshop 2: Leadership Overview (2 Days)

This workshop is an overview of leadership principles, a way to set norms for future leadership workshops, and an examination of personal leadership skills, attitudes, and behaviors. Participants should gain a good understanding of who they are as leaders.

Day 1

8 to 11 A.M.

- Introduction and Overview
- Activity 1.1—Forming Groups: Group Puzzles
- Activity 1.2—Forming Groups: Name Tags
- Activity 1.3—Learning Names
- Activity 1.4—Learning Some Facts About Each Other
- Activity 1.6—Rules We Can Live By

Short Break at End of Activity 1.6

- Activity 1.9—Working Together: A Ball Game
- Activity 1.11—Distinguishing Types of Intelligence
- Activity 1.13—The Tree of Me

11 to 11:30 A.M.

- Lunch

11:30 A.M. to 3 P.M.

- Activity 3.1—Taking a Leadership Self-Inventory
  - □ Integrity
  - □ Compassion
  - □ Belonging
  - □ Aspiring
  - □ Self-Reflection

Day 2

8 to 11 A.M.

- Activity 3.1—Taking a Leadership Self-Inventory (continued)
  - □ Decisiveness
  - □ Curiosity and Creativity
  - □ Fun and Humor
  - □ Role Model
  - □ Confidence
  - □ Goal-Setting Worksheet
  - □ My Goals

11 to 11:30 A.M.

- Lunch

11:30 A.M. to 3 P.M.

- Activity 6.1—Wellness Wheel: Personal Health Self-Assessment
- Activity 6.2—When Am I in My Power?
- Activity 6.4—Personal Transformation

- Activity 6.5—Affirmations
- Closure

Workshop 3: Leading Groups (3 Days)

The focus of this 3-day experience is to demonstrate the stages of team development, the roles leaders play on teams, leadership styles, how to run a meeting, team agreements, and action plans and action groups.

Day 1

8 to 11 A.M.

- Overview
- Establishing Rules of the Day

Note: Prior to the retreat, leaders may want to decide on general rules for the retreat. Activity 1.6 might be helpful for that purpose. Some rules might be related specifically to the retreat setting (rules related to smoking, drinking, drugs, sexual activities, texting, and cell phones). Some general guidelines also include confidentiality and a willingness to participate. Three easy-to-remember rules are take care of yourself, take care of each other, and take care of this place.

- Activity 5.1—Understanding the Team-Building Process
- Activity 5.2—Guiding the Team Through Stages: Strategies
- Activity 5.3—Understanding Leadership Roles
- Team Challenges:
  - Activity 5.4—Card Towers
  - Activity 5.5—Silent Puzzles
  - Activity 5.6—Great Escape

11 to 11:30 A.M.
Lunch

11:30 A.M. to 3 P.M.

- Team Challenges continue from morning session, if necessary
- Activity 5.7—Identifying Leadership Styles
- Activity 5.8—Experiencing Types of Leadership Styles

Day 2

8 to 11 A.M.

- Activity 5.9—Making Team Agreements
- Activity 5.10—Understanding Levels of Agreement
- Activity 5.11—Holding Effective Meetings
- Activity 5.12—Holding Effective Meetings: Practice

11 to 11:30 A.M.
- Lunch

11:30 A.M. to 3:00 P.M.
- Activity 5.16—Developing a Compelling Vision

Day 3

8 to 11 A.M.
- Activity 5.17—Moving from Vision to Plan
- Activity 5.18—Identifying and Solving Constraints
- Activity 5.19—Creating Action Plans
- Activity 5.20—Scheduling Activities

11 to 11:30 A.M.
- Lunch

11:30 A.M. to 3:00 P.M.
- Action Group Planning Meetings: Groups meet, arrange activities in priority order, fully design the first project, and suggest additional projects.

About the Author

Ric Stuecker, M.A., has taught school at every level—elementary through college. For more than 20 years, he has been a nationally recognized educational trainer, consultant, and speaker. He is author of the books *Reviving the Wonder: 76 Activities That Touch the Inner Spirit of Youth* (2001) and *Cultivating Kindness in School: Activities That Promote Integrity, Respect, and Compassion in Elementary and Middle School Students* (2004). Ric has led workshops in leadership, personal growth, study skills, and communication skills throughout the United States. He has trained adults who teach and work with youth in resiliency and asset building, nonverbal communication, and presentation skills. He has directed a treatment center for drug-dependent youth. In addition, he has been a consultant to a number of schools and school districts, holding grants from the Office of Safe and Drug-Free Schools. Ric lives in Louisville, Kentucky, with his wife, Barbara. He has two grown daughters and two grandchildren.

To contact Ric, email him at ricatteal@aol.com.